Numbers That Preach Study Manual

Troy Brewer

DESTINY IMAGE

Take note that the name satan and related names are not capitalized. We choose not to acknowledge him, even to the point of violating grammatical rules.

DESTINY IMAGE® PUBLISHERS, INC.

P.O. Box 310, Shippensburg, PA 17257-0310

"Publishing cutting-edge prophetic resources to supernaturally empower the body of Christ"

This book and all other Destiny Image and Destiny Image Fiction books are available at Christian bookstores and distributors worldwide.

For more information on foreign distributors, call 717-532-3040.

Reach us on the Internet: www.destinyimage.com.

ISBN 13 TP: 979-8-8815-0247-8

ISBN 13 eBook: 979-8-8815-0248-5

For Worldwide Distribution, Printed in the U.S.A.

1 2 3 4 5 6 7 8 /30 29 28 27 26

Contents

CHAPTER 1

THE NUMBER ONE

UNITY

And Adam said, "This is now bone of my bones and flesh of my flesh; she shall be called Woman, because she was taken out of Man." Therefore a man shall leave his father and mother and be joined to his wife, and they shall become one flesh. (Genesis 2:23–24, NKJV)

When God first made Adam, it wasn't long before He introduced the need for Eve. From Adam's rib, God formed a companion not from his head to be dominated, nor from his feet to be trampled, but from his side, close to his heart and under his arm. This divine act wasn't just about creating a helper; it was a sermon preached through a number—one. Unity was stamped on humanity from the beginning.

This story echoes through Scripture and human history. Unity is God's number one priority, and He teaches us that placing Him first is the foundation of true oneness. The first commandment places Him above all else, and the very first words of the Bible begin with Him. All order, intimacy, and harmony flow from this reality.

Jesus demonstrated this unity perfectly. As a boy, He declared His devotion to His Father's business, and His final words on the Cross confirmed that commitment completed. In Him, the ultimate picture of oneness between God and man is fulfilled. Through Christ, curses are turned into blessings, and disorder becomes harmony.

The challenge for us is clear: if God's number is one, and His message through it is unity, how are we living it out? Where do we resist putting God first, and how might disunity in our lives and relationships reveal a deeper misalignment with Him?

Focus Point

I and My Father are one. (John 10:30, NKJV)

This verse embodies the divine unity that Christ models for us. Jesus was not independent from the Father, but in perfect agreement with Him. That unity is the same to which we are called—oneness with God, with Christ, and with each other. It is not mere agreement but a deep alignment of heart, purpose, and relationship.

Main Theme

The theme of this chapter is unity as God's highest priority. From the creation of Eve to the ministry of Christ, Scripture consistently shows that oneness with God brings peace, intimacy, and blessing. When humanity strays, division and death follow; when Christ enters, unity and grace abound. Unity is not a suggestion but the very foundation of God's Kingdom order.

"Unity is God's fingerprint on creation and His invitation into intimacy."

Key Scriptures

- *In the beginning God created the heavens and the earth.* (Genesis 1:1, NKJV)
- *Let the peace of God rule in your hearts, to which also you were called in one body; and be thankful.* (Colossians 3:15, NKJV)
- *In the beginning was the Word, and the Word was with God, and the Word was God.* (John 1:1, NKJV)

Key Points

- **Unity in Creation** God created Eve from Adam's rib to symbolize love, intimacy, and unity from the very beginning.
- **God First in Priority** The Bible opens with "In the beginning God," teaching us that all order starts with Him first.

- **Jesus Modeled Unity** Christ lived and died making His Father's will number one, showing the fullness of divine oneness.
- **Peace Through Oneness** True peace flows when believers live as one body under God's rule, not in division.
- **Unity in History** Events like the year 1898 and the Rough Riders at San Juan Hill highlight God's fingerprint of "oneness" even in history.
- **The Beloved Marked by One** David's life shows how the stamp of one signifies eternity and intimacy with God.
- **Eternity and Unity** Scripture ties "eternity" to God's oneness, reminding us that His unity is everlasting.

JOURNALING QUESTIONS

Journaling gives us a way to sit with the truths of unity and bring them into our daily walk. When we write, we slow down enough to notice where God is calling us to put Him first and where disunity may be pulling us away. It is a spiritual mirror that allows us to see alignment or misalignment with His Word. Unity cannot be faked—it must be cultivated, and journaling helps bring those hidden things into the light.

By responding to the journaling prompts, readers can uncover personal barriers to unity and open themselves to transformation. Writing honest answers will lead to revelations of where God is at work, where His peace is missing, and where intimacy with Him can grow stronger. This process leads not only to deeper understanding but to realignment with God's number one priority: unity with Him and with others.

UNITY IN MARRIAGE AND RELATIONSHIPS

Where have I seen God's design for unity reflected in my relationships, and where is it lacking?

____

____

____

____

____

____

____

Putting God First

What areas of my life are competing for "first place" that belongs only to God?

Living as One Body

How do I contribute to unity—or disunity—in the body of Christ?

Curses to Blessings

Where have I witnessed Jesus transform brokenness into unity and blessing in my life?

Eternity in My Heart

How does knowing God has set eternity in my heart affect the way I pursue unity today?

____

____

____

____

____

____

Actionable Steps

Put God First Daily
Commit each day to seeking God's will before your own, through prayer and Scripture, allowing Him to order your priorities.

Pursue Reconciliation
Take practical steps to mend a relationship where division exists, choosing humility and forgiveness as Christ modeled.

Cultivate Unity in Community
Engage actively in your church or fellowship, not just attending but contributing to the unity of the body with encouragement, service, and love.

Personal Reflection

Unity is not a vague ideal but a call to live in step with God and others. As you reflect on this chapter, consider where your life reflects the oneness God has stamped into creation, and where disunity reveals areas of misalignment. Putting God first is the pathway to intimacy and peace.

This is not an easy call—it requires surrender, humility, and commitment. Yet the rewards are eternal. Every moment we yield to God's authority is a step into deeper intimacy, just as Jesus modeled. His oneness with the Father is our invitation into a life of alignment.

Where am I resisting unity with God? How can I realign my priorities with His? What step will I take today to live in the blessing of oneness?

____
____
____
____
____
____
____
____
____
____
____
____
____
____
____
____
____
____
____
____
____
____
____
____
____
____

Closing Prayer: *Lord, thank You for revealing Your heart through the number one. Teach me to put You first in every part of my life. Where I have pursued my own way, draw me back into unity with You. Let peace rule in my heart as I walk in oneness with You and with those You've placed in my life. May my life echo the unity Jesus modeled, bringing glory to You in all things. Amen.*

Chapter 2

The Number Two

A Faithful Witness and Being Set Apart

And I will give power to my two witnesses, and they will prophesy one thousand two hundred and sixty days, clothed in sackcloth. (Revelation 11:3, NKJV)

When God stamped the number two upon His creation, He was already declaring something about separation and witness. From the very beginning, on the second day, He divided the waters, establishing the truth that where light appears, there must also be division. Division is not always destructive—it can be divine, drawing a clear line between what belongs to God and what belongs to darkness.

This theme carries forward into the lives of God's people. Cain and Abel, Jacob and Esau, Isaac and Ishmael—each pair carries a testimony of separation, one chosen and one rejected, one a faithful witness and one representing what God calls His people to stand against. In this way, the number two becomes a mark of identity: God's people are set apart not by blending in but by contrasting with the world.

Jesus affirmed this when He sent His disciples out "two by two," giving them authority over unclean spirits. Noah's Ark, too, was filled with creatures entering "two by two," declaring both preservation and witness to God's promises. These pairs reveal that testimony is strengthened in agreement, and that truth requires two or three witnesses to be established.

The challenge for believers today is to see themselves as faithful witnesses, set apart in a world that prefers compromise. Are we willing to be distinct, even if it means standing in contrast to those around us? God still stamps His number two on those who are willing to testify of His goodness and remain steadfast in separation from darkness.

FOCUS POINT

And He called the twelve to Himself, and began to send them out two by two, and gave them power over unclean spirits. (Mark 6:7, NKJV)

This verse highlights the power of testimony in unity. Jesus chose not to send His disciples alone but in pairs, emphasizing the biblical principle that witness is strengthened through agreement. The number two reminds us that separation from the world is not isolation—it is a calling to stand together in faithful testimony.

MAIN THEME

The number two signifies the divine principle of separation and faithful witness. From Genesis to Revelation, God establishes truth through two witnesses, confirms His Word with pairs, and calls His people to live distinctly from the world. Faithful witness requires courage to stand apart, and strength is found in agreement with others who walk in God's truth.

"To be a faithful witness means to be set apart, yet never alone."

KEY SCRIPTURES

- *And God said, "Let there be a firmament in the midst of the waters, and let it divide the waters from the waters."* (Genesis 1:6, NKJV)
- *And they went into the ark to Noah, two by two, of all flesh in which is the breath of life.* (Genesis 7:15, NKJV)
- *By the mouth of two or three witnesses every word shall be established.* (Matthew 18:16, NKJV)

KEY POINTS

- **Separation on the Second Day** God divided the waters on the second day, establishing the principle of divine separation.

- **Pairs Throughout Scripture** Cain and Abel, Jacob and Esau, Isaac and Ishmael all reveal the truth of separation and witness.
- **The Power of Two Witnesses** Revelation reveals two witnesses who will testify during the Tribulation with divine authority.
- **Jesus Sent Them Two by Two** Christ affirmed the power of paired witness by sending His disciples in twos with authority.
- **Noah's Ark and Preservation** Animals entered the Ark two by two, declaring God's preservation through faithful obedience.
- **Witness in Major Events** At critical moments, God provided at least two witnesses—at Sinai, the Crucifixion, the Resurrection, and the Ascension.
- **History Confirms the Pattern** Even figures like George Washington bore the mark of two, born on the 22nd day of the second month, a faithful witness in history.

Journaling Questions

Journaling in this chapter helps uncover how we are called to be faithful witnesses in our everyday lives. Writing allows us to identify where compromise has blurred the line between light and darkness and where God is calling us to stand set apart. The act of reflection reveals whether our testimony points others toward Christ or leaves them uncertain of our allegiance.

Through journaling, readers will discover the strength that comes from agreement with others and the courage required to remain distinct. Answering these questions will bring clarity to what it means to be a witness, not just in words but in lifestyle. This practice helps align hearts with God's call to live faithfully as those stamped with the number two.

God's Call to Separation

Where is God asking me to separate from worldly influences to strengthen my testimony?

____

____

____

____

____

____

____

TWO BY TWO

Who has God placed in my life to partner with me in faithful witness, and how am I nurturing that relationship?

THE WITNESS OF MY LIFE

Does my daily life testify of Christ in a way that others can clearly see?

FAITHFUL IN CONTRAST

Am I willing to stand in contrast to the culture, even when it brings discomfort or criticism?

Historic Witness

What can I learn from faithful witnesses in Scripture and history about courage in separation?

____

____

____

____

____

____

Actionable Steps

Identify Areas of Compromise
Examine where you have blended into the world's ways and take steps to realign with God's standards.

Strengthen a Partnership
Commit to walking with another believer in accountability, prayer, and witness, just as Jesus sent disciples two by two.

Live as a Testimony
Choose one area of your life where your actions can more clearly reflect Christ and begin practicing faithful witness there.

Personal Reflection

Being a faithful witness means allowing God to set us apart for His purposes. As you reflect on this chapter, consider where He may be inviting you to stand distinct in your faith. Unity with the world often comes at the cost of truth, but unity with Christ requires separation from darkness.

This journey will not always be easy. Standing apart means surrendering comfort and risking misunderstanding, but it also means stepping into the authority and power God gives His witnesses. Faithfulness is never about blending in—it is about standing firm.

Am I living as a faithful witness to Christ? Where is God calling me to separate more fully from the world? How will I partner with others to testify of His truth?

Closing Prayer: *Father, thank You for the gift of being called as a faithful witness. Give me courage to stand apart from the world and strength to live as a testimony of Your truth. Surround me with partners in faith who will walk with me in agreement, and may my life bear witness to Your goodness and power. Amen.*

Chapter 3

The Number Three

Perfect Completion

For on the third day the Lord will come down upon Mount Sinai in the sight of all the people.
(Exodus 19:11, NKJV)

On the third day of creation, God commanded the earth to rise out of the waters, establishing the first hint that the number three would carry a divine message of fullness and life. Later, when Abraham was commanded to sacrifice Isaac, it was on the third day that he lifted his eyes and saw the place of sacrifice—foreshadowing Christ's work at Calvary nearly 2,000 years later.

This theme of the third day continued when Israel, freshly delivered from Egypt, camped at Sinai. God instructed them to consecrate themselves, and on the third day He revealed His presence in power. The message was clear: the third day is when God shows Himself in fullness, completion, and resurrection.

The resurrection of Jesus Christ is surrounded by threes. He rose on the third day, He hung between three crosses, and three hours of darkness covered the land. Peter denied Him three times before the resurrection and declared his love three times after. Even the words "It is finished" are three in Greek. All of these threes are God's way of stamping His divine completion upon the sacrifice of His Son.

The challenge for us is this: if God's number three declares perfect completion, are we living as those who have been raised with Christ into the fullness of life? Or do we still linger in partial surrender, resisting the completeness He has made available to us?

Focus Point

Then on the third day Abraham lifted his eyes and saw the place afar off. (Genesis 22:4, NKJV)

This verse embodies prophetic revelation. Abraham saw Calvary not only as a location but as a promise fulfilled in Christ. On the third day, God revealed the fullness of His redemptive plan, showing that His work is never partial—it is always complete.

Main Theme

The number three is stamped throughout Scripture to reveal God's message of resurrection, divinity, and fullness. From creation to Calvary, the third day represents the moment when God brings His work to completion. Jesus' resurrection is the ultimate declaration that His sacrifice was perfect and eternal.

"Three is God's signature of resurrection and the fullness of His work."

Key Scriptures

- *For on the third day the Lord will come down upon Mount Sinai in the sight of all the people.* (Exodus 19:11, NKJV)
- *He was crucified in the third hour, and there was darkness over the whole land until the ninth hour.* (Mark 15:25, 33, NKJV)
- *Jesus answered and said to him, "Most assuredly, I say to you, unless one is born again, he cannot see the kingdom of God."* (John 3:3, NKJV)

Key Points

- **Third Day Glory** God revealed His power on the third day at creation, at Sinai, and ultimately through Christ's resurrection.
- **Foreshadowing at Moriah** Abraham's third-day vision of sacrifice pointed directly to Calvary and God's perfect Lamb.

- **Resurrection Proclaimed** Jesus rose on the third day, declaring God's plan fully accomplished.
- **Threes at the Cross** Three crosses, three hours of darkness, and three denials all carry the divine watermark of completion.
- **Fullness Revealed** Scripture speaks of the fullness of God, Christ, and the Godhead—all tied to the number three.
- **Marked by New Birth** The term "born again" appears three times in Scripture, each emphasizing resurrection life.
- **Completion in Eternity** God's pattern of threes points believers toward the eternal completeness found only in Him.

Journaling Questions

Journaling around the number three helps us uncover areas of life where we settle for partial obedience instead of fullness. Writing about these patterns allows us to recognize God's call to live in resurrection power. Journaling creates space to see the connections between Scripture's threes and our own spiritual maturity.

By answering the prompts, readers will encounter the Holy Spirit's invitation to live as complete, not fractured; to stand in the fullness of Christ's sacrifice, not in fragments of faith. These reflections will press us to embrace resurrection power as a present reality, not just a historical event.

Third Day Revelation

What "third day" moments in my life has God used to reveal His power and completion?

____

____

____

____

____

____

____

Patterns of Three

Where do I see threes in Scripture or in my own life that point me toward God's fullness?

____

____

____

____

____

____

Living in Fullness

Am I walking in the fullness of Christ, or holding back parts of my life from His resurrection power?

____

____

____

____

____

____

Completion Versus Compromise

Where have I settled for partial surrender instead of embracing God's complete plan?

____

____

____

____

____

____

Resurrection Reality

How does the truth of Christ's resurrection transform the way I face challenges today?

____

____

____

____

____

____

Actionable Steps

Embrace Full Obedience
Commit to obeying God in areas where you've only given partial surrender, trusting His completion.

Mark a Third Day
Choose a specific day to consecrate as a reminder of resurrection power—fast, pray, and realign with God's promises.

Live Out Resurrection Power
Actively declare and demonstrate the reality of Christ's resurrection in your daily life, bringing hope and faith to others.

Personal Reflection

Perfect completion is God's design for His people. The number three whispers to us through Scripture, reminding us that His work is not partial but whole. As you reflect, consider whether you are walking in the fullness Christ has provided or settling for less.

This journey into completion requires surrender and faith. The resurrection proves that what looks finished in defeat is actually complete in victory. God calls us to live out that reality daily.

Where am I resisting God's completion in my life? How will I embrace resurrection power today? What step can I take to live fully in the fullness of Christ?

***Closing Prayer:** Lord, thank You for the revelation of Your perfect completion through the number three. Teach me to walk in the fullness of Christ's resurrection. Where I have lived in fragments, bring wholeness. Where I have resisted, bring surrender. Let my life testify that Your work is complete and eternal. Amen.*

Chapter 4

The Number Four

God's Creation

And this gospel of the kingdom will be preached in all the world as a witness to all the nations, and then the end will come. (Matthew 24:14, NKJV)

God stamped His creation with the number four. From the very beginning, this number became a mark upon the material world, a reminder that everything seen and unseen is crafted by His hand. On the first day, we see a rhythm of God saying, seeing, dividing, and calling, setting the stage for a world that reflects His order and design. Four represents creation, structure, and the fullness of what God has made.

We see this number woven into the fabric of our natural world: four elements, four regions of the earth, four seasons, four lunar cycles, and four divisions of the day. This repetition isn't random—it's a declaration that the physical world is under the imprint of divine purpose. The number four is God's way of reminding us that everything He made is meant to point us back to Him.

Jesus used the natural order to teach spiritual truths. In the Parable of the Sower, He described four kinds of soil, each representing the heart's condition in receiving the Word. The harvest is determined by whether the heart is hard, shallow, crowded, or receptive. Just as creation bears the number four, so too does our spiritual response to God's Word carry this divine stamp.

The question remains: how do we engage with God's creation as faithful stewards? The world around us bears His fingerprint, but will we recognize His work and respond to His truth? Are we living as those who honor His creation or as those entangled in the unredeemed systems of the world?

Focus Point

The earth is the Lord's, and all its fullness, the world and those who dwell therein. (Psalm 24:1, NKJV)

This verse captures the truth of the number four. Everything in the physical world belongs to God. The seasons, elements, and nations are not accidents but reflections of His sovereignty. To recognize the number four is to recognize that creation itself is a testimony to the Creator.

Main Theme

The number four represents creation and the systems God established for the world. It reveals His order, His sovereignty, and His intent to reach all nations through His creation. At the same time, it reminds us that the world's systems can be corrupted and must be redeemed.

"Creation bears God's fingerprint, declaring His order, His presence, and His purpose in all the world."

Key Scriptures

- *And this gospel of the kingdom will be preached in all the world as a witness to all the nations, and then the end will come.* (Matthew 24:14, NKJV)
- *The earth is the Lord's, and all its fullness, the world and those who dwell therein.* (Psalm 24:1, NKJV)
- *Then I looked, and behold, a whirlwind was coming out of the north, a great cloud with raging fire engulfing itself; and brightness was all around it and radiating out of its midst like the color of amber, out of the midst of the fire. Also from within it came the likeness of four living creatures.* (Ezekiel 1:4–5, NKJV)

Key Points

- **The World Number** Four is God's stamp upon creation, marking the material world with His order.

- **The Elements of Creation** Earth, air, fire, and water reveal the divine imprint of four upon the natural world.
- **The Four Directions** North, south, east, and west represent the whole earth under God's reign.
- **The Four Seasons** Spring, summer, fall, and winter testify to God's rhythm of life and harvest.
- **The Four Soils** Jesus described four heart conditions in the Parable of the Sower, tying creation to spiritual response.
- **The Four Faces of the Cherubim** The creatures around God's throne bear four faces, representing His sovereignty over the kingdoms of the world.
- **The Four Gospels** Matthew, Mark, Luke, and John reveal Christ to all the world, mirroring the number four's message of completeness in creation and redemption.

Journaling Questions

Journaling about the number four helps us see how deeply creation points us back to God. Writing reflections allows us to notice the seasons, the rhythms, and the structures of our lives where God is speaking through His design. Just as creation reveals His hand, journaling opens our eyes to the ways He orders our steps.

When answering these questions, readers will discover how their lives are connected to God's created order and how they are called to steward His world. Reflection will draw out gratitude for His creation and a renewed sense of responsibility to live as witnesses in the world He so carefully crafted.

Creation's Fingerprint

Where do I see God's fingerprint in the natural world, and how does it strengthen my faith?

Seasons of Life

How have different "seasons" in my life reflected God's order and purpose?

The Soil of My Heart

Which of the four soils best describes the current condition of my heart?

Stewardship and Witness

How am I stewarding God's creation in my daily life as an act of worship?

All the World

What is my personal role in spreading the gospel to all nations?

____

____

____

____

____

____

Actionable Steps

Honor Creation
Take intentional steps to appreciate and care for the natural world as God's handiwork.

Examine Your Soil
Evaluate the condition of your heart in light of the Parable of the Sower and invite God to cultivate fruitfulness.

Be a Global Witness
Engage in prayer, giving, or missions that extend the gospel to "all the world," reflecting the global scope of God's plan.

Personal Reflection

Creation is not random; it is divinely ordered. The number four is a reminder that God has stamped His presence on the world around us. As you reflect, consider how your life aligns with His order and purpose.

To live in step with creation is to recognize God's sovereignty in the seasons of life and in the structures He designed. It means living as a witness in the world He made, not conformed to its systems but redeemed for His glory.

Am I honoring God in how I engage with His creation? What season am I in, and how is He calling me to respond? How can I live as a faithful witness to His order in all the world?

Closing Prayer: *Creator God, thank You for stamping Your number on the world and reminding me through creation of Your presence and order. Teach me to honor the seasons of life, to be a faithful steward of what You have made, and to live as a witness in all the earth. May my life reflect the beauty and purpose of Your creation. Amen.*

Chapter 5

The Number Five

Grace of God

Moreover the law entered that the offense might abound. But where sin abounded, grace abounded much more, so that as sin reigned in death, even so grace might reign through righteousness to eternal life through Jesus Christ our Lord. (Romans 5:20–21, NKJV)

Grace has always carried the mark of God's number five. Israel marched out of Egypt in ranks of five, declaring it was not by their power but by God's grace that they were set free. David picked up five smooth stones to face Goliath, demonstrating that victory was not found in military strength but in the grace of God. The anointing oil, made with five ingredients, symbolized God's ability to set apart and empower for His purposes.

Grace is more than unmerited favor—it is divine ability. Like a bullied child suddenly rising up with superhero strength, grace is God-given power to overcome what otherwise cannot be defeated. It is the underdog's secret weapon, the power that turns weakness into triumph. Jesus Himself bore five wounds on the Cross, stamping grace on the very act that secured our salvation.

In the New Testament, Paul spoke of preferring to share five clear words of understanding rather than ten thousand in tongues. Even in speech, the number five preaches of clarity given by grace. At Bethesda's pool with its five porches, a lame man was made whole, showing that walking in Christ is possible only through grace. Again and again, Scripture preaches that grace is the power to overcome, progress, and stand strong.

The question is whether we are living in this grace or trying to overcome in our own strength. Grace is not something to admire from a distance but something to walk in daily.

God stamps it on our hands, feet, and senses as a reminder that everything we do, everywhere we walk, and all we perceive are marked by His power to overcome.

Focus Point

And with great power the apostles gave witness to the resurrection of the Lord Jesus. And great grace was upon them all. (Acts 4:33, NKJV)

This verse shows that power and grace are inseparable. Grace is not passive—it fuels the witness of God's people. When the apostles walked in great power, it was because great grace was upon them. The number five reminds us that grace equips us to overcome, testify, and live victoriously.

Main Theme

The number five represents grace as God's divine empowerment to overcome. It marks Israel's deliverance, David's victory, the anointing oil, and the wounds of Christ. Grace is not weakness—it is God's supernatural strength working through us to triumph where human effort fails.

"Grace is God's gift of power to the powerless, stamped with His number five."

Key Scriptures

- *Yet in the church I would rather speak five words with my understanding, that I may teach others also, than ten thousand words in a tongue.* (1 Corinthians 14:19, NKJV)
- *As you therefore have received Christ Jesus the Lord, so walk in Him.* (Colossians 2:6, NKJV)
- *These things I have spoken to you, that in Me you may have peace. In the world you will have tribulation; but be of good cheer, I have overcome the world.* (John 16:33, NKJV)

Key Points

- **Grace as Overcoming Power** Grace gives the supernatural ability to rise above what is otherwise impossible to defeat.
- **Israel in Fives** The Exodus reveals grace's power to deliver God's people from bondage in ranks of five.
- **David's Five Stones** Victory over Goliath came not through might, but through God's grace symbolized by five stones.
- **Five Words of Clarity** Paul emphasized five clear words of teaching over thousands in tongues, showing grace brings clarity.
- **The Five Ingredients of Oil** Anointing oil with five components symbolizes God's power to set apart and empower for service.
- **The Five Porches of Bethesda** Healing came at the pool with five porches, showing grace enables us to walk in Christ.
- **The Five Wounds of Christ** Jesus bore five wounds on the Cross, marking salvation as the ultimate act of grace.

Journaling Questions

Journaling about grace helps us to see where we've relied on our own efforts instead of leaning on God's power. It gives us space to remember that grace is not earned—it is received. As we write, we can uncover moments when God's grace sustained us in weakness and equipped us to stand in victory.

By reflecting on these truths, readers will recognize God's grace as active in their lives today, not just a theological concept. Journaling will highlight the reality that grace touches every part of life—what we do, where we walk, and how we perceive. It helps us embrace grace as God's gift of power for every challenge.

Grace in My Weakness

Where has God's grace given me strength when I was powerless?

____

____

____

Overcoming Through Five

How does the imagery of Israel in fives or David's five stones encourage me to trust grace in battle?

____
____
____
____
____
____

Anointed for Purpose

In what ways has God's grace set me apart for His calling?

____
____
____
____
____
____

Walking in Christ

Where do I need grace to help me walk in greater obedience and faith?

____
____
____
____
____
____

Marked by the Cross

How does the truth of Christ's five wounds deepen my understanding of grace?

____
____
____
____
____
____

Actionable Steps

Receive God's Empowerment
Consciously surrender areas of weakness and ask God to release His grace as strength.

Practice Grace in Speech
Like Paul, choose clarity and edification in your words, allowing grace to guide your communication.

Walk in Grace Daily
Begin each day by declaring dependence on God's grace, asking Him to empower your steps, actions, and perceptions.

Personal Reflection

The number five preaches loudly: grace is God's gift of overcoming power. As you reflect, consider where you may still be trying to conquer in your own strength. Grace is the key to freedom, victory, and fruitfulness.

Living in grace means letting God's strength be perfected in your weakness. It is the assurance that even when the battle is fierce, you are not fighting alone. His grace is more than enough.

Where do I need to stop striving and start receiving grace? How will I apply God's gift of grace to my challenges today? What step of faith can I take that demonstrates I am walking in His grace?

Closing Prayer: *Father, thank You for the gift of grace marked by Your number five. Teach me to rely on Your strength instead of my own. Anoint me to walk in Your power, to speak with clarity, and to overcome every challenge. May my life testify that grace is not weakness but Your divine ability working in me. Amen.*

Chapter 6

The Number Six

The Flesh

This I say then: Walk in the Spirit, and you shall not fulfill the lust of the flesh. For the flesh lusts against the Spirit, and the Spirit against the flesh; and these are contrary to one another, so that you do not do the things that you wish. (Galatians 5:16–17, NKJV)

The number six is God's watermark upon the flesh. From the beginning, man was created on the sixth day, and the sixth character in Scripture is the serpent. It is the number that preaches man's weakness, imperfection, and opposition to God. While five points to grace and seven to the Spirit, six sits between them, symbolizing human effort that falls short without God's power.

Goliath bore the mark of six. He stood six cubits tall, wore six pieces of armor, and even fathered descendants with six fingers and six toes. His spear weighed six hundred shekels. He embodied human arrogance and fleshly strength in defiance of God. Yet the Spirit always holds the advantage—the armor of God in Ephesians 6 is capped with prayer, a seventh piece that ensures victory over flesh.

The number six belongs to man. Six days of labor are given to mankind, but the seventh is God's. Fields could be worked for six years, but the seventh was to rest. Six dispensations mark man's attempts at ruling himself, but the seventh belongs to Christ. Even the infamous number 666, the mark of the beast, is the ultimate representation of flesh—man, man, man—fully opposed to God and destined for destruction.

The question is clear: will we walk according to the weakness of the flesh, or will we allow the Spirit to overcome? Six preaches man's insufficiency, but it also points us toward God's sufficiency. Where flesh fails, grace abounds, and the Spirit reigns.

Focus Point

Here is wisdom. Let him who has understanding calculate the number of the beast, for it is the number of a man: His number is six hundred threescore and six. (Revelation 13:18, NKJV)

This verse declares that six, when multiplied, becomes the ultimate mark of man apart from God. The number 666 is the picture of flesh exalted to its fullest, the beastly opposition to God. It warns us that man without God is doomed to corruption, but it also points to the necessity of the Spirit's victory.

Main Theme

The number six represents the flesh—humanity's weakness, opposition, and inability to fulfill God's law. It reminds us that without grace and the Spirit, man is enslaved to imperfection. But in Christ, we are empowered to overcome the flesh and walk in victory.

"Six preaches man's weakness, but the Spirit preaches God's victory."

Key Scriptures

- *This I say then: Walk in the Spirit, and you shall not fulfill the lust of the flesh.* (Galatians 5:16, NKJV)
- *Man was created on the sixth day.* (Genesis 1:26–31, NKJV)
- *Here is wisdom. Let him who has understanding calculate the number of the beast, for it is the number of a man: His number is 666.* (Revelation 13:18, NKJV)

Key Points

- **The Flesh Stamped with Six** Man was created on the sixth day, showing that six is tied to humanity and its weakness.
- **Goliath and the Sixes** Goliath bore six cubits, six pieces of armor, and six hundred shekels, marking fleshly arrogance.

- **The Rival of the Spirit** The six pieces of Goliath's armor contrast with the armor of God in Ephesians 6, completed by prayer.
- **The Number of Man** Six days belong to man for labor, but the seventh belongs to the Lord, teaching man's limits.
- **Six Dispensations** Man attempts to rule through six dispensations, but the seventh reveals Christ's perfect reign.
- **The Mark of the Beast** The number 666 represents flesh at its fullest, man in total rebellion against God.
- **The Spirit's Victory** Though six points to man's insufficiency, the Spirit always "has one up" on the flesh, bringing triumph.

Journaling Questions

Journaling about the number six helps us to identify the areas where the flesh has too much influence. Writing allows us to see patterns of self-reliance, pride, or weakness that oppose God's Spirit. By recording these reflections, we make space for the Spirit to reveal how to overcome the flesh.

Through journaling, readers will recognize that the number six is not just about failure but about learning dependence on God. These questions invite us to confront where the flesh is active and to invite the Spirit to reign. The result is a deeper walk of victory and surrender.

The Flesh at Work

Where do I see the influence of fleshly thinking or behavior in my life?

____

____

____

____

____

____

____

Lessons from Goliath

What "giants" of the flesh do I need to confront with God's Spirit?

____
____
____
____
____
____

Six Days, One Lord

How do I balance my labor with giving God His rightful place of rest and rule?

____
____
____
____
____
____

The Warning of 666

What does the reality of the mark of the beast teach me about resisting the pull of the world's systems?

____
____
____
____
____
____

Walking in the Spirit

What specific step can I take to walk more consistently in the Spirit's power rather than the flesh?

____

____

____

____

____

____

Actionable Steps

Confront the Giants
Name one area where the flesh is dominant and actively bring it before God in prayer for deliverance.

Honor the Seventh
Set aside intentional time of rest and worship, remembering that six belongs to man but the seventh belongs to God.

Choose the Spirit Daily
Make it a daily practice to invite the Holy Spirit to guide your steps and empower you against the pull of the flesh.

Personal Reflection

The number six reminds us of our humanity and our frailty. It preaches that flesh cannot win against the Spirit, but it also invites us to rely on God. As you reflect, consider whether you are living in your own strength or by the Spirit's power.

Victory is not found in resisting the flesh by human effort but by yielding to the Spirit. God's number seven always triumphs over six. The mark of the beast may represent rebellion, but the mark of Christ is victory and life.

Where is the flesh still ruling in my life? How will I surrender these areas to the Spirit? What daily step can I take to ensure I walk in the Spirit's triumph?

Closing Prayer: *Lord, thank You for showing me through the number six the weakness of my flesh. Teach me to walk in Your Spirit, not relying on my own strength. Deliver me from pride, self-reliance, and rebellion, and clothe me in Your power. May my life declare the victory of the Spirit over the weakness of the flesh. Amen.*

Chapter 7

The Number Seven

The Spirit of God

Grace to you and peace from Him who is and who was and who is to come, and from the seven Spirits who are before His throne, and from Jesus Christ, the faithful witness, the firstborn from the dead, and the ruler over the kings of the earth. (Revelation 1:4–5, NKJV)

The number seven first appeared in creation when God rested on the seventh day. Not because He was tired, but because His work was complete. From that moment forward, the seventh day was set apart as holy, and it became a divine marker of perfection, completion, and sanctification. Seven is the number that preaches God's Spirit bringing things into fullness.

We see sevens all throughout Scripture: the seven Spirits of God, the seven churches in Revelation, the seven seals, the seven trumpets, and the seven bowls of judgment. These are not random but deliberate, showing God's perfection in justice, mercy, and order. The Spirit lacks nothing—He is wisdom, counsel, power, knowledge, and the fear of the Lord in perfect harmony.

The number seven reminds us that God completes what He starts. He is not random; His plans are whole, holy, and sufficient. Whenever we see seven in Scripture, it is a whisper that something belongs entirely to Him. From forgiveness to protection, from sanctification to justice, seven declares that God's Spirit is present, working, and bringing His people to completion.

The challenge is this: are we living as though His Spirit is enough? Do we trust in His completion, or do we still attempt to finish things in our own strength? Seven preaches perfection, but it also calls us to rest in what God has already made whole.

FOCUS POINT

Then came Peter to Him and said, "Lord, how often shall my brother sin against me, and I forgive him? Up to seven times?" Jesus said to him, "I do not say to you, up to seven times, but up to seventy times seven." (Matthew 18:21–22, NKJV)

This verse shows how seven embodies forgiveness and perfection. Jesus expands Peter's notion of limited mercy into limitless forgiveness, revealing that the Spirit's work is always complete and abundant, never partial or lacking.

MAIN THEME

The number seven is God's signature of spiritual perfection, completion, and sanctification. From creation to Revelation, it points to the fullness of His Spirit and the certainty that what He begins, He will complete.

"Seven is the Spirit's signature, marking everything He perfects as holy and complete."

KEY SCRIPTURES

- *By the seventh day God completed His work which He had done, and He rested on the seventh day from all His work which He had done.* (Genesis 2:2, NASB)
- *Seven lamps of fire were burning before the throne, which are the seven Spirits of God.* (Revelation 4:5, NKJV)
- *Then came Peter to Him and said, "Lord, how often shall my brother sin against me, and I forgive him? Up to seven times?"* (Matthew 18:21, NKJV)

KEY POINTS

- **Creation Completed** God's rest on the seventh day established seven as the number of completion and sanctification.
- **Seven Spirits of God** Isaiah 11 describes the fullness of the Spirit—wisdom,

understanding, counsel, might, knowledge, fear of the Lord, and the Spirit of the Lord Himself.

- **Seven Churches** In Revelation, Jesus addressed seven churches, showing the complete spectrum of spiritual conditions in His people.
- **Seven Judgments** Seven seals, seven trumpets, and seven bowls declare God's perfect justice and mercy.
- **Sevenfold Forgiveness** Jesus taught limitless mercy through the image of seventy times seven, revealing perfection in forgiveness.
- **Sevenfold Protection** Deuteronomy declares that enemies who come one way will flee seven ways, showing God's Spirit brings complete victory.
- **Seven in Revelation** Over 50 sevens are woven through Revelation, stamping the Spirit's perfection upon the final story of history.

Journaling Questions

Journaling about the number seven invites us to recognize God's perfection in our lives. Writing allows us to see where we have been striving in our own strength and to rest instead in His completion. It is a way of acknowledging that God finishes what He starts and that His Spirit lacks nothing.

By reflecting on these truths, readers can uncover areas of life where they need to trust God's completion. Journaling will help highlight where His Spirit has already been at work and where we are called to stop striving and start resting in His sufficiency.

Completion in My Life

Where have I seen God finish something in my life perfectly, even when I doubted?

____

____

____

____

____

____

____

THE SEVENFOLD SPIRIT

Which aspect of the Spirit described in Isaiah 11 do I most need to embrace today?

THE CHURCHES' EXAMPLE

Which of the seven churches in Revelation reflects my current spiritual condition?

SEVENFOLD FORGIVENESS

Am I practicing the kind of limitless forgiveness Jesus taught with seventy times seven?

Trusting His Completion

Where am I still trying to finish in my own strength what God has already made complete?

____

____

____

____

____

____

____

Actionable Steps

Rest in His Work
Set aside intentional time to rest in God's presence, acknowledging His work is finished.

Practice Sevenfold Forgiveness
Choose one relationship where you can extend mercy beyond what feels reasonable.

Trust His Perfection
Declare God's promises over an unfinished area of your life, trusting that He will bring it to completion.

Personal Reflection

Seven is God's way of stamping His Spirit on what belongs to Him. It is the whisper of completion and the assurance of perfection. As you reflect, ask yourself where you are still striving in the flesh rather than resting in the Spirit's sufficiency.

Perfection is not about never failing—it is about allowing the Spirit to bring everything into completion. The same God who sanctified the seventh day is still sanctifying your life today.

Where do I need to trust God's Spirit to finish what He started? How can I rest more fully in His sufficiency? What step can I take to live in the perfection of His Spirit?

Closing Prayer: *Holy Spirit, thank You for marking my life with Your perfection. Teach me to rest in Your completion and to trust that You finish what You start. Help me to walk in the fullness of Your wisdom, power, and presence, and may my life reflect Your holiness and completion. Amen.*

Chapter 8

The Number Eight

New Beginnings

Then He who sat on the throne said, "Behold, I make all things new." And He said to me, "Write, for these words are true and faithful." (Revelation 21:5, NKJV)

From the very beginning, the number eight has preached newness. In Genesis, the first words promise life and order, but the book ends with death—a coffin in Egypt. Humanity's story without God always collapses into ruin. Yet God interrupts with new beginnings. Jesus enters the story as the true "new sheriff in town," bringing not just renewal but an entirely new covenant. He turns curses into blessings and death into life.

Throughout Scripture, God stamps His number eight on new seasons. There were eight people in Noah's Ark, preserved for a fresh start after the flood. Circumcision, the mark of covenant identity, was commanded on the eighth day. King David, the eighth son of Jesse, rose to reign as a man after God's heart. Each example points to God's love for resurrection, renewal, and redemption.

The New Testament amplifies this message. Jesus rose on the first day of the week—often called the "eighth day." It was not merely another morning; it was the dawn of eternal salvation, a brand-new creation. In His ministry, the word *born* appears eight times in His conversation with Nicodemus, and the word *water* eight times with the Samaritan woman. These echoes of eight proclaim rebirth and renewal in Christ.

The question becomes whether we will step into the "eighth day" reality of new beginnings. Are we clinging to the old cycles of brokenness, or are we embracing the resurrection life Jesus offers? God's number eight calls us to trust that no matter how final the coffin seems, His Spirit speaks life beyond it.

Focus Point

Therefore, if anyone is in Christ, he is a new creation; old things have passed away; behold, all things have become new. (2 Corinthians 5:17, NKJV)

This verse reveals the essence of eight: Christ transforms the old into something brand new. It is not a patch on the past but a resurrection into new life. The number eight preaches that God's promise of renewal is both personal and eternal.

Main Theme

Eight is God's number for resurrection, redemption, and new beginnings. It appears whenever He brings His people out of death into life, out of bondage into covenant, and out of despair into hope. The eighth day is the dawn of something never seen before—a fresh start that only God can provide.

"Eight is God's promise that every ending in Him is a new beginning."

Key Scriptures

- *And he that sat upon the throne said, "Behold, I make all things new."* (Revelation 21:5, NKJV)
- *And Jesus said to them, "I am the bread of life. He who comes to Me shall never hunger, and he who believes in Me shall never thirst."* (John 6:35, NKJV)
- *Circumcise the flesh of your foreskins, and it shall be a sign of the covenant between Me and you. He who is eight days old among you shall be circumcised.* (Genesis 17:11–12, NKJV)

Key Points

- **New Covenant** Jesus fulfills the old covenant and inaugurates the new, marking the ultimate new beginning.

- **Eight People in the Ark** God preserved eight lives through the flood to restart humanity with fresh hope.
- **The Eighth Day Circumcision** The covenant of God was sealed on the eighth day, signifying identity and belonging.
- **David the Eighth Son** Chosen from obscurity, David's kingship testified to God's pattern of fresh beginnings.
- **Resurrection on the Eighth Day** Jesus rose up on the "eighth day," the first day of the week, declaring victory over death and the dawn of eternal life.
- **Eightfold Conversations** The words *born* and *water* appearing eight times in key dialogues underline the message of rebirth.
- **Eight Things to Think On** Philippians 4:8 outlines eight virtues, guiding believers into a renewed mind and lifestyle.

JOURNALING QUESTIONS

Journaling about the number eight opens our hearts to see where God is inviting us into renewal. Writing reflections allows us to identify areas where old patterns still rule and where the Spirit is calling us to step into resurrection life. It reminds us that in Christ, endings are never final—they are doorways to new beginnings.

Answering these questions will help readers recognize God's hand of renewal at work in their lives. Journaling leads us to embrace His new covenant, His new promises, and His eternal life. It helps us move from clinging to old identities into fully living as new creations.

OLD VERSUS NEW

What "old things" in my life is God asking me to release so He can bring renewal?

____

____

____

____

____

____

____

EIGHTH DAY LIVING

How am I embracing resurrection life as a present reality rather than a distant hope?

COVENANT IDENTITY

What does it mean to me personally that covenant identity began on the eighth day?

FRESH STARTS

Where has God given me a new beginning, and how have I responded to it?

Renewed Mind

Which of the eight virtues in Philippians 4:8 do I most need to meditate on today?

____

____

____

____

____

____

Actionable Steps

Release the Old
Intentionally let go of one area of your life where the past still holds sway, and trust God for renewal.

Embrace the Eighth Day
Mark a fresh start with prayer, fasting, or worship as a declaration of stepping into resurrection life.

Think on the Eight
Practice daily meditation on the eight virtues of Philippians 4:8 to renew your mind with God's truth.

Personal Reflection

The number eight resounds through Scripture as God's declaration of resurrection and renewal. It whispers that no matter how final death or despair appears, His Spirit brings fresh life. As you reflect, consider where you need to step out of the coffin of the old and into the promise of the new.

This is not simply about change—it is about transformation. Jesus is the God of new beginnings, and His resurrection proves that every ending in Him is a new dawn.

Where is God inviting me into new beginnings? How will I release the old to step into His renewal? What daily practice will help me live as a new creation?

Closing Prayer: *Lord Jesus, thank You for being the God of new beginnings. Thank You for rising on the eighth day to bring me new life. Teach me to release the old and step fully into Your renewal. Let my life testify that in You, every ending is the beginning of something greater. Amen.*

Chapter 9

The Number Nine

Divine Judgment

Now thanks be to God who always leads us in triumph in Christ, and through us diffuses the fragrance of His knowledge in every place. For we are to God the fragrance of Christ among those who are being saved and among those who are perishing. To the one we are the aroma of death leading to death, and to the other the aroma of life leading to life.
(2 Corinthians 2:14–16, NKJV)

The number nine preaches a double message: fruit in the redeemed and judgment in the unredeemed. It is one of the hardest numbers to summarize because its meaning changes depending on the context. Nine months of pregnancy bring forth new life, while nine biblical sieges of Jerusalem highlight God's severe judgment. The same Spirit that brings life also brings finality when rebellion persists.

Scripture shows nine as a pivot between blessing and judgment. There are nine gifts of the Spirit, manifesting life and forward movement, and nine fruits of the Spirit, revealing character shaped by God. Yet Jesus died at the ninth hour, a sign of judgment being poured out so that eternal life might be released. Even the Hebrew day known as the Ninth of Av carries the weight of tragedy—both temples were destroyed on that same day, and countless disasters followed.

History also bears this imprint. From expulsions to wars, the Ninth of Av has marked Israel with loss and judgment. Yet nine also carries redemption: Christ became the firstfruits at His resurrection, and the Spirit brings forth fruit that lasts. The number nine proclaims that judgment is not only about punishment but also about separating life from death, fruitfulness from barrenness.

The challenge for us is whether we will be found fruitful or judged. Nine calls us to embrace the Spirit's life so that we become the aroma of Christ, not the stench of rebellion.

Focus Point

But now Christ is risen from the dead, and has become the firstfruits of those who have fallen asleep. (1 Corinthians 15:20, NKJV)

This verse ties together the dual meaning of nine. Christ died at the ninth hour, a picture of judgment, but He rose as the firstfruits, the picture of life. Nine is God's reminder that judgment is real, but in Christ, it leads to fruit and resurrection.

Main Theme

The number nine reveals God's divine judgment—life when surrendered to the Spirit and death when resisting Him. It is the Spirit who decides whether judgment produces fruit or finality. Nine presses us to align with the Spirit so that our lives bear lasting fruit rather than fall under destruction.

"Nine is the Spirit's dividing line—judgment that brings either fruit or finality."

Key Scriptures

- *Now thanks be to God who always leads us in triumph in Christ... to the one we are the aroma of death leading to death, and to the other the aroma of life leading to life.* (2 Corinthians 2:14–16, NKJV)
- *But now Christ is risen from the dead, and has become the firstfruits of those who have fallen asleep.* (1 Corinthians 15:20, NKJV)
- *Now from the sixth hour until the ninth hour there was darkness over all the land. And Jesus cried out again with a loud voice and yielded up His spirit.* (Matthew 27:45,50, NKJV)

Key Points

- **Double Meaning of Nine** Nine represents both fruit and judgment, depending on whether the Spirit brings life or finality.
- **Pregnancy and Birth** Nine months of gestation show God's number tied to life, birth, and fruitfulness.
- **Gifts and Fruits of the Spirit** There are nine gifts and nine fruits of the Spirit, preaching life when judgment produces growth.
- **The Ninth Hour** Jesus died at the ninth hour, judgment poured out to bring forth resurrection life.
- **Judgment in History** The Ninth of Av marks tragedies from the destruction of the temples to expulsions and wars.
- **999 and Death** Forms of the word *death* appear 999 times in Scripture, underscoring judgment's finality.
- **Nine as a Divider** This number separates life from death, blessing from curse, and fruitfulness from barrenness.

Journaling Questions

Journaling about the number nine helps us reflect on how we respond to the Spirit's judgment. Writing reveals whether our lives carry the fruit of surrender or the finality of rebellion. Journaling gives space to see how God's Spirit has separated us from death and called us to life.

By engaging these questions, readers will gain clarity on where they are bearing fruit and where the Spirit is calling for repentance. Journaling leads us to embrace judgment as the Spirit's gift, ensuring that our lives are marked by fruit, not destruction.

Fruit or Finality

In what areas of my life is the Spirit producing fruit, and where is He warning of finality?

____

____

____

____

____

Nine Months of New Life

What spiritual "births" has God brought about in me after a season of waiting?

____

____

____

____

____

____

The Ninth Hour

How does Jesus' death at the ninth hour shape my understanding of judgment and grace?

____

____

____

____

____

____

Historic Warnings

What lessons do I learn from the tragedies of the Ninth of Av about disobedience and its consequences?

____

____

____

____

____

____

Living as Firstfruits

How am I living as a firstfruit of Christ's resurrection in my daily walk?

____

____

____

____

____

____

____

Actionable Steps

Embrace the Spirit's Fruit
Commit to cultivating the nine fruits of the Spirit, asking God to grow them in your life.

Respond to Judgment
Identify one area where the Spirit has been convicting you and take practical steps toward repentance and renewal.

Mark a Ninth-Hour Prayer
Choose a regular time to pray at nine o'clock, remembering Christ's sacrifice and aligning your life with His Spirit.

Personal Reflection

The number nine stands as both warning and promise. It tells us that judgment is inevitable, but the outcome depends on whether we yield to the Spirit. As you reflect, consider whether your life is fragrant with fruit or marked by finality.

God's Spirit calls us to life. To ignore His judgment is to invite destruction, but to surrender is to bear eternal fruit.

Where am I resisting the Spirit's judgment? How will I embrace His call to fruitfulness? What step will I take today to live as the aroma of Christ?

Closing Prayer: *Lord, thank You for the number nine that preaches both fruit and judgment. Teach me to yield to Your Spirit so that my life bears fruit that remains. Deliver me from rebellion and finality, and let me live as a testimony of resurrection life in Christ. Amen.*

Chapter 10

The Number Ten

Perfect Order

The steps of a good man are ordered by the Lord, and He delights in his way.
(Psalm 37:23, NKJV)

The number ten is God's signature of perfect order. From the beginning, it has been tied to the establishment of His Kingdom and His plan for humanity. Ten is one of the four "perfect numbers," representing God's way of putting things into alignment with His will. When Pharaoh exalted himself as god, ten plagues revealed who the true Boss was. When Israel attempted to live without divine leadership, God gave them Ten Commandments. Time and again, when humanity strayed into disorder, God sent His number ten to restore balance.

This truth echoes through generations. Noah, the tenth from Adam, was chosen to reset the world through the flood. Abraham, the tenth from Noah, became the father of faith, initiating a covenant that ordered the nations. King David, the tenth from Judah, was chosen to establish a kingdom after God's own heart. In every cycle of ten, God reveals His authority, His plan, and His order.

Perfect order is not human control but divine alignment. Jesus' parables and teachings consistently reveal that humility brings us into order, while pride invites judgment. Whether through the Ten Commandments, the tithe of one-tenth, or the ten generations that mark new beginnings, God uses the number ten to preach His message: submit to His order, and life flourishes; resist His order, and chaos reigns.

The challenge for us is to examine our own lives. Are our steps ordered by the Lord, or are we resisting His design? Ten calls us back to the reality that Christ is not our "copilot" but our

King. Only when He is the head do our lives come into true alignment with His Kingdom order.

Focus Point

And build an altar unto the Lord your God on top of this rock in the ordered place. (Judges 6:26, KJV)

This verse highlights the principle of ten: God's order requires an "ordered place." Worship, obedience, and daily living must align with His design. When we bring our lives into order under Him, He establishes His Kingdom in and through us.

Main Theme

Ten represents God's perfect order and Kingdom alignment. It appears in the commandments, in generations, and in tithes, reminding us that everything belongs to Him. Perfect order is not optional; it is the foundation of God's plan for creation and redemption.

"Ten is God's seal of perfect order, calling us to align our lives under His Kingdom rule."

Key Scriptures

- *The steps of a good man are ordered by the Lord, and He delights in his way.* (Psalm 37:23, NKJV)
- *So the Lord said to Moses: "Go in to Pharaoh; for I have hardened his heart... and that you may tell in the hearing of your son and your son's son the mighty things I have done in Egypt."* (Exodus 10:1–2, NKJV)
- *"Bring all the tithes into the storehouse, that there may be food in My house, and try Me now in this," says the Lord of hosts, "If I will not open for you the windows of heaven and pour out for you such blessing that there will not be room enough to receive it."* (Malachi 3:10, NKJV)

Key Points

- **Ten as Kingdom Order** The number ten always signals God's authority and perfect alignment with His will.
- **Noah the Tenth** God reset creation through Noah, the tenth generation from Adam, establishing new order.
- **Abraham the Tenth** The covenant was set in motion with Abraham, the tenth from Noah, as the father of faith.
- **David the Tenth** The tenth from Judah, David, was chosen to establish God's kingdom after His own heart.
- **Ten Plagues, Ten Commandments** God displayed His sovereignty through ten plagues and established His covenant through ten laws.
- **The Tithe of Ten** Giving one-tenth back to God acknowledges His ownership and establishes financial order.
- **Ten in Creation** Genesis 1 repeats "God said" ten times, declaring that His Word orders the universe.

Journaling Questions

Journaling about the number ten helps us evaluate where our lives are aligned—or misaligned —with God's order. Writing down these reflections makes us aware of areas where pride resists His authority and where humility invites His Kingdom rule. It reminds us that order is not about control but about submitting to His headship.

Answering these questions will help readers see God's hand in their timelines, finances, and daily walk. Journaling brings clarity on whether their lives reflect His perfect order or drift toward self-rule. It provides an opportunity to surrender again to His design.

Perfect Order in My Life

Where do I see God's perfect order at work, and where do I resist it?

____

____

____

____

The Generations of Ten

How does God's use of ten through Noah, Abraham, and David encourage me about His plan for my own timeline?

____

____

____

____

____

____

The Ten Commandments

What do the commandments reveal about God's desire for order in my life today?

____

____

____

____

____

____

The Tithe Test

Am I trusting God with my resources by honoring Him with the tithe?

____

____

____

____

____

____

Ordered Steps

What practical steps can I take to bring my life into greater alignment with God's order?

____

____

____

____

____

____

____

Actionable Steps

Surrender to His Headship
Consciously declare Christ as King, not merely helper, aligning your life under His rule.

Honor God with the Tithe
Commit to giving the first tenth of your income to God, trusting Him to bless the rest.

Establish Ordered Practices
Build spiritual disciplines—prayer, worship, and Scripture—that bring order and structure to your walk with Him.

Personal Reflection

The number ten declares loudly that God is a God of order. It calls us to align with His design rather than pursue our own way. As you reflect, consider whether Christ is truly head of your life or if He has been reduced to a secondary role.

When our lives are out of order, chaos follows. But when we align with His plan, blessing flows, and His Kingdom is revealed. Ten is God's seal that He is the Boss, and we are called to trust His perfect order.

Where have I resisted God's order? How will I surrender control and align with His Kingdom? What step will I take today to live under His perfect order?

Closing Prayer: *Father, thank You for the number ten and its message of perfect order. Align my life with Your will and teach me to walk in Your Kingdom design. Help me to surrender every area where I resist You, and let my life reflect the order and blessing of living under Your headship. Amen.*

Chapter 11

The Number Eleven

Valor or Disorder

Now faith is the substance of things hoped for, the evidence of things not seen. For by it the elders obtained a good testimony. (Hebrews 11:1–2, NKJV)

The number eleven carries a paradox—it can represent heroic valor when redeemed or disastrous disorder when unredeemed. Eleven sits between ten, the number of perfect order, and twelve, the number of perfect government. When man's weakness (six) is added into God's order (ten), but short of God's government (twelve), the result is disorder. Yet, when redeemed, God stamps the number eleven on acts of courage, faith, and sacrifice.

The Bible's "Faith Hall of Fame" in Hebrews 11 is the clearest example. This chapter celebrates men and women who stood against impossible odds through faith, and it is marked with the number eleven. Likewise, history echoes the same pattern—Veterans Day falls on 11/11, commemorating the 11th hour of the 11th day of the 11th month when World War I ended. In moments of great courage, God stamps eleven to honor heroes.

On the other hand, eleven also marks disorder. Canaan, cursed for his father's rebellion, had eleven sons. Samson, betrayed for 1,100 pieces of silver, fell into chaos because he failed to honor God's calling. Even the phrase "the 11th hour" reminds us of urgency and finality—it is the last chance before order is restored. Eleven warns that being out of order invites judgment, whether for nations, churches, or individuals.

The challenge is to decide whether our lives bear the redeemed mark of valor or the unredeemed mark of disorder. Eleven is a dividing line between collapse and courage, between chaos and faith.

Focus Point

But the people who know their God shall be strong, and carry out great exploits. (Daniel 11:32, NKJV)

This verse captures the redeemed meaning of eleven. Those who know their God rise in valor and perform mighty deeds. Eleven is not just a number of chaos but also a banner of courage, marking lives that testify of faith and endurance.

Main Theme

Eleven preaches a dual message: unredeemed, it speaks of disorder and collapse; redeemed, it celebrates valor, faith, and courage. It warns against rebellion while inspiring believers to rise as heroes of faith.

"Eleven is God's paradox—disorder in rebellion or valor in redemption."

Key Scriptures

- *Now faith is the substance of things hoped for, the evidence of things not seen. For by it the elders obtained a good testimony.* (Hebrews 11:1–2, NKJV)
- *But the people who know their God shall be strong, and carry out great exploits.* (Daniel 11:32, NKJV)
- *And about the eleventh hour he went out and found others standing idle, and said to them, "Why have you been standing here idle all day?"* (Matthew 20:6, NKJV)

Key Points

- **Disorder Defined** Eleven represents disintegration, falling short of God's order and government.
- **Heroes of Faith** Hebrews 11 celebrates men and women who bore the redeemed mark of eleven through faith.

- **Veterans Day and Valor** 11/11 marks remembrance of courageous soldiers and the prophetic sign of valor.
- **Samson's Failure** Betrayed for 1,100 pieces of silver, Samson's life demonstrates eleven as judgment on disorder.
- **Canaan's Curse** Canaan, with eleven sons, reveals rebellion's fruit—disorder and judgment.
- **The Urgency of the Eleventh Hour** The eleventh hour speaks of urgency, finality, and the last chance before God's order comes.
- **Christ and Completion** Jesus, living 33 years (3 × 11), reveals how eleven, when redeemed, points to the ultimate victory of the Cross.

Journaling Questions

Journaling about eleven helps us discern whether our lives reflect valor or disorder. Writing invites us to confront where rebellion has produced chaos and where faith has produced courage. It gives space to see how God's number works both as warning and as encouragement.

Through these reflections, readers will find clarity on whether they are aligned with God's order or drifting toward collapse. Journaling presses us to embrace the redeemed meaning of eleven—living as heroes of faith who rise in courage for God's Kingdom.

Disorder in My Life

Where have I seen signs of disorder in my life that need to be brought under God's order?

____

____

____

____

____

____

____

Acts of Valor

What is one way I have stood in faith when it would have been easier to shrink back?

The Eleventh Hour

Where is God calling me to act urgently, rather than delaying obedience?

Learning from Samson

What lessons can I learn from Samson's failure to honor his calling?

Living as a Hero of Faith

What does it look like for me to live as one marked by valor in today's world?

____
____
____
____
____
____

Actionable Steps

Bring Disorder Into Order
Identify one area of your life that feels unstable and intentionally surrender it to God's authority.

Stand in Valor
Step into a situation requiring courage, trusting God to empower your faith as He did the heroes of Hebrews 11.

Respond at the Eleventh Hour
Take immediate action in an area where you have delayed obedience, treating this moment as urgent.

Personal Reflection

The number eleven is a prophetic paradox. It warns us of disorder when we resist God but also honors us with valor when we walk in faith. As you reflect, ask yourself whether your life bears the redeemed mark of eleven.

Faith requires courage, and disorder is defeated when we yield to God's authority. Eleven challenges us to live as heroes of faith, rising in the urgency of the eleventh hour.

Am I living in valor or disorder? Where do I need to act urgently in faith? How can I become a hero of faith marked by God's redeemed number eleven?

Closing Prayer: *Father, thank You for the lesson of the number eleven. Expose the areas of disorder in my life and teach me to walk in Your order. Give me courage to rise in valor and faith, standing as one marked by Your Spirit. May my life honor You as a testimony of courage and victory. Amen.*

Chapter 12

The Number Twelve

Perfect Government

And he hath on his vesture and on his thigh a name written, KING OF KINGS, AND LORD OF LORDS. (Revelation 19:16, KJV)

The number twelve is God's seal of perfect government. It proclaims His rulership, His control, and His divine order over nations and individuals alike. While we often think of government as human rule, twelve reminds us that even kings, presidents, and emperors are governed by God. He uses this number to declare that His authority is supreme and His plan is unshakable.

Throughout history and Scripture, twelve appears whenever God reveals His order in leadership. There were twelve tribes of Israel, each carrying a distinct place in His covenant plan. Jesus chose twelve disciples to establish the foundation of the Church. The New Jerusalem is described with twelve gates, twelve angels, twelve foundations, and dimensions marked by twelve, showing God's eternal government in His Kingdom.

Even earthly rulers acknowledge this truth, knowingly or not. George Washington, in his farewell address, declared, "It is impossible to govern the world without God and the Bible." From Nebuchadnezzar, whom God called "My servant," to modern leaders, the message is the same: God rules over all. Authority is permitted only because it is given from above, and it will one day be brought into full submission under Christ.

The challenge of twelve is for us to live as those under God's perfect government. Are our lives aligned with His authority, or are we fighting against His order? Twelve reminds us that Christ is King of kings and Lord of lords, and every throne must bow before Him.

Focus Point

Then cometh the end, when he shall have delivered up the kingdom to God, even the Father; when he shall have put down all rule and all authority and power. (1 Corinthians 15:24, KJV)

This verse captures the heart of twelve: God will put down all authority that resists Him. His government is perfect, eternal, and final. The number twelve teaches us to trust His plan and to live as citizens of His Kingdom even now.

Main Theme

Twelve preaches God's perfect government. It declares that all leadership is subject to Him, that His plan is eternal, and that His Kingdom is unshakable. Twelve reminds us that there is order, there is purpose, and there is a King whose rule is perfect.

"Twelve is God's seal of perfect government, declaring His authority is final and eternal."

Key Scriptures

- *And he hath on his vesture and on his thigh a name written, KING OF KINGS, AND LORD OF LORDS.* (Revelation 19:16, KJV)
- *On the east three gates; on the north three gates; on the south three gates; and on the west three gates. And the wall of the city had twelve foundations, and in them the names of the twelve apostles of the Lamb.* (Revelation 21:13–14, KJV)
- *Jesus answered, "Thou couldest have no power at all against me, except it were given thee from above."* (John 19:11, KJV)

Key Points

- **The Twelve Tribes** God's covenant people were divided into twelve tribes, revealing divine order in community.

- **The Twelve Disciples** Jesus appointed twelve apostles to establish His Kingdom work on earth.
- **The New Jerusalem** Heaven's city is marked with twelve gates, twelve angels, and twelve foundations.
- **Twelve in Miracles** Jesus fed the multitude and twelve baskets of fragments remained, testifying of divine sufficiency.
- **The First Words of Jesus** At age twelve, Jesus first spoke in the temple, showing alignment with His Father's government.
- **Authority Permitted** All rulers, even wicked ones, are under God's hand and used to fulfill His plan.
- **Final Authority** One day all governments will be brought down, and Christ's rule alone will remain.

Journaling Questions

Journaling about the number twelve invites us to reflect on God's authority over every area of life. Writing helps us see whether we are living as citizens of His Kingdom or resisting His government. It presses us to surrender control and align with His order.

Through these reflections, readers will recognize that life under God's government is not oppressive but liberating. It is the assurance that His rule is good, perfect, and eternal. Journaling helps us embrace His order with trust and faith.

The Twelve Tribes

How does the story of the twelve tribes remind me that God has a place and purpose for me?

____

____

____

____

____

____

____

Living as a Disciple

What can I learn from the twelve disciples about living under Christ's authority?

New Jerusalem Vision

How does the vision of twelve gates and twelve foundations inspire my hope in God's Kingdom?

Authority in My Life

Where am I resisting God's government, and how can I submit to His rule?

Trusting God's Plan

What areas of my life need to come into alignment with God's order?

____

____

____

____

____

____

Actionable Steps

Surrender Control
Acknowledge areas where you resist God's authority and submit them to Him in prayer.

Live as a Kingdom Citizen
Choose one daily action that reflects life under God's rule—integrity, service, or faithfulness.

Honor God's Order
Commit to honoring leaders in your life, remembering that their authority is permitted by God.

Personal Reflection

The number twelve proclaims loudly that God rules. It challenges us to bring every part of life under His authority. As you reflect, consider whether you are living aligned with His government or resisting His order.

God's Kingdom is not chaos—it is perfect government. Christ's rule is not temporary—it is eternal. Twelve reminds us that His plan is final and His authority unshakable.

Where am I resisting God's rule? How will I live as a citizen of His Kingdom? What step will I take to align with His perfect government?

____

____

Closing Prayer: *Father, thank You for the number twelve and its message of perfect government. Teach me to live under Your authority and to trust Your plan. Align my life with Your order, and help me to honor You as King of kings and Lord of lords. Amen.*

Chapter 13

The Number Thirteen

Rebellion

But the men of Sodom were wicked and sinners before the Lord exceedingly. (Genesis 13:13, KJV)

Thirteen is the Bible's number of rebellion. It represents apostasy, the rejection of truth once received, and the stubborn insistence on defiance against God. From the very first pages of Scripture, the thirteenth verse of the thirteenth chapter of Genesis declares the rebellion of Sodom. Nimrod, whose name means "rebel," is the thirteenth from Adam, and he founded Babylon—the root of all false religion and idolatry. Thirteen shows us that when man rises against God, destruction follows.

The Bible connects thirteen again and again to rebellion. Jesus declared in Matthew 13:13 that He spoke in parables because the rebellious hearts of people refused to understand. In Mark 7, thirteen rebellious things are listed that come from within the heart of man, including blasphemy, pride, and foolishness. Even Judas, the betrayer, appears in John 13, where Jesus announces His treason at the Last Supper. The entire thirteenth chapter of Revelation is devoted to the Antichrist and the beast, the ultimate rebellion against God.

History also bears this imprint. Haman decreed the extermination of the Jews on the thirteenth day of the first month. Words tied to rebellion—rebel, treason, dragon, carnal—each appear thirteen times in Scripture. Even the constellation Draco the Dragon, a symbol of satanic rebellion, carries thirteen stars. Again and again, the number preaches its message: rebellion brings ruin.

The lesson of thirteen is sobering. While the world celebrates rebellion as strength, Scripture exposes it as a path to destruction. Yet even here, God offers redemption. Jesus bore thirty-nine stripes—thirteen times three—to break the curse of rebellion and bring healing. Thirteen warns us of the cost of sin but also points to the hope found in Christ, who redeems even the most rebellious heart.

Focus Point

For rebellion is as the sin of witchcraft, and stubbornness is as iniquity and idolatry. (1 Samuel 15:23, NKJV)

This verse reveals the danger of rebellion—it is not a small misstep but a sin as serious as witchcraft. Thirteen exposes rebellion as destructive, but God offers grace to those who turn back. His mercy is greater than our defiance.

Main Theme

Thirteen preaches rebellion, apostasy, and the dangers of resisting God's authority. It marks the actions of Nimrod, Sodom, Judas, and the Antichrist, but it also points us to redemption through Christ's stripes.

"Thirteen warns: rebellion destroys, but Christ redeems."

Key Scriptures

- *But the men of Sodom were wicked and sinners before the Lord exceedingly.* (Genesis 13:13, KJV)
- *Therefore I speak to them in parables, because seeing they do not see, and hearing they do not hear, nor do they understand.* (Matthew 13:13, NKJV)
- *But He was wounded for our transgressions, He was bruised for our iniquities; the chastisement for our peace was upon Him, and by His stripes we are healed.* (Isaiah 53:5, NKJV)

Key Points

- **Thirteen and Apostasy** Thirteen is tied to falling away from truth, showing rebellion's devastating cost.
- **Nimrod the Rebel** The thirteenth from Adam, Nimrod founded Babylon and all false religion.
- **Thirteen Things of the Heart** Mark 7 lists thirteen evils proceeding from man's heart, exposing human depravity.
- **John 13 and Judas** The betrayal of Christ is recorded in John 13, where Judas falls into rebellion.
- **Revelation 13 and the Beast** The Antichrist rises in Revelation 13 as the ultimate picture of defiance.
- **Thirteen in History** From Haman's decree to Draco's constellation, thirteen marks rebellion in history.
- **Redemption from Rebellion** Christ bore thirty-nine stripes, completing the curse of rebellion and offering healing.

Journaling Questions

Journaling about the number thirteen challenges us to confront rebellion in our own lives. Writing about these themes helps us identify areas of stubbornness or resistance to God's authority. It presses us to see rebellion not as harmless independence but as a destructive path.

By reflecting on these truths, readers will see both the danger of rebellion and the hope of redemption. Journaling creates space to surrender areas of defiance to Christ, allowing His healing stripes to restore and redeem what rebellion has broken.

Rebellion Exposed

Where have I seen rebellion in my life, and what has it cost me spiritually or relationally?

____

____

____

____

____

Thirteen Things of the Heart

Which of the thirteen rebellious traits listed in Mark 7 am I most vulnerable to, and how can I surrender it?

____

____

____

____

____

____

Judas's Lesson

What does Judas' betrayal teach me about the dangers of rebellion in the heart?

____

____

____

____

____

____

Redeemed from Stripes

How does the truth that Jesus bore thirty-nine stripes for rebellion bring hope to my life?

____

____

____

____

____

____

RESISTING BABYLON

Where am I tempted to align with the "Babylon" systems of this world rather than with God's Kingdom?

____

____

____

____

____

____

ACTIONABLE STEPS

Identify Rebellion
Name one area of your life where you've resisted God's authority and bring it into prayerful submission.

Repent and Return
Choose repentance where rebellion has taken root, asking God for forgiveness and restoration.

Embrace Healing
Declare by faith that Christ's stripes have broken the curse of rebellion and walk in His healing power.

PERSONAL REFLECTION

Thirteen is a sobering number. It warns of rebellion's destructive power, but it also points to redemption through Christ. As you reflect, ask whether your life bears the mark of rebellion or the mark of healing.

God does not leave us in rebellion—He offers stripes for healing, forgiveness for sin, and restoration for brokenness. Thirteen preaches destruction, but it also whispers hope through Jesus Christ.

Where am I still resisting God's authority? How will I surrender rebellion to Him today? What step can I take to embrace His healing and redemption?

____

____

____

____

____

____

____

____

____

____

____

____

____

____

____

____

____

____

____

____

____

____

____

____

____

____

____

____

____

____

Closing Prayer: *Father, thank You for the lesson of the number thirteen. Expose any rebellion in my heart and lead me into repentance. Thank You that Jesus bore stripes for my healing and redemption. Deliver me from the curse of rebellion and align me fully with Your Kingdom. Amen.*

Chapter 14

The Number Fourteen

Promises and Fear

So all the generations from Abraham to David are fourteen generations, from David until the captivity in Babylon are fourteen generations, and from the captivity in Babylon until the Christ are fourteen generations. (Matthew 1:17, NKJV)

The number fourteen carries the weight of generational promises and the reverence of holy fear. When God spoke of deliverance, it was on the fourteenth day of the month that Israel was set free from Egypt, fulfilling a promise over four hundred years old. Fourteen preaches that God does not forget His word; His promises may seem delayed, but they are certain.

Generations echo this message. From Abraham to David, David to Babylon, and Babylon to Christ—three sets of fourteen generations declare the unbroken line of God's faithfulness. Matthew ties this lineage to the name David, whose numerical value is fourteen. It was no accident. The promises of God are not left in ambiguity; they are sealed in numbers, names, and generations.

The fear of the Lord is tied to this same number. The phrase appears fourteen times in Proverbs, reminding us that true wisdom begins with reverence for God. The moon, waxing and waning in its fourteen-day cycle, preaches promises reflected from God's light. Even the Stations of the Cross, numbering fourteen, speak of the suffering Christ endured on the fourteenth day of Nisan during Passover, a reminder that promises are costly and fear of God is necessary.

The question is whether we will live in the certainty of God's promises and the humility of

His fear. Fourteen reminds us that God will keep His word across generations, but it also warns us that promises are received in reverence, not presumption.

Focus Point

By humility and the fear of the Lord are riches and honor and life. (Proverbs 22:4, NKJV)

This verse reveals that the fear of the Lord is not terror but reverence. It brings blessing, honor, and life. The number fourteen declares that promises are secure, but they are accessed through holy fear.

Main Theme

Fourteen is God's number of generational promises and holy fear. It points to His covenant faithfulness across time and warns that His promises are held by those who walk in reverence.

"Fourteen preaches God's faithfulness through generations and the fear that keeps us aligned with His promises."

Key Scriptures

- *So all the generations from Abraham to David are fourteen generations...* (Matthew 1:17, NKJV)
- *Now you shall keep it until the fourteenth day of the same month....It is the Lord's Passover.* (Exodus 12:6,11, NKJV)
- *By humility and the fear of the Lord are riches and honor and life.* (Proverbs 22:4, NKJV)

Key Points

- **The Day of Deliverance** On the fourteenth day, God delivered Israel from Egypt, proving His promises never fail.

- **Three Fourteens in Generations** Matthew marks Christ's arrival through three sets of fourteen, showing generational faithfulness.
- **The Name of David** Fourteen is the numerical value of "David," tying the promise of the Messiah to God's covenant.
- **The Fourteen Stations of the Cross** Christ's suffering on the fourteenth day of Nisan fulfills promises through sacrifice.
- **The Moon's Witness** Fourteen-day cycles of the moon reflect the promises of God's faithfulness to His bride.
- **The Fear of the Lord** The phrase appears fourteen times in Proverbs, teaching reverence as the path to wisdom.
- **Promises Across Generations** Fourteen proclaims that God keeps covenant promises not just for a season but for generations.

Journaling Questions

Journaling about the number fourteen encourages us to trace God's promises in our own lives and families. Writing reflections helps us see the ways God has kept His word through generations, even when fulfillment seemed delayed. It reminds us that His timing is precise, and His promises never fail.

By answering these questions, readers will embrace both the faithfulness of God's promises and the reverence of fearing Him. Journaling creates space to remember His generational blessings and to live humbly, aware that promises are fulfilled through faith and fear.

Generational Faithfulness

Where do I see God's promises kept across generations in my family or community?

___

___

___

___

___

___

___

Day of Deliverance

How does the first fourteenth-day Passover in Exodus remind me to trust God's timing?

Fear of the Lord

What does it mean for me to live with reverence, not presumption, toward God's promises?

The Cross and Promises

How does the suffering of Christ on Passover deepen my trust in God's covenant?

Moon and Reflection

How do the cycles of creation, like the moon, remind me of God's unchanging promises?

____

____

____

____

____

____

Actionable Steps

Remember His Promises
Write down one generational promise God has fulfilled in your life and give Him thanks.

Practice Holy Fear
Commit to daily humility before God, inviting His wisdom into your decisions.

Trust His Timing
Identify one area where you're impatient and choose to trust God's precise timing.

Personal Reflection

The number fourteen resounds with God's covenant faithfulness and the call to reverence. It invites us to live as those who trust His promises across generations and walk humbly in the fear of the Lord. As you reflect, consider where His promises are unfolding in your life and whether reverence is shaping your response.

Promises without fear lead to presumption, but fear without promises leads to despair. Fourteen binds the two together—hope in His promises and humility in His presence.

Where am I trusting God's promises? How am I living in reverence before Him? What step will I take to align myself with His covenant faithfulness today?

____

____

Closing Prayer: *Faithful God, thank You for the number fourteen that reminds me of Your generational promises and the call to fear You. Teach me to trust Your timing, to honor You with reverence, and to remember that You keep covenant across the ages. Let my life reflect both faith in Your promises and humility before Your throne. Amen.*

Chapter 15

The Number Fifteen

Rest and Overcoming Death

There remains therefore a rest for the people of God. (Hebrews 4:9, NKJV)

The number fifteen preaches grace perfectly completed. It is three times five—three representing perfect completion and five representing grace. Together, they declare that rest is found when grace has done its perfect work. Fifteen is tied to consecration, to being set apart for God, and to overcoming death itself.

Israel rested on the fifteenth day three times each year during the feasts. This date marked moments of holy visitation, consecration, and rest in God's presence. The feasts were not just traditions; they were prophetic markers pointing to the truth that ultimate rest comes only in Him. By His grace, death itself is overcome, and His people enter into the eternal Sabbath of God.

Scripture overflows with illustrations of this number. The waters of Noah's flood rose fifteen cubits above the highest mountain before the Ark rested, declaring that what destroyed the world could not touch those preserved by God. The Jews overcame annihilation on the fifteenth day in the time of Esther, turning death into celebration. Hezekiah was given fifteen extra years of life, a personal victory over the grave. Even Bethany, where Jesus raised Lazarus from the dead, is fifteen furlongs from Jerusalem—a reminder that resurrection life is never far away.

Fifteen is God's number that whispers hope: rest is not weakness but victory, and death is not final but conquered. The challenge is whether we will live consecrated, resting in His grace, and confident in His promise of eternal life.

FOCUS POINT

However, Jesus spoke of his death: but they thought that He was speaking about taking rest in sleep. (John 11:13, NKJV)

This verse connects death and rest, showing that in Christ, even death is only a form of rest. The number fifteen declares that God's grace is sufficient to carry us beyond death into eternal life.

MAIN THEME

Fifteen preaches rest and the overcoming of death through God's grace. It proclaims consecration, victory, and hope. Where others see endings, fifteen testifies of new beginnings and the eternal Sabbath of God.

"Fifteen is God's number of rest—grace perfected to overcome even death."

KEY SCRIPTURES

- *There remains therefore a rest for the people of God.* (Hebrews 4:9, NKJV)
- *However, Jesus spoke of his death: but they thought that He was speaking about taking rest in sleep.* (John 11:13, NKJV)
- *Thus says the Lord, "I have heard your prayer, I have seen your tears; surely I will heal you...and will add to your days fifteen years."* (2 Kings 20:5-6, NKJV)

KEY POINTS

- **Grace Perfected** Fifteen is three times five, showing grace brought to perfect completion and rest.
- **Feasts on the Fifteenth** God's people rested on the fifteenth day during feasts, consecrated for holy visitation.
- **Noah's Fifteen Cubits** The floodwaters rose fifteen cubits before the Ark rested safely on Ararat.

- **Esther's Fifteenth Day** The Jews overcame death and turned defeat into victory on the fifteenth day.
- **Hezekiah's Fifteen Years** God granted fifteen more years of life, showing victory over death's decree.
- **Bethany and Resurrection** Bethany, fifteen furlongs from Jerusalem, was the place where Lazarus rose to life.
- **Rest Beyond Death** Fifteen connects rest with overcoming death, pointing us to eternal life in Christ.

Journaling Questions

Journaling about the number fifteen helps us recognize where God is calling us to enter His rest. It reminds us that grace is not just for survival but for victory—even over death. Writing about these truths presses us to live consecrated and to see death not as defeat but as transition into eternal rest.

By answering these prompts, readers will learn to embrace rest as a mark of victory, to see God's grace as their strength, and to live with the confidence that even death is conquered in Christ. Journaling creates space to surrender to His rest and celebrate His overcoming power.

Grace to Rest

Where do I need to let God's grace lead me into true rest?

___

___

___

___

___

___

___

THE FIFTEENTH DAY

How do the feasts on the fifteenth day teach me about consecration and holy visitation?

____
____
____
____
____
____

OVERCOMING DEATH

What do Hezekiah's added years or Esther's deliverance teach me about victory over death?

____
____
____
____
____
____

MY ARK OF REST

What "floods" has God carried me above, giving me rest when others were overwhelmed?

____
____
____
____
____
____

Resurrection Hope

How does the story of Lazarus remind me to live with faith in God's power over death?

____

____

____

____

____

____

Actionable Steps

Enter His Rest
Set aside intentional time to rest in God's presence, trusting His grace to carry you.

Celebrate Victory
Mark a day of thanksgiving for ways God has delivered you from death or destruction.

Live Consecrated
Dedicate an area of your life afresh to God, setting it apart as holy unto Him.

Personal Reflection

The number fifteen resounds with the promise that God's grace is enough to overcome death itself. It calls us into rest, not as an escape but as a victory. As you reflect, consider whether you are striving in your own strength or resting in His grace.

Rest is not inactivity—it is reigning with Christ. Fifteen preaches that even in death, we find rest, because in Him, death is swallowed up in victory.

Where am I resisting God's rest? How can I live consecrated in His grace? What does it mean for me to see death not as an end but as rest in Christ?

____

____

Closing Prayer: *Father, thank You for the number fifteen that preaches rest and overcoming death. Teach me to live consecrated and to trust Your grace as sufficient. Let me walk in the victory of Your rest, confident that even death has been defeated by Christ. Amen.*

Chapter 16

The Number Sixteen

The Love of God

Beloved, let us love one another, for love is of God; and everyone who loves is born of God and knows God. (1 John 4:7, NKJV)

Sixteen is God's number of love. It is most clearly seen in the "Love Chapter" of 1 Corinthians 13, where sixteen distinct attributes of love are listed. These are not sentimental feelings or shallow affections but the deep, sacrificial, God-kind of love that never fails. In a world that confuses love with desire or convenience, sixteen reminds us that God's love is steadfast, patient, kind, and eternal.

Throughout Scripture, sixteen reappears to preach the message of love. There are sixteen Jehovah titles that reveal God's character—our Provider, Healer, Shepherd, Banner, and more—each face of His nature testifying to His love. The Bible also contains powerful 3:16 verses, each revealing some facet of God's love. John 3:16 is the most famous, declaring God's gift of His Son. But 1 John 3:16 reminds us that this same love calls us to lay down our lives for others. Love is not passive; it is action, sacrifice, and covenant.

Even Psalm 91, long known as the chapter of divine protection, carries sixteen verses declaring how God's love preserves those who dwell in Him. Sixteen baptisms, sixteen commands given to Israel, and sixteen judges raised up in the Old Testament all carry the imprint of this number. Sixteen insists that to know God is to know love, and to grow in love is to grow in Him.

The challenge of sixteen is simple yet profound: are we reflecting the love of God, or are we content with shallow imitations? Sixteen does not allow us to stay lukewarm; it calls us to love as He loves, to live as He lived, and to reveal His love to a world desperate for it.

FOCUS POINT

By this we know love, because He laid down His life for us. And we also ought to lay down our lives for the brethren. (1 John 3:16, NKJV)

This verse declares the true nature of love—sacrificial, selfless, and rooted in Christ's example. Sixteen teaches us that love is not simply received; it must also be given.

MAIN THEME

Sixteen preaches the love of God—sacrificial, covenantal, and eternal. It reminds us that to know Him is to love Him, and to love Him is to love others.

"Sixteen is God's number of love, revealing His character, His covenant, and His call to lay down our lives."

KEY SCRIPTURES

- *Beloved, let us love one another, for love is of God; and everyone who loves is born of God and knows God.* (1 John 4:7, NKJV)
- *For God so loved the world that He gave His only begotten Son, that whoever believes in Him should not perish but have everlasting life.* (John 3:16, NKJV)
- *By this we know love, because He laid down His life for us. And we also ought to lay down our lives for the brethren.* (1 John 3:16, NKJV)

KEY POINTS

- **Sixteen Attributes of Love** 1 Corinthians 13 lists sixteen traits of true love, showing it as patient, kind, humble, and enduring.
- **Sixteen Jehovah Titles** From Jehovah Jireh to Jehovah Shalom, sixteen names reveal His loving character to His people.
- **The Famous 3:16s** Verses like John 3:16 and 1 John 3:16 center the Bible's message on God's sacrificial love.

- **Psalm 91's Sixteen Verses** This protection chapter highlights sixteen promises tied to dwelling in God's love.
- **Sixteen Judges** Even in times of rebellion, God raised sixteen judges, proving His love never abandoned Israel.
- **Sixteen Baptisms and Commands** Scripture's patterns of sixteen affirm love's role in covenant, obedience, and relationship with God.
- **Love as Action** Sixteen preaches that love is not mere words but selfless action rooted in Christ's example.

JOURNALING QUESTIONS

Journaling about the number sixteen helps us measure our love against God's standard. Writing reminds us that love is not simply emotion but obedience and sacrifice. It presses us to reflect on how well we embody the sixteen attributes of 1 Corinthians 13 in our daily walk.

By answering these prompts, readers will see where God's love is flowing freely in their lives and where it is lacking. Journaling invites us to embrace His call to love sacrificially, to live generously, and to reveal His character in every relationship.

WHERE DO I STAND?

Which of the sixteen descriptions of love in 1 Corinthians 13 is God calling me to grow in most right now?

____

____

____

____

____

____

____

Jehovah's Love Revealed

Which of the sixteen Jehovah titles has been most personal to me in this season?

____

____

____

____

____

____

John 3:16 vs. 1 John 3:16

How do these two verses together challenge me to both receive and give God's love?

____

____

____

____

____

____

Psalm 91's Love

How do the sixteen promises of Psalm 91 encourage me to dwell in God's love daily?

____

____

____

____

____

____

Love in Action

What is one practical way I can lay down my life in love for someone else this week?

____
____
____
____
____
____

Actionable Steps

Practice a Love Attribute
Choose one of the sixteen descriptions of love and intentionally practice it each day.

Claim a Jehovah Title
Pray using one of the sixteen Jehovah titles, declaring His love in that area of your life.

Live Sacrificially
Identify one opportunity to lay down your own comfort for the sake of loving someone else.

Personal Reflection

The number sixteen reminds us that God is love and that His love is not abstract but deeply personal. As you reflect, ask yourself whether your life reflects the fullness of His love or if you've settled for lesser versions.

God's love is eternal, covenantal, and sacrificial. Sixteen calls us to embrace that love, live in it, and share it boldly.

Am I truly reflecting the sixteenfold love of God? How will I demonstrate His love to others this week? What step can I take to live out the fullness of His covenant love?

____
____

Closing Prayer: *Father, thank You for the number sixteen that reveals Your love. Teach me to live out the attributes of true love, to know You more deeply through Your names, and to reflect Your love in every part of my life. Let my life be a testimony of Your covenant love that never fails. Amen.*

Chapter 17

The Number Seventeen

Overcoming Victory

But thanks be to God, who gives us the victory through our Lord Jesus Christ.
(1 Corinthians 15:57, NKJV)

Seventeen is the number of overcoming victory. It marks the moments when God's people prevail against impossible odds, not by human effort but by His power. When the Ark rested on Ararat on the seventeenth day of the month, it proclaimed that judgment had passed and victory had come. When Israel crossed the Red Sea on the seventeenth day, it declared deliverance from bondage and triumph over their enemies.

Seventeen is woven into the lives of God's people as a testimony of His faithfulness. Jacob lived in Egypt for seventeen years, showing the grace of completion in a foreign land. Jeremiah prayed seventeen times before sealing his faith with a land purchase of seventeen shekels, a prophetic act of hope. Most profoundly, Jesus was resurrected on the seventeenth day of the month, securing the greatest victory in human history—death defeated, life eternal secured.

The book of Revelation ties this number to the promises for overcomers. Seventeen distinct promises are given to those who conquer by faith: eating from the tree of life, escaping the second death, receiving hidden manna, a white stone with a new name, power over nations, and eternal inheritance as God's sons. These are not empty metaphors but divine guarantees for those who remain faithful.

Seventeen is God's assurance that victory is not optional but promised. It challenges us to see obstacles as opportunities for His glory and to remember that in Christ, overcoming is our inheritance.

Focus Point

He who overcomes shall inherit all things, and I will be his God and he shall be My son. (Revelation 21:7, NKJV)

This verse summarizes the message of seventeen: the promises of God belong to the overcomer. Victory is not merely surviving but inheriting all that Christ secured through His resurrection.

Main Theme

Seventeen preaches overcoming victory through Christ. It reminds us that every trial has a promised triumph and that in Jesus, we are more than conquerors.

"Seventeen is God's banner of victory—declaring that every obstacle is already overcome in Christ."

Key Scriptures

- *But thanks be to God, who gives us the victory through our Lord Jesus Christ.* (1 Corinthians 15:57, NKJV)
- *Now the Ark rested in the seventh month, the seventeenth day of the month, on the mountains of Ararat.* (Genesis 8:4, NKJV)
- *He who overcomes shall inherit all things, and I will be his God and he shall be My son.* (Revelation 21:7, NKJV)

Key Points

- **The Ark's Rest** On the seventeenth day, the Ark rested, marking victory over the flood and preservation of life.
- **Crossing the Red Sea** Israel crossed the Red Sea on the seventeenth, declaring deliverance from bondage.
- **Jacob's Seventeen Years** Seventeen years in Egypt symbolized grace and fulfillment for God's people.

- **Jeremiah's Seventeen Prayers** The prophet sealed his faith with seventeen prayers and a land purchase of seventeen shekels.
- **Christ's Resurrection** Jesus rose on the seventeenth, forever conquering death and offering eternal life.
- **Seventeen Promises in Revelation** The overcomer is promised life, power, inheritance, and identity through Christ.
- **Victory Multiplied** The number thirty-four (seventeen doubled) magnifies God's overcoming power that results in miraculous manifestations.

JOURNALING QUESTIONS

Journaling about the number seventeen helps us recognize God's victory in our lives. Writing presses us to identify where He has brought deliverance and where He is still calling us to trust for triumph. It gives us perspective to see obstacles as places where His overcoming power will be revealed.

By answering these prompts, readers will learn to live as overcomers, claiming the promises of Revelation and walking in confidence that victory belongs to them in Christ. Journaling transforms trials into testimonies of His faithfulness.

THE ARK'S REST

Where has God given me rest and victory after a season of trial or judgment?

Crossing Over

What "Red Sea" moment in my life has revealed God's power to deliver me?

____

____

____

____

____

____

Resurrection Power

How does knowing Jesus rose on the seventeenth give me hope in my own battles?

____

____

____

____

____

____

The Seventeen Promises

Which of the promises to overcomers in Revelation speaks most to me right now?

____

____

____

____

____

____

Living as an Overcomer

How can I shift my mindset from struggling to overcoming in Christ?

____

____

____

____

____

____

Actionable Steps

Declare Victory
Identify one battle in your life and declare God's victory over it by faith.

Claim a Promise
Choose one of the seventeen promises of Revelation and pray it into your life daily.

Live as an Overcomer
Adopt an attitude of overcoming by speaking and acting in alignment with Christ's triumph.

Personal Reflection

Seventeen is God's signature of overcoming. It tells us that in Christ, victory is not uncertain but guaranteed. As you reflect, ask whether you are living as a struggler or as an overcomer.

God has already written your victory in Christ. Seventeen preaches that no Red Sea, no flood, no grave, and no enemy can withstand His power.

Where am I still living as though defeat is possible? How can I embrace Christ's resurrection victory daily? What promise of Revelation will I claim as my inheritance?

____

____

____

____

Closing Prayer: *Lord Jesus, thank You for the victory of the number seventeen. Teach me to live as an overcomer, to claim Your promises, and to walk in the triumph of Your resurrection. Let every obstacle in my life become a testimony of Your overcoming power. Amen.*

Chapter 18

The Number Eighteen

Abundant Life/Sin Bondage

The thief does not come except to steal, and to kill, and to destroy. I have come that they may have life, and that they may have it more abundantly. (John 10:10, NKJV)

The number eighteen preaches a double message—abundant life in Christ or bondage to sin without Him. In Jewish tradition, the Hebrew word *chai*, meaning "life," equals eighteen. It is such a central theme that Jewish communities give gifts in multiples of eighteen, declaring blessings of life. A rabbi once explained that this number signifies God's gift of multiplied life. For believers, it points to the abundant life found in Christ, overflowing with grace and vitality.

Scripture reinforces this meaning. Abraham was promised in Genesis 18:18 that all nations would be blessed through him. Jesus declared in Matthew 18:18 that what is bound on earth will be bound in heaven, showing authority over both bondage and freedom. Even creation reflects this pattern—the average person breathes eighteen times a minute, a constant rhythm of life given by God.

Yet, unredeemed, the number eighteen warns of bondage. The Bible lists eighteen traitors, records eighteen questions demanded of Jesus, and recounts eighteen judges who ruled during Israel's disorder. In gematria, eighteen also equals 3 × 6—"man, man, man"—a picture of fleshly bondage when life is lived apart from God. The number exposes humanity's pull toward sin and the destruction it brings when grace is rejected.

The challenge of eighteen is whether we will embrace Christ's life or remain in bondage. It asks us to choose between the breath of life in Him or the suffocation of sin in our own strength.

Focus Point

Assuredly, I say to you, whatever you bind on earth will be bound in heaven, and whatever you loose on earth will be loosed in heaven. (Matthew 18:18, NKJV)

This verse highlights the dual power of eighteen—bondage or freedom. In Christ, we are given authority to break chains and release abundant life, but apart from Him, we remain bound by sin.

Main Theme

Eighteen preaches the abundance of life in Christ and the reality of bondage without Him. It is both a number of hope and a warning, declaring that the breath of life is only truly free when surrendered to God.

"Eighteen declares: In Christ there is abundant life; in the flesh there is bondage to sin."

Key Scriptures

- *Abraham shall surely become a great and mighty nation, and all the nations of the earth shall be blessed in him.* (Genesis 18:18, NKJV)
- *Assuredly, I say to you, whatever you bind on earth will be bound in heaven, and whatever you loose on earth will be loosed in heaven.* (Matthew 18:18, NKJV)
- *The thief does not come except to steal, and to kill, and to destroy. I have come that they may have life, and that they may have it more abundantly.* (John 10:10, NKJV)

Key Points

- **Life in Eighteen** The Hebrew word *chai* equals eighteen, symbolizing life and blessing.

- **Abundant Life in Christ** John 10:10 declares the fullness of life Jesus came to give.
- **Authority to Bind and Loose** Matthew 18:18 shows the believer's authority to break free from bondage and live in His liberty.
- **Eighteen in Creation** The human breath cycle—eighteen per minute—points to God's sustaining life.
- **Eighteen Traitors** Scripture lists eighteen traitors, warning of the pull toward betrayal and bondage.
- **Eighteen Judges and Questions** Periods of disorder highlight the dangers of rejecting God's rule.
- **Man, Man, Man** Eighteen as 3 × 6 warns of fleshly bondage when life is lived apart from God.

Journaling Questions

Journaling about the number eighteen invites us to examine whether we are living in the abundance of Christ or trapped in cycles of bondage. Writing helps us see how God breathes His life into our daily rhythms and where sin still suffocates us. It challenges us to claim His promise of abundant life.

By reflecting on these truths, readers will identify areas where God has multiplied His blessings and areas that need His deliverance. Journaling reminds us that abundant life is not automatic—it is chosen by surrendering to Christ's authority.

Breath of Life

Where do I recognize God's sustaining breath giving me daily life?

Abundant Living

What does abundant life in Christ look like for me right now?

____
____
____
____
____
____

Bondage Identified

What "man, man, man" cycles of the flesh still hold me in bondage?

____
____
____
____
____
____

Authority to Loose

How am I using the authority of Matthew 18:18 to walk in freedom?

____
____
____
____
____
____

Life or Bondage

Which areas of my life testify of God's life, and which reveal the bondage of sin?

____

____

____

____

____

____

____

Actionable Steps

Embrace Abundant Life
Consciously receive Christ's promise of life more abundantly by declaring it in prayer and action.

Break Chains
Identify one area of bondage and intentionally apply God's Word to loose it in His authority.

Multiply Life
Give generously—financially or through service—in multiples of eighteen as a prophetic act of life-giving.

Personal Reflection

The number eighteen presses us to decide: abundant life or sin's bondage? It reminds us that every breath is a gift from God and every day an opportunity to walk in His freedom. As you reflect, consider whether you are living bound or alive.

Christ's invitation is clear—He came to give life, and not just enough to survive but overflowing abundance.

Where am I still bound by the flesh? How will I claim Christ's abundant life today? What step can I take to walk fully in His freedom?

Closing Prayer: *Lord, thank You for the number eighteen that declares both abundant life and bondage. Teach me to choose Your life daily and to walk in the freedom of Your Spirit. Break every chain of sin, and let my life testify of the abundance only found in You. Amen.*

Chapter 19

The Number Nineteen

Covenant Order / Godless Chaos

For God is not the author of confusion but of peace, as in all the churches of the saints.
(1 Corinthians 14:33, NKJV)

The number nineteen is a paradox. Redeemed, it preaches covenant order—God's structure, faith, and divine timing. Unredeemed, it warns of godless chaos, the collapse that comes when man refuses God's authority. Scripture and history alike echo this tension. Hebrews 11 lists nineteen heroes of faith, men and women who ordered their lives under God's covenant. Yet, nineteen also appears in times of judgment, chaos, and rebellion.

Ed Vallowe, in *Biblical Mathematics*, notes the significance of nineteen in relation to both divine order and fruitfulness. The number combines ten, the symbol of order, with nine, the symbol of judgment and fruit. When redeemed, nineteen speaks of faith producing fruit through God's perfect order. But when unredeemed, it marks chaos—judgment against those who reject His covenant.

History reinforces this pattern. The northern kingdom of Israel had nineteen kings before collapsing into captivity under Assyria. Each king drifted further into disobedience, and their lack of faith destroyed the nation. In our own time, the number nineteen marks global shaking: the 9/11 attacks, carried out by nineteen hijackers, and the Covid-19 pandemic, named for its emergence in 2019. Both moments became prophetic reminders of what happens when God's order is rejected and chaos reigns.

Even creation preaches nineteen. The Hebrew calendar is ordered around a 19-year cycle to keep solar and lunar time aligned. Joshua 19 records God's fulfillment of His promise to allot land to Israel, showing that even in apparent chaos, His covenant order stands firm.

The question for us is whether we live under God's covenant order or in the chaos of our own ways. Nineteen reminds us that God will not author confusion. He invites us into His peace, His order, and His covenant faithfulness.

FOCUS POINT

Blessed is the man who walks not in the counsel of the ungodly... but his delight is in the law of the Lord, and in His law he meditates day and night. (Psalm 1:1–2, NKJV)

This verse highlights covenant order. To reject God's way is to enter chaos; to embrace His Word is to bear fruit. Nineteen challenges us to choose wisely.

MAIN THEME

Nineteen preaches the stark contrast between covenant order and godless chaos. It warns of destruction when faith is abandoned but promises fruitfulness when lives are ordered under God's covenant.

"Nineteen divides the line—God's covenant order brings peace, but rejecting Him invites chaos."

KEY SCRIPTURES

- *For God is not the author of confusion but of peace, as in all the churches of the saints.* (1 Corinthians 14:33, NKJV)
- *Now faith is the substance of things hoped for, the evidence of things not seen.* (Hebrews 11:1, NKJV)
- *So they left all the commandments of the Lord their God... and sold themselves to do evil in the sight of the Lord, to provoke Him to anger.* (2 Kings 17:16–17, NKJV)

Key Points

- **Nineteen Heroes of Faith** Hebrews 11 lists nineteen heroes, preaching covenant order through faith.
- **Ten Plus Nine** Nineteen combines order (ten) and judgment/fruit (nine), offering life when redeemed.
- **Nineteen Kings of Israel** The northern kingdom's nineteen kings led to collapse through disobedience.
- **Chaos in History** Events like 9/11 and Covid-19 reveal the destructive nature of godless chaos.
- **Nineteen-Year Cycle** The Hebrew calendar's 19-year cycle demonstrates God's order in creation.
- **Joshua 19** God fulfilled His covenant promise by allotting land to Israel, showing His faithfulness.
- **Redeemed or Unredeemed** Nineteen asks whether we walk in covenant order or in chaos of rebellion.

Journaling Questions

Journaling about the number nineteen helps us examine whether we live under God's order or in self-made chaos. Writing down reflections on history, Scripture, and personal experiences can reveal patterns of obedience or rebellion in our own lives.

By answering these prompts, readers will discover where God is inviting them into covenant alignment. Journaling presses us to confront areas of confusion and invite His peace and order to reign.

Heroes of Faith

Which of the nineteen heroes of faith most inspires me to live in covenant order?

____

____

____

____

____

Kings of Chaos

What lessons can I learn from the downfall of Israel's nineteen kings?

Chaos in My Life

Where do I see confusion ruling in my life, and how can I invite God's order?

Historical Warnings

How do events like 9/11 or Covid-19 challenge me to examine where I've trusted man instead of God?

COVENANT ALIGNMENT

What practical steps can I take to walk more fully in God's covenant order?

____

____

____

____

____

____

ACTIONABLE STEPS

Embrace God's Word
Commit to daily meditation on Scripture, aligning your life with His order.

Reject Confusion
Identify one area of chaos in your life and surrender it to God's peace.

Mark God's Faithfulness
Celebrate a moment where God brought order out of chaos in your life.

PERSONAL REFLECTION

The number nineteen is a dividing line. It shows us the fruit of covenant order and the devastation of chaos. As you reflect, consider where your life stands—aligned with God's faithfulness or caught in disorder.

God calls us to peace, not confusion. Nineteen invites us to live as people of covenant, walking in His order even in a chaotic world.

Where is God calling me to leave behind chaos? How will I embrace His covenant order? What fruit will my obedience bear in His Kingdom?

____

____

Closing Prayer: *Father, thank You for the lesson of the number nineteen. Teach me to reject chaos and to live in Your covenant order. Bring peace where there has been confusion and let my life bear fruit that glorifies You. Amen.*

CHAPTER 20

THE NUMBER TWENTY

WAITING AND EXPECTANCY

So you, by the help of your God, return; observe mercy and justice, and wait on your God continually. (Hosea 12:6, NKJV)

The number twenty is associated with waiting, expectancy, and prophetic fulfillment. It preaches of patience, prayer, and the assurance that God has ordered something to come to pass. It is 10 × 2, combining God's order with witness, declaring that what God has promised is sure, though it may require waiting for manifestation.

Scripture offers many patterns of twenty. Israel waited twenty years for deliverance through Samson. The Ark of the Covenant remained twenty years in Kirjath-jearim until David restored it. Solomon spent twenty years completing the temple and his house, marking fulfillment after decades of expectancy. Jeremiah prophesied for twenty years before Jerusalem fell, a sobering reminder that not all waiting is easy—it can involve groaning, discipline, or judgment before God's purpose is revealed.

The prophetic side of twenty is also tied to dreams and visions. There are twenty recorded dreams in the Bible and twenty visions, each one marking God's voice breaking through human uncertainty. These moments were not random; they revealed God's plan, often during seasons of waiting. Like twenty-twenty vision, this number also speaks of clarity, seeing what God intends even before it appears.

The challenge of twenty is learning to live in expectancy without losing faith. Waiting is not passive—it is active trust, continued prayer, and the humility to believe God's timing is perfect. Twenty preaches hope: that what God has ordered, He will bring to pass, and those who wait on Him will not be disappointed.

Focus Point

Believe in the Lord your God, and you shall be established; believe His prophets, and you shall prosper. (2 Chronicles 20:20, NKJV)

This verse reveals that waiting is tied to faith in God's Word and the testimony of His prophets. Twenty challenges us to hold fast in prayer and expectancy until the promise is fulfilled.

Main Theme

Twenty preaches waiting and expectancy. It assures us that God has ordered His plans and that through prayer and patience, His promises will be revealed.

"Twenty reminds us: waiting is not delay, it is expectancy for God's ordered promise."

Key Scriptures

- *So you, by the help of your God, return; observe mercy and justice, and wait on your God continually.* (Hosea 12:6, NKJV)
- *Believe in the Lord your God, and you shall be established; believe His prophets, and you shall prosper.* (2 Chronicles 20:20, NKJV)
- *Hallow My Sabbaths, and they will be a sign between Me and you, that you may know that I am the Lord your God.* (Ezekiel 20:20, NKJV)

Key Points

- **Twenty Years of Waiting** Israel, the Ark, Solomon, and Jeremiah each highlight seasons of twenty-year waiting for God's purpose.
- **Dreams and Visions** There are twenty recorded dreams and twenty visions in Scripture, preaching expectancy of God's revelation.
- **Twenty-Twenty Vision** The number twenty is linked to clarity—seeing spiritually what God has already ordered.

- **Order and Witness** Twenty combines God's order (ten) with witness (two), assuring that promises are certain.
- **Prophetic Waiting** Twenty calls us to expect God to fulfill His Word through prayer and prophecy.
- **Fulfillment After Delay** Though long in coming, God's promises—like Solomon's temple—are worth the wait.
- **Active Expectancy** Waiting is not passive but an act of trust, prayer, and alignment with God's timing.

Journaling Questions

Journaling about the number twenty invites us to reflect on how we respond in seasons of waiting. Writing gives us perspective on whether our expectancy is filled with faith or frustration. It helps us recognize that waiting is part of God's process, not a sign of abandonment.

Through these reflections, readers will learn to hold fast to God's promises, embrace prophetic words, and treat waiting as a season of preparation rather than delay. Journaling transforms waiting into worship and expectancy into faith.

Seasons of Waiting

What twenty-year seasons or long waits in my life have taught me about God's timing?

____

____

____

____

____

____

____

Dreams and Visions

What has God revealed to me in dreams or visions during seasons of waiting?

____

____

____

____

____

____

Clarity in Waiting

How does the image of "twenty-twenty vision" inspire me to see God's promises clearly?

____

____

____

____

____

____

Prophetic Trust

How am I holding on to God's Word and the witness of prophecy in this season?

____

____

____

____

____

____

Active Waiting

What steps can I take to turn passive waiting into active expectancy?

____
____
____
____
____
____

Actionable Steps

Embrace Waiting as Worship
Choose one area of delay and turn it into an opportunity for worship and prayer.

Record Promises
Write down promises God has given you, treating them as prophetic declarations to wait on.

Practice Expectant Faith
Daily declare God's faithfulness while waiting, speaking hope instead of frustration.

Personal Reflection

The number twenty preaches expectancy and waiting with faith. It calls us to believe that God has already ordered His plan and that His timing is perfect. As you reflect, ask yourself if your waiting is marked by trust or impatience.

Waiting does not diminish the promise—it strengthens it. Twenty assures us that what God has spoken, He will bring to pass.

Am I waiting in faith or frustration? How can I live in expectancy rather than despair? What promise will I choose to actively wait on today?

____
____
____

Closing Prayer: *Father, thank You for the message of the number twenty. Teach me to wait in faith, to live in expectancy, and to trust Your timing. Let my waiting be filled with prayer, hope, and active trust in Your promises. Amen.*

Chapter 21

The Number Twenty-One

Manifest Spirit

But he who does the truth comes to the light, that his deeds may be clearly seen, that they have been done in God. (John 3:21, NKJV)

The number twenty-one is formed by seven times three. Seven represents the Spirit, and three represents completion. Together, they declare the Spirit's perfect work brought into manifestation. Twenty-one is the number of exposure—when light shines, all things are revealed for what they truly are. It brings truth into the open, whether good or evil.

Scripture shows that twenty-one often reveals hidden darkness. Paul lists twenty-one sins that will be manifest in the last days (2 Timothy 3:2–5). The solstices, occurring around the twenty-first of June and December, mark the extremes of light and darkness in creation, preaching the same truth: light exposes, darkness is uncovered. We are living in the 21st century, an era where hidden things—both corruption and revival—are being revealed on an unprecedented scale.

Twenty-one also carries an angelic dimension. Daniel's prayer was delayed twenty-one days as the prince of Persia resisted the messenger angel until Michael came to assist (Daniel 10:13). Even Jesus used the word *angels* twenty-one times, always in the plural, highlighting spiritual realities revealed through angelic activity. Twenty-one reminds us that the unseen realm is real and that spiritual battles bring truth to the surface.

The number is also woven into the very structure of Scripture. Obadiah has twenty-one verses, Judges and John each have twenty-one chapters, and twenty-one of the New Testament books are epistles. The book of Hebrews references twenty-one Old Testament books, and the

Gospel of John alone contains twenty-one distinct numbers. All of this underscores that twenty-one preaches revelation—truth manifested through the Spirit, Scripture, and history.

Focus Point

For nothing is secret that will not be revealed, nor anything hidden that will not be known and come to light. (Luke 8:17, NKJV)

This verse captures the heart of twenty-one. The Spirit brings hidden things to light, manifesting truth and exposing both darkness and glory.

Main Theme

Twenty-one preaches manifestation by the Spirit. It reveals that light uncovers hidden things, that spiritual battles expose reality, and that Scripture itself is structured to declare truth.

"Twenty-one is the number of manifestation—where the Spirit brings truth into the light."

Key Scriptures

- *But he who does the truth comes to the light, that his deeds may be clearly seen, that they have been done in God.* (John 3:21, NKJV)
- *For nothing is secret that will not be revealed, nor anything hidden that will not be known and come to light.* (Luke 8:17, NKJV)
- *But the prince of the kingdom of Persia withstood me twenty-one days; and behold, Michael, one of the chief princes, came to help me.* (Daniel 10:13, NKJV)

Key Points

- **Seven Times Three** Twenty-one reveals the Spirit's perfect work completed and manifested.
- **Exposure of Darkness** Paul lists twenty-one sins in 2 Timothy, warning of last-days corruption revealed.

- **Solstices as Signs** The 21st marks extremes of light and dark, symbolizing manifestation of hidden things.
- **Angelic Resistance** Daniel's twenty-one-day delay shows the unseen battles tied to manifestation.
- **Jesus and Angels** Jesus used "angels" twenty-one times, always plural, affirming spiritual realities.
- **Scriptural Patterns** Books like Obadiah, Judges, and John reinforce twenty-one as a number of revelation.
- **Century of Manifestation** The 21st century itself is a prophetic picture of exposure, truth, and manifestation.

Journaling Questions

Journaling about the number twenty-one invites us to consider what God is revealing in our lives. Writing helps us confront areas of hidden darkness and embrace the light of His Spirit. It also challenges us to see delays in prayer not as denials but as spiritual battles in the unseen realm.

Through these reflections, readers will recognize that the Spirit brings truth to light for both correction and encouragement. Journaling allows us to track what God is manifesting in our lives, moving us from secrecy to revelation.

Hidden Things Revealed

What has God recently exposed in my life that I need to bring into the light?

____

____

____

____

____

____

____

Spiritual Battles

Where have I experienced delays that might be tied to unseen battles like Daniel's?

____

____

____

____

____

____

The Solstice Pattern

How does creation's cycle of light and darkness remind me of the Spirit's work of exposure?

____

____

____

____

____

____

Angelic Reality

How do I see angelic activity affirming God's truth in Scripture and my life?

____

____

____

____

____

____

Living in the Light

What practical steps can I take to walk transparently in God's truth?

____

____

____

____

____

____

Actionable Steps

Expose Darkness
Confess and confront hidden sin, choosing to walk in light.

Wait in Faith
Persist in prayer even during delays, trusting that God is working in the unseen.

Declare Revelation
Speak truth boldly, manifesting God's Word in your life and community.

Personal Reflection

The number twenty-one reminds us that nothing remains hidden forever. It preaches that the Spirit brings all things into the light—whether sin, truth, or glory. As you reflect, ask whether you are living openly in His truth or hiding in shadows.

God calls His people to manifest His Spirit in word, deed, and transparency. Twenty-one is His invitation to let truth shine through us.

What is God exposing in my life? How will I respond to delays in prayer? Am I living as one who manifests the Spirit's truth?

____

____

____

Closing Prayer: *Holy Spirit, thank You for the message of the number twenty-one. Shine Your light in my life and expose anything hidden. Teach me to live openly, transparently, and truthfully before You. Let my life manifest Your Spirit and bring glory to Christ. Amen.*

Chapter 22

The Number Twenty-Two

Personal Revelation / Disorder Manifestation

Arise, shine; for your light has come! And the glory of the Lord is risen upon you. For behold, the darkness shall cover the earth, and deep darkness the people; but the Lord will arise over you, and His glory will be seen upon you. (Isaiah 60:1–2, NKJV)

The number twenty-two preaches two powerful themes: redeemed, it speaks of personal revelation; unredeemed, it manifests disorder. At its core are the twenty-two letters of the Hebrew alphabet—the very foundation of God's written Word. Every revelation He gave Israel, every prophecy, and every promise was communicated through those twenty-two letters. Revelation, the Bible's final book, has twenty-two chapters, showing how God's Word brings light to the very end.

Twenty-two also appears in prophetic imagery. The book of Isaiah records the word *light* twenty-two times, particularly in the context of God's glory rising amidst darkness. This number symbolizes truth breaking forth in times of deep despair. Yet, unredeemed, twenty-two marks chaos. It is the product of eleven and two—valor or disorder joined with witness—meaning it can represent a manifested testimony of disorder. History illustrates this: both Ahab and Jeroboam reigned twenty-two years in disobedience, their governments remembered more for idolatry than righteousness.

Even modern events bear this mark. President John F. Kennedy was assassinated on 11/22/1963, a tragic disruption remembered around the world. Such moments highlight the duality of this number: it can carry light and revelation, or it can manifest deep disorder. Twenty-two is a dividing line, challenging us to ask whether our lives reflect God's revelation or human rebellion.

The lesson is this: twenty-two presses us to embrace God's Word and light as personal revelation, while warning us of the dangers of disorder when truth is rejected.

Focus Point

Your word is a lamp to my feet and a light to my path. (Psalm 119:105, NKJV)

This verse captures the redeemed meaning of twenty-two. God's Word, composed from twenty-two letters of the Hebrew alphabet, brings revelation, guidance, and order in a world filled with disorder.

Main Theme

Twenty-two preaches revelation and exposure. Redeemed, it gives light and personal insight through God's Word. Unredeemed, it manifests disorder and chaos in the absence of truth.

"Twenty-two divides light from darkness: it is revelation when embraced, or disorder when rejected."

Key Scriptures

- *Arise, shine; for your light has come! And the glory of the Lord is risen upon you.* (Isaiah 60:1, NKJV)
- *Your word is a lamp to my feet and a light to my path.* (Psalm 119:105, NKJV)
- *So Ahab the son of Omri reigned over Israel in Samaria twenty-two years.* (1 Kings 16:29, NKJV)

Key Points

- **Twenty-Two Letters** The Hebrew alphabet's twenty-two letters form the foundation of God's revelation to His people.
- **Revelation's Final Word** The book of Revelation has twenty-two chapters, testifying of God's Word to the very end.

- **Light in Isaiah** The word *light* appears twenty-two times, symbolizing revelation breaking into darkness.
- **Witness of Disorder** Twenty-two is 11 × 2, showing how rebellion can manifest as visible chaos.
- **Kings of Chaos** Ahab and Jeroboam reigned twenty-two years, each remembered for idolatry and disorder.
- **Modern Tragedy** The date 11/22 marks the assassination of John F. Kennedy, a global moment of disorder.
- **Choice of Alignment** Twenty-two asks whether we will embrace light and revelation or manifest disorder.

JOURNALING QUESTIONS

Journaling about twenty-two invites us to ask whether God's Word is bringing light into our lives or whether we are allowing disorder to rule. Writing helps us recognize where His revelation is speaking and where rebellion has left chaos. It is an opportunity to embrace Scripture as personal revelation and to align with His order.

Through these reflections, readers will learn that revelation is not abstract but personal. God reveals Himself through His Word and through the Spirit, bringing clarity where there was confusion. Twenty-two challenges us to live as people of revelation rather than disorder.

THE WORD'S LIGHT

How has God's Word been a lamp and light to me recently?

____

____

____

____

____

____

____

Twenty-Two Chapters

What does it mean that the book of Revelation, with twenty-two chapters, is God's final Word to us?

____
____
____
____
____
____

Light vs. Darkness

Where do I see God's revelation breaking into dark places in my life?

____
____
____
____
____
____

Kings of Disorder

What lessons do I learn from Ahab or Jeroboam's twenty-two years of failed leadership?

____
____
____
____
____
____

Living in Revelation

How can I choose revelation over disorder in a specific area of my life this week?

____

____

____

____

____

____

Actionable Steps

Commit to the Word
Read a passage daily, remembering that God's revelation comes through His Word.

Identify Disorder
Recognize one area of your life marked by confusion and invite God's light into it.

Walk in Revelation
Share a testimony of how God's Word has brought revelation to you, giving light to others.

Personal Reflection

Twenty-two is a number of choice. It offers revelation when God's Word is embraced and warns of disorder when it is ignored. As you reflect, consider whether you are living aligned with His Word or drifting into confusion.

God has given His Word as light, not for scholars alone but for every believer. Twenty-two asks us: will we walk in that light, or will we manifest disorder?

Where is God calling me into deeper revelation? What area of my life needs His light? How will I choose revelation over disorder today?

____

____

____

Closing Prayer: *Father, thank You for the number twenty-two and the revelation it brings. Teach me to walk in Your Word as light, to embrace revelation, and to reject disorder. Let my life shine with Your truth and bring glory to Your name. Amen.*

Chapter 23

The Number Twenty-Three

Death or God's Presence

For the wages of sin is death, but the gift of God is eternal life in Christ Jesus our Lord.
(Romans 6:23, NKJV)

The number twenty-three preaches a sobering duality: unredeemed, it speaks of death; redeemed, it proclaims the presence of God. It is formed from ten plus thirteen—God's perfect order combined with rebellion. Left unredeemed, twenty-three marks judgment upon rebellion, the wages of sin being death. Redeemed, however, it declares life in God's presence.

Romans 1:28–32 lists twenty-three sins that lead to death, underscoring the destructive path of rebellion. Luke 23:23 records the crowd demanding Jesus' crucifixion, while Romans 6:23 reveals the wages of sin. Even in language patterns, words like "hell" appear twenty-three times in the New Testament, emphasizing this number's link to death. Yet Scripture does not leave us in despair. Psalm 23 declares that even in the valley of death, God's presence comforts us. Zechariah 8:23 prophesies that in the last days, people will cling to God's people, saying, "We have heard that God is with you."

History and testimony reinforce this pattern. The martyr Polycarp was burned alive on February 23, A.D. 155, boldly confessing Christ. James Dean, who famously owned a Porsche nicknamed "Little Bastard," died after a prophetic warning on the 23rd. Even cultural artifacts like Bill Wiese's testimony *23 Minutes in Hell* reflect how deeply this number has been tied to mortality. Yet, equally, believers testify of the nearness of God's presence marked by this number.

The message of twenty-three is that without Christ, death is the outcome of sin, but with Him, death is swallowed up in life, and His presence becomes our eternal reality.

FOCUS POINT

We are confident, yes, well pleased rather to be absent from the body and to be present with the Lord. (2 Corinthians 5:8, NKJV)

This verse shows the redeemed meaning of twenty-three. While death looms in a fallen world, for the believer it ushers in the immediate presence of God.

MAIN THEME

Twenty-three preaches the wages of sin as death and the gift of grace as life in God's presence. It challenges us to face mortality with hope in Christ.

"Twenty-three divides the line: unredeemed it is death, redeemed it is God's presence."

KEY SCRIPTURES

- *For the wages of sin is death, but the gift of God is eternal life in Christ Jesus our Lord.* (Romans 6:23, NKJV)
- *Yea, though I walk through the valley of the shadow of death, I will fear no evil; for You are with me.* (Psalm 23:4, NKJV)
- *Thus says the Lord of hosts: "In those days ten men from every language of the nations shall grasp the sleeve of a Jewish man, saying, 'Let us go with you, for we have heard that God is with you.'"* (Zechariah 8:23, NKJV)

KEY POINTS

- **Twenty-Three Sins** Romans 1 lists twenty-three sins, each ending in death without repentance.
- **Crucifixion Declared** Luke 23:23 records the crowd calling for Christ's death, the ultimate miscarriage of justice.
- **Psalm 23's Comfort** Even in death's shadow, God's presence offers assurance and peace.

- **Zechariah's Prophecy** The 23,000th verse of Scripture (Zechariah 8:23) proclaims God's presence with His people.
- **Polycarp's Martyrdom** On February 23, A.D. 155, Polycarp's faith revealed death as a doorway to presence.
- **Judgment in History** Dates and events tied to twenty-three often reveal mortality and divine warnings.
- **Life Through Christ** Redeemed, twenty-three is no longer a number of death but of God's abiding presence.

Journaling Questions

Journaling about the number twenty-three presses us to confront mortality while embracing God's presence. Writing about these truths reminds us that death is not the final word for believers. Instead, it becomes the doorway to being with Christ forever.

By reflecting on these themes, readers will identify areas where fear of death lingers and learn to rest in the promise of God's presence. Journaling becomes a way to process mortality with hope.

Facing Death

How do I respond to the reality that sin leads to death?

____

____

____

____

____

____

____

Psalm 23 Assurance

How does the promise of God's presence comfort me in fearful seasons?

____
____
____
____
____
____

Zechariah's Promise

What does Zechariah 8:23 reveal about God's presence in the last days?

____
____
____
____
____
____

Martyrdom's Witness

What does Polycarp's story teach me about faith and God's presence in suffering?

____
____
____
____
____
____

REDEEMED DEATH

How does the assurance of eternal life in Christ change the way I view death?

____

____

____

____

____

____

ACTIONABLE STEPS

Embrace Eternal Life
Confess daily that eternal life in God's presence is your hope in Christ.

Reject Fear of Death
Identify one fear of mortality and surrender it to God's promise of life.

Walk in His Presence
Choose to live with an awareness of His nearness, making every moment sacred.

PERSONAL REFLECTION

The number twenty-three preaches both warning and hope. It warns that sin ends in death, but it assures that Christ brings us into God's presence. As you reflect, consider whether you are living in fear of death or in faith for eternal life.

Death without Christ is final, but in Him, it is only transition into His presence.

Do I live in fear of death or in hope of His presence? How will I embrace God's nearness today? What eternal perspective will shape the way I live now?

____

____

____

____

Closing Prayer: *Father, thank You for the message of the number twenty-three. Teach me to face mortality with faith and to live in the assurance of Your presence. Let my life testify of hope, not fear, and may I live prepared for eternity in Christ. Amen.*

Chapter 24

The Number Twenty-Four

Perfect Government

Around the throne were twenty-four thrones, and on the thrones I saw twenty-four elders sitting, clothed in white robes; and they had crowns of gold on their heads. (Revelation 4:4, NKJV)

The number twenty-four preaches perfect government made manifest. It is twelve doubled—government and authority multiplied and confirmed by witness. In heaven, John saw twenty-four elders circling the throne, each falling down in worship, proclaiming that government is not about human control but divine order under the King of kings. Worship and government are inseparable in this number: when God rules, His people respond in reverence.

Twenty-four is also connected to priesthood. David divided the sons of Aaron into twenty-four courses for priestly service (1 Chronicles 24), ensuring that worship and intercession continued in order and rhythm. In the same way, twenty-four divisions of musicians (1 Chronicles 25) sang before the Lord, showing that praise and prayer uphold God's government. The picture is of a Kingdom ruled through worship, priesthood, and the presence of God.

Even creation preaches this number. The earth is encircled by 24,000 miles, divided into twenty-four time zones, declaring that God governs time and space. Each day contains twenty-four hours, reminding us that every moment is under His authority. Luke's Gospel, which emphasizes Christ as the perfect Son of Man, contains twenty-four chapters, aligning divine government with the life of Jesus.

Twenty-four is not about oppressive rule but about order, worship, and priestly alignment with God's authority. It reveals that perfect government is made manifest not in chaos but in harmony with the King of kings and Lord of lords.

Focus Point

And has made us kings and priests to His God and Father, to Him be glory and dominion forever and ever. Amen. (Revelation 1:6, NKJV)

This verse shows the connection between government and priesthood. The redeemed are called kings and priests, sharing in Christ's perfect government through worship and service.

Main Theme

Twenty-four preaches perfect government as established by God. It declares that His authority governs time, creation, worship, and priesthood.

"Twenty-four is the number of perfect government—God's authority manifested through worship and priesthood."

Key Scriptures

- *Around the throne were twenty-four thrones, and on the thrones I saw twenty-four elders sitting, clothed in white robes; and they had crowns of gold on their heads.* (Revelation 4:4, NKJV)
- *These were the divisions of the sons of Aaron... the heads of the fathers' houses, as they were divided, were twenty-four in number.* (1 Chronicles 24:1, 4–5, NKJV)
- *And has made us kings and priests to His God and Father, to Him be glory and dominion forever and ever. Amen.* (Revelation 1:6, NKJV)

Key Points

- **Twelve Doubled** Twenty-four is 12 × 2, showing government and authority confirmed by witness.
- **Elders Around the Throne** The twenty-four elders worship continually, linking government with reverence.

- **Priestly Divisions** David appointed twenty-four priestly courses to ensure constant worship.
- **Musical Divisions** Twenty-four groups of singers upheld praise as part of God's government.
- **God Governs Time** The earth's 24,000-mile circumference and twenty-four time zones reveal His order.
- **Hours of the Day** Twenty-four hours preach that every moment belongs to His authority.
- **Luke's Gospel** The twenty-four chapters of Luke declare Christ's perfect humanity under divine government.

Journaling Questions

Journaling about twenty-four reminds us that God governs every detail of life. Writing about this number helps us see worship as central to government and order. It challenges us to examine whether our lives are aligned with His authority or caught in self-rule.

Through these reflections, readers will learn that to live under perfect government is to walk in harmony with Christ as both King and High Priest. Journaling invites us to see worship, intercession, and daily rhythms as part of God's Kingdom order.

Witness of Authority

How does twenty-four as twelve doubled challenge me to confirm God's authority in my life?

____

____

____

____

____

____

____

Elders in Worship

What does the image of twenty-four elders teach me about the link between worship and government?

____

____

____

____

____

____

Priesthood and Service

How can I live daily as both king and priest unto God?

____

____

____

____

____

____

Time Under His Rule

How do twenty-four hours remind me to live every moment under God's authority?

____

____

____

____

____

____

Perfect Government

What area of my life needs to come under His perfect government today?

____
____
____
____
____
____
____

Actionable Steps

Submit to His Rule
Identify an area of life you've held in self-rule and submit it to His authority.

Live as Priest and King
Engage daily in both prayer (priesthood) and action (kingship) to reflect His Kingdom.

Redeem the Day
Consciously dedicate all twenty-four hours to God's purposes, inviting Him into every moment.

Personal Reflection

The number twenty-four resounds with the truth that God governs in perfect order. It calls us to live as kings and priests, aligned with His authority and surrendered to His rule. As you reflect, ask yourself if your life mirrors heavenly government or earthly confusion.

Perfect government is not oppression—it is the order of God revealed in worship and priesthood.

Am I living as one who reflects God's government? How do I align my hours and days with His authority? What step will I take to live as both priest and king in His Kingdom?

Closing Prayer: *Lord, thank You for the message of the number twenty-four. Teach me to live in alignment with Your perfect government. Make me a faithful king and priest, devoted to worship and service. Let every hour of my life reflect Your authority and glory. Amen.*

Chapter 25

The Number Twenty-Five

Grace for Grace

And of His fullness we have all received, and grace for grace. For the law was given through Moses, but grace and truth came through Jesus Christ. (John 1:16–17, NKJV)

The number twenty-five preaches grace multiplied—five times five, a picture of God's abundant provision beyond measure. It represents not just grace but grace heaped upon grace, the kind that sustains faith across long seasons of waiting. Abraham and Sarah lived this truth when they waited twenty-five years for the fulfillment of God's promise. At seventy-five, Abraham received God's word that he would have a son. At one hundred years old, with Sarah at ninety, Isaac was born. The twenty-five years of waiting did not diminish God's promise but instead strengthened Abraham's faith, preparing him to trust God fully, even when asked to lay Isaac on the altar.

This number carries both promise and patience. It testifies that grace is not merely for a moment but for the long journey of faith. Grace upon grace sustains us when the promise tarries and gives us the strength to trust that God will complete what He has begun. Twenty-five reminds us that what He has given grace for, He will bring to pass. It is the assurance that every word He speaks is backed by multiplied grace until fulfillment.

Grace for grace also speaks of Christ's fullness. The law came through Moses, but grace and truth came through Jesus. His life, death, and resurrection released an unending flow of grace to those who believe. This grace not only forgives but empowers, not only pardons but sustains. Twenty-five is the picture of grace compounded, eternal, and overflowing.

The challenge is whether we are willing to trust the multiplied grace of God through seasons of waiting and testing. Twenty-five asks us to believe that His grace is sufficient, not just once, but continually, layer upon layer, until the promise is complete.

Focus Point

Now the Lord was gracious to Sarah as He had said, and the Lord did for Sarah what He had promised. (Genesis 21:1,NIV)

This verse ties the twenty-five years of waiting to God's faithfulness. Grace carried Abraham and Sarah until the promise was fulfilled, showing that God's timing is always perfect.

Main Theme

Twenty-five preaches grace upon grace. It is God's multiplied provision, sustaining faith through waiting and fulfilling promises in His perfect time.

"Twenty-five is grace multiplied—God's provision compounding until His promise is fulfilled."

Key Scriptures

- *And of His fullness we have all received, and grace for grace.* (John 1:16, NKJV)
- *Now the Lord was gracious to Sarah as He had said, and the Lord did for Sarah what He had promised.* (Genesis 21:1, NIV)
- *By faith Abraham, when he was tested, offered up Isaac...concluding that God was able to raise him up, even from the dead.* (Hebrews 11:17, 19, NKJV)

Key Points

- **Grace Multiplied** Twenty-five is five times five, symbolizing grace compounded beyond measure.
- **Waiting for Isaac** Abraham and Sarah's twenty-five-year wait preaches patience sustained by grace.

- **Strength in Testing** The long wait prepared Abraham to trust God when asked to sacrifice Isaac.
- **Christ's Fullness** Grace and truth came through Jesus, supplying grace upon grace for all.
- **Grace for the Long Journey** Twenty-five shows grace not only forgives but also sustains faith over time.
- **Promise Fulfilled** When grace carries us, the promise always comes to pass.
- **Grace Eternal** Grace upon grace flows endlessly from Christ's fullness to His people.

Journaling Questions

Journaling about the number twenty-five invites us to reflect on seasons of waiting and the sustaining grace that carries us through. Writing helps us recognize how God's grace multiplies, layer upon layer, until His promises are fulfilled. It also helps us process times when waiting feels endless, reminding us that His provision is always enough.

By reflecting on these truths, readers will see grace not as a one-time event but as a continual supply. Journaling calls us to remember past testimonies of grace and to expect multiplied grace for the present and future.

Grace Multiplied

Where have I experienced God's grace compounded beyond what I expected?

Waiting Faith

What promise have I been waiting for, and how is His grace sustaining me?

____

____

____

____

____

____

Tested Trust

How has a long wait prepared me for deeper trust in God?

____

____

____

____

____

____

Christ's Fullness

What does it mean to me that Jesus provides grace upon grace?

____

____

____

____

____

____

Fulfilled Promises

Where can I celebrate a testimony of God's grace fulfilled after a long season?

Actionable Steps

Remember Past Grace
Record testimonies of how God's grace has carried you through delays.

Receive Fresh Grace
Ask God daily for new layers of grace to sustain your faith.

Declare His Fulfillment
Speak life over promises still waiting, declaring that His grace will complete them.

Personal Reflection

The number twenty-five calls us to trust in multiplied grace. It assures us that God's provision is not exhausted in one moment but continues until the promise is fulfilled. As you reflect, ask whether you are resting in His sufficiency or striving in your own strength.

Grace upon grace flows endlessly in Christ. Twenty-five preaches that His faithfulness sustains us through years, tests, and promises yet to come.

Where am I relying on my own strength instead of His grace? How is God multiplying grace in my life right now? What promises am I trusting Him to fulfill through grace upon grace?

Closing Prayer: *Father, thank You for the multiplied grace revealed in the number twenty-five. Teach me to rest in Your sufficiency, to trust through waiting, and to celebrate the grace that sustains me until Your promises are fulfilled. Amen.*

Chapter 26

The Number Twenty-Six

Beloved

This is My beloved Son, in whom I am well pleased.
(Matthew 3:17, NKJV)

The number twenty-six preaches beloved identity. It carries the weight of both covenant and intimacy, pointing us to the relationship between David, the "beloved" king, and Jesus, the "beloved" Son. In the genealogy of Luke, there are twenty-six generations from David to Christ, testifying that God's promise through David's line was not forgotten but fulfilled in Jesus. The number also marks the span from Adam to Moses, highlighting God's faithfulness across history.

The word *beloved* itself appears twenty-six times in the Song of Solomon, written by Solomon, the son of David. This connection weaves intimacy and covenant love into the meaning of twenty-six. David's very name means "beloved," and in Scripture, only David and Jesus are directly called "beloved." The number declares that belovedness is not just affection—it is divine identity.

Even deeper, twenty-six carries God's very name. The Hebrew letters *Yod* (10), *He* (5), *Vav* (6), and *He* (5) spell YHWH, which totals twenty-six. The tetragrammaton, God's covenant name, is a declaration of His presence and His love for His people. From Adam to Yahweh in Genesis 4, the span of twenty-six marks the divine thread weaving humanity to God.

The message of twenty-six is this: to be beloved is to be known by God, chosen by Him, and named as His own. It calls us to live from identity, not performance, and to embrace the truth that in Christ, we are His beloved children.

FOCUS POINT

Behold what manner of love the Father has bestowed on us, that we should be called children of God! (1 John 3:1, NKJV)

This verse reveals the essence of twenty-six. Beloved identity is bestowed, not earned. It is the declaration of God's covenant love over His children.

MAIN THEME

Twenty-six preaches belovedness as divine identity. It reminds us that God's covenant love names us as His own, just as David and Jesus were called beloved.

"Twenty-six is God's number of belovedness—our identity as chosen and cherished in Him."

KEY SCRIPTURES

- *This is My beloved Son, in whom I am well pleased.* (Matthew 3:17, NKJV)
- *Behold what manner of love the Father has bestowed on us, that we should be called children of God!* (1 John 3:1, NKJV)
- *So all the generations from Abraham to David are fourteen generations, from David until the captivity in Babylon are fourteen generations, and from the captivity in Babylon until the Christ are fourteen generations.* (Matthew 1:17, NKJV)

KEY POINTS

- **David the Beloved** The name David means "beloved," revealing the identity God gave His chosen king.
- **Jesus the Beloved** Only David and Jesus are directly called "beloved" in Scripture, linking covenant and identity.
- **Twenty-Six Generations** From David to Christ, twenty-six generations testify of God's faithfulness to His promise.

- **Beloved in Song of Solomon** The word *beloved* appears twenty-six times in the Song of Solomon, echoing intimacy.
- **The Name of Yahweh** YHWH equals twenty-six, declaring God's covenant presence and love.
- **From Adam to Moses** Twenty-six generations link the beginning of humanity to the lawgiver, marking God's plan.
- **Identity, Not Performance** Twenty-six preaches that belovedness is who we are in God, not what we achieve.

Journaling Questions

Journaling about twenty-six invites us to reflect on our identity as God's beloved. Writing helps us move from striving for approval to resting in His covenant love. It reminds us that belovedness is not a title for the few but the inheritance of all who belong to Him.

By answering these prompts, readers will see how deeply God has named them as His beloved. Journaling creates a sacred space to embrace divine intimacy and to reject the lie of performance-driven worth.

Beloved Identity

How does knowing I am God's beloved change the way I see myself?

____

____

____

____

____

____

____

David's Example

What does David's identity as "beloved" teach me about God's covenant love?

Jesus the Beloved Son

How does Jesus' beloved identity shape my understanding of being a child of God?

God's Name YHWH

What does it mean that God's covenant name (YHWH = 26) ties to belovedness?

Living as Beloved

What practical step can I take to live each day as God's beloved, not as a performer?

Actionable Steps

Rest in Identity
Take time daily to remind yourself you are beloved, not because of performance but because of God's choice.

Speak Belovedness
Affirm others by reminding them of their beloved identity in Christ.

Embrace Intimacy
Set aside time in prayer to experience God's covenant love as His beloved child.

Personal Reflection

The number twenty-six is God's declaration of belovedness. It calls us to live from the identity of being chosen, cherished, and named as His own. As you reflect, ask whether you are striving for approval or resting in His love.

Belovedness is more than affection; it is covenant identity.

Am I living as God's beloved? How will I embrace belovedness as my identity? What step will I take to rest in His love today?

Closing Prayer: *Father, thank You for the message of the number twenty-six. Teach me to live as Your beloved, resting in covenant love and walking in the identity You have given me. Let my life reflect the truth that I am chosen and cherished by You. Amen.*

CHAPTER 27

THE NUMBER TWENTY-SEVEN

TADA!

The Lord is my light and my salvation; whom shall I fear? The Lord is the strength of my life; of whom shall I be afraid? (Psalm 27:1, NKJV)

The number twenty-seven preaches unveiling and revelation—when the light comes on, God says, "Tada!" It represents the moment truth is revealed in God's presence. While not a prolific number in the Bible, its message is unmistakable. The term "candlestick" appears twenty-seven times in Scripture, symbolizing the light of truth that shines when God manifests His presence.

Abraham's story is unveiled through twenty-seven books in the Bible, showing how God's promise was progressively revealed. Matthew records twenty-seven generations from David to Christ, culminating in Jesus' arrival—the ultimate "Tada!" of God's plan. Even the structure of Scripture reflects this: the New Testament contains twenty-seven books, and the last one, Revelation, unveils Jesus Christ.

The feast of Saint John is celebrated on December 27, linking this number to the apostle who carried the revelation of Christ. Scripture further confirms its meaning with verses like Genesis 1:27, declaring humanity created in God's image, and John 10:27, where Jesus says His sheep hear His voice. Romans 8:27 assures that the Spirit searches hearts, making intercession according to God's will. Twenty-seven, three cubed (3 × 3 × 3), is the revelation of all things Jesus, emphasizing progressive light, truth, and manifestation.

The message of twenty-seven is simple but profound: when God reveals truth, it is always His "Tada!" moment, bringing light into darkness and unveiling His purposes.

FOCUS POINT

My sheep hear My voice, and I know them, and they follow Me. (John 10:27, NKJV)

This verse embodies twenty-seven's theme. Revelation is not just light but intimacy—hearing His voice and responding in trust and obedience.

MAIN THEME

Twenty-seven preaches revelation, unveiling, and the light of truth in Christ. It marks the moments when God's purposes are revealed with clarity and glory.

"Twenty-seven is God's 'Tada!'—the unveiling of truth and light in His presence."

KEY SCRIPTURES

- *So God created man in His own image; in the image of God He created him; male and female He created them.* (Genesis 1:27, NKJV)
- *My sheep hear My voice, and I know them, and they follow Me.* (John 10:27, NKJV)
- *He who searches the hearts knows what the mind of the Spirit is, because He makes intercession for the saints according to the will of God.* (Romans 8:27, NKJV)

KEY POINTS

- **Candlestick of Light** The word *candlestick* appears twenty-seven times, symbolizing God's manifest light.
- **Generations to Christ** Matthew records twenty-seven generations from David to Jesus, God's ultimate unveiling.
- **Twenty-Seven Books** The New Testament's twenty-seven books culminate in Revelation, the unveiling of Christ.
- **Saint John's Feast** Celebrated on December 27, affirming the link between twenty-seven and revelation.

- **Scriptural Echoes** Genesis 1:27, Psalm 27, John 10:27, and Romans 8:27 all reinforce themes of creation, identity, and revelation.
- **Three Cubed** Twenty-seven is 3 × 3 × 3, symbolizing complete revelation in Christ.
- **Progressive Revelation** Twenty-seven preaches that truth unfolds layer by layer in God's timing.

Journaling Questions

Journaling about twenty-seven invites us to reflect on how God has unveiled truth in our lives. Writing helps us recognize His "Tada!" moments—when His presence illuminates hidden things, when His promises come to pass, and when His Word comes alive in fresh revelation.

Through these reflections, readers will see that twenty-seven calls us to expect God to reveal His purposes continually. Journaling becomes a way to trace the light of truth breaking into our personal journeys.

Light Revealed

What recent moment has felt like God's "Tada!" unveiling in my life?

____
____
____
____
____
____

Hearing His Voice

How have I recognized and responded to God's voice, as in John 10:27?

____
____
____
____
____

Scriptural Revelation

Which verse marked with twenty-seven speaks most to me about God's revelation?

Progressive Unveiling

What truths has God revealed layer by layer in my walk with Him?

Living in the Light

How can I practically walk in the unveiled truth of Christ each day?

Actionable Steps

Expect Revelation
Pray daily with expectancy for God's "Tada!" moments of revelation.

Follow His Voice
Respond quickly to the Spirit's leading, living in intimacy and obedience.

Celebrate Light
Mark testimonies of God's unveiling in your life as memorials of His faithfulness.

Personal Reflection

The number twenty-seven reminds us that God delights in unveiling His truth. It is His "Tada!" moment when light breaks into darkness and His purposes are revealed. As you reflect, consider where you are waiting for His light and where He has already revealed it.

God is faithful to unveil His truth in His time. Twenty-seven preaches that His revelation always brings clarity, joy, and transformation.

Where do I need God's light unveiled? How will I respond to His voice when He reveals truth? What step will I take to live in His "Tada!" today?

Closing Prayer: *Lord, thank You for the unveiling truth of twenty-seven. Shine Your light into my life, reveal what is hidden, and let me walk in intimacy with You. Teach me to expect and celebrate Your "Tada!" moments of revelation. Amen.*

Chapter 28

The Number Twenty-Eight

Times and Seasons

To everything there is a season, a time for every purpose under heaven. (Ecclesiastes 3:1, NKJV)

The number twenty-eight preaches times and seasons. It represents beginnings and endings, declaring that every purpose unfolds within God's divine order. Ecclesiastes 3 lists twenty-eight times and seasons, starting with birth and ending with peace, proclaiming that every moment of life is governed by His sovereignty. The sequence reminds us that God holds all transitions in His hands, from laughter to weeping, from planting to uprooting, from war to peace.

Scripture and creation echo this truth. The word *weeks* appears twenty-eight times in Scripture, symbolizing cycles of time. The phrase "day and night" appears twenty-eight times, anchoring rhythm in God's design. The lunar month holds twenty-eight days, marking time by the heavens. Even the Gregorian calendar is built on a twenty-eight-year cycle, showing God's imprint on human order. February, the shortest month, bears twenty-eight days, underscoring the completeness of His design.

The cross itself is tied to this number. The word *cross* appears twenty-eight times in the New Testament, pointing us to Christ's finished work as the center of every season. No matter what time we are in—joy, mourning, gain, or loss—the cross guarantees victory and redemption. And in Matthew 28, Jesus promises to be with us always, "even to the end of the world," assuring us that no season is without His presence.

The message of twenty-eight is clear: every season has a purpose, every time is measured, and every cycle is overseen by the God who orders all things.

FOCUS POINT

Lo, I am with you always, even to the end of the age. (Matthew 28:20, NKJV)

This verse affirms that Christ is present in every season. Whether in beginning or ending, His promise anchors us through the cycles of life.

MAIN THEME

Twenty-eight preaches divine timing and God's sovereignty over seasons. It assures us that nothing is random; every moment is ordered with purpose and infused with Christ's presence.

"Twenty-eight declares: God is Lord of every time, season, and cycle."

KEY SCRIPTURES

- *To everything there is a season, a time for every purpose under heaven.* (Ecclesiastes 3:1, NKJV)
- *Mark the blameless man, and observe the upright; for the future of that man is peace.* (Psalm 37:37, NKJV)
- *Lo, I am with you always, even to the end of the age.* (Matthew 28:20, NKJV)

KEY POINTS

- **Twenty-Eight Times** Ecclesiastes lists twenty-eight times and seasons, marking life's divine order.
- **Scriptural Cycles** The words *weeks* and *day and night* appear twenty-eight times, testifying of God's rhythm.
- **Lunar and Calendar Order** A lunar month contains twenty-eight days; the Gregorian calendar follows a twenty-eight-year cycle.
- **The Shortest Month** February's twenty-eight days show God's completeness even in brevity.

- **The Cross for Every Season** *Cross* appears twenty-eight times in the New Testament, centering all seasons on Christ's work.
- **Christ's Promise in Matthew 28** Jesus assures His presence in every time and season, even to the end.
- **Peaceful Ending** The sequence in Ecclesiastes begins with birth and ends with peace, pointing to God's ultimate plan.

JOURNALING QUESTIONS

Journaling about twenty-eight allows us to identify the season we are in and how God is working through it. Writing reminds us that times of sorrow are not without meaning and times of joy are not without purpose. Every season reveals His hand and leads us toward peace.

Through reflection, readers will recognize God's sovereignty over their personal cycles and learn to trust that His timing is perfect. Journaling helps us embrace both beginnings and endings as part of His eternal plan.

RECOGNIZING MY SEASON

What season am I currently in, and how do I see God's purpose in it?

____

____

____

____

____

____

SCRIPTURAL CYCLES

How does the repetition of "weeks" and "day and night" affirm God's order in my life?

____

____

____

____

____

The Cross and My Season

How does Christ's cross give meaning to the season I am walking through now?

____

____

____

____

____

____

Shortest Month Lesson

What does February's twenty-eight days teach me about completeness in brevity?

____

____

____

____

____

____

Christ's Presence

How does Matthew 28:20 encourage me to trust Him in every season?

____

____

____

____

____

____

Actionable Steps

Identify Your Season
Take time to prayerfully discern what season of Ecclesiastes 3 you are living in.

Anchor in the Cross
Connect your current season to the cross, seeing redemption in every circumstance.

Trust His Timing
Commit to trusting God's timeline instead of forcing your own.

Personal Reflection

The number twenty-eight reminds us that life is a cycle of God-ordained seasons. Each moment carries His purpose, and no time is wasted. As you reflect, ask whether you see your season through the lens of frustration or faith.

God is the Lord of beginnings and endings, of days and nights, of sorrow and joy. Twenty-eight preaches His sovereignty over every season.

Do I see God's hand in my season? How will I anchor myself in His timing? What step will I take to embrace His presence in this moment?

Closing Prayer: *Father, thank You for the message of twenty-eight. Teach me to trust Your timing, to embrace every season with faith, and to rest in the assurance that Jesus is with me always. Let every cycle of my life testify of Your sovereignty. Amen.*

Chapter 29

The Number Twenty-Nine

Mountains

I will lift up my eyes to the hills—from whence comes my help? My help comes from the Lord, who made heaven and earth. (Psalm 121:1–2, NKJV)

The number twenty-nine preaches mountains—places of encounter, worship, and the voice of God. Throughout Scripture, mountains are where God reveals Himself: Moses received the Ten Commandments on Sinai, Elijah heard the still small voice on Carmel, and Jesus was transfigured on a high mountain. Mountains represent both majesty and intimacy, awe and instruction.

There are twenty-nine mountains specifically mentioned in the Bible. From Ararat, where the Ark rested after the flood, to Zion, the dwelling place of God's presence, each mountain carries prophetic weight. These high places remind us that God often calls His people upward, out of the ordinary, to meet Him in a place of revelation.

Psalm 29 ties directly to this number, resounding with the theme of God's voice: "The voice of the Lord is powerful; the voice of the Lord is full of majesty." Mountains symbolize that voice—steady, immovable, and commanding. They are the places where heaven touches earth, where human weakness meets divine strength.

The message of twenty-nine is clear: God calls us to the mountain to hear His voice. It is both a challenge and an invitation—to climb higher, to step away from the noise, and to encounter Him in majesty and instruction.

Focus Point

The voice of the Lord is powerful; the voice of the Lord is full of majesty. (Psalm 29:4, NKJV)

This verse captures the essence of twenty-nine. Mountains are not just physical—they are prophetic symbols of God's voice, strength, and authority.

Main Theme

Twenty-nine preaches mountains as places of revelation and God's voice. They remind us that God calls us higher to hear Him and to experience His presence.

"Twenty-nine is the number of mountains—where God's voice resounds and His presence is revealed."

Key Scriptures

- *So God created man in His own image; in the image of God He created him; male and female He created them.* (Genesis 1:27, NKJV)
- *Now it came to pass, as He prayed on the mountain, that the appearance of His face was altered, and His robe became white and glistening.* (Luke 9:29, NKJV)
- *The voice of the Lord is powerful; the voice of the Lord is full of majesty.* (Psalm 29:4, NKJV)

Key Points

- **Twenty-Nine Mountains** There are twenty-nine mountains in Scripture, each tied to God's voice and presence.
- **Ararat's Rest** The Ark rested on Ararat, symbolizing new beginnings after judgment.
- **Sinai's Law** God gave His law on Sinai, teaching that mountains are places of instruction.
- **Carmel's Fire** Elijah called down fire on Carmel, revealing God's supremacy.

- **Transfiguration Mountain** Jesus was unveiled in glory on the mountain, affirming His divine Sonship.
- **Zion's Dwelling** Zion represents God's presence with His people, the ultimate mountain of worship.
- **Psalm 29's Voice** The psalm links this number to the powerful, majestic voice of the Lord.

Journaling Questions

Journaling about twenty-nine invites us to consider the mountains in our lives—those places where God calls us higher to hear His voice. Writing helps us identify moments of revelation and the need to step out of the ordinary to encounter Him.

Through these reflections, readers will recognize that mountains are both places of testing and of glory. Journaling will reveal how God uses these "high places" to teach, strengthen, and reveal His majesty.

Mountains of Encounter

What mountain moments in my life has God used to reveal His presence?

____

Hearing His Voice

Where do I need to step away from the noise to hear God's voice more clearly?

____

Mountains of Rest

How does Ararat's message of rest after the flood encourage me today?

____
____
____
____
____
____

Instruction on Sinai

What commandments or instructions has God spoken to me in mountain seasons?

____
____
____
____
____
____

Zion's Presence

How do I live daily in the reality of Zion—God's dwelling with His people?

____
____
____
____
____
____

ACTIONABLE STEPS

Seek the Mountain
Dedicate intentional time to meet God in prayer, away from distraction.

Hear and Obey
Write down what God reveals in "mountain moments" and walk it out in obedience.

Celebrate His Majesty
Reflect on past encounters with God and testify of His presence and power.

PERSONAL REFLECTION

The number twenty-nine reminds us that God speaks from the mountain. He calls us upward, not for escape but for encounter. As you reflect, ask yourself whether you are willing to climb higher to hear His voice.

God's voice is majestic, powerful, and full of life. Twenty-nine preaches that mountains are not obstacles—they are invitations to revelation.

What mountain is God calling me to climb? How will I listen for His voice there? What step will I take to dwell in His presence on the mountain?

Closing Prayer: *Lord, thank You for the number twenty-nine and its message of mountains. Call me higher to hear Your voice, to rest in Your presence, and to see Your majesty. Teach me to embrace every mountain as an invitation to encounter You. Amen.*

Chapter 30

The Number Thirty

Redemption and Service

Now Jesus Himself began His ministry at about thirty years of age, being (as was supposed) the son of Joseph, the son of Heli. (Luke 3:23, NKJV)

The number thirty preaches redemption and service. It marks the point when one steps into priestly duty, kingly rule, or prophetic fulfillment. In the Old Testament, Levites entered temple service at thirty, the age at which strength and maturity aligned for responsibility. David became king at thirty, beginning his reign over Israel. Jesus was baptized and began His ministry at thirty, stepping fully into His redemptive calling.

Thirty also connects to the value of life and redemption. Leviticus placed the price of a female servant at thirty shekels in her prime, and Zechariah prophesied the betrayal of Christ for thirty pieces of silver—fulfilled when Judas sold Him to the chief priests. What man used as a price of betrayal, God used as the cost of redemption. Thirty thus preaches both the gravity of service and the depth of Christ's sacrifice.

Ezekiel's prophetic ministry also began in his thirtieth year, marked by visions of God's glory by the River Chebar. The wheel within the wheel vision revealed God's presence and sovereignty. This pattern of thirty emphasizes that significant Kingdom ventures—whether service, rule, or redemption—often carry this divine stamp.

The message of thirty is this: God appoints seasons where service and redemption intersect. It is the number of stepping into calling with maturity and of seeing God redeem what the enemy meant for harm.

FOCUS POINT

And I will bring the blind by a way they did not know; I will lead them in paths they have not known. I will make darkness light before them, and crooked places straight. These things I will do for them, and not forsake them. (Isaiah 42:16, NKJV)

This verse echoes thirty's meaning. Redemption is God's work, and service is our response. He redeems us to serve Him and serve others in His strength.

MAIN THEME

Thirty preaches redemption through Christ and service empowered by maturity and calling. It declares that God appoints times when His people step fully into His purposes.

"Thirty is the number of redemption and service—where calling and sacrifice meet."

KEY SCRIPTURES

- *Now Jesus Himself began His ministry at about thirty years of age, being (as was supposed) the son of Joseph, the son of Heli.* (Luke 3:23, NKJV)
- *So David was thirty years old when he began to reign, and he reigned forty years.* (2 Samuel 5:4, NKJV)
- *So they weighed out for my wages thirty pieces of silver. And the Lord said to me, "Throw it to the potter"—that princely price they set on me.* (Zechariah 11:12–13, NKJV)

KEY POINTS

- **Levite Service** Levites entered service at thirty, marking readiness for priestly responsibility.
- **David's Kingship** David began to reign at thirty, stepping into his divine authority.

- **Jesus' Ministry** Christ began His redemptive ministry at thirty, the age of fullness and calling.
- **Ezekiel's Vision** The prophet Ezekiel received visions in his thirtieth year, entering service as God's messenger.
- **Price of Redemption** Thirty shekels marked the value of a servant, later fulfilled in Christ's betrayal and redemption.
- **Stamp of Calling** Kingdom ventures often carry the stamp of thirty, showing God's divine timing.
- **Intersection of Service and Sacrifice** Thirty preaches that true service flows from God's redemption.

JOURNALING QUESTIONS

Journaling about thirty invites us to reflect on the maturity of our calling and the depth of God's redemption. Writing helps us identify moments when God called us into greater service and where His redemption has transformed betrayal into blessing.

Through these reflections, readers will see that service is not obligation but the overflow of redemption. Journaling captures the intersection where calling meets sacrifice, showing us God's purpose in our story.

SERVICE AT THIRTY

What does the pattern of service beginning at thirty teach me about maturity and readiness?

David's Example

How does David's kingship at thirty inspire me to step into my calling?

Jesus' Ministry

What does Christ beginning His ministry at thirty reveal about redemption and timing?

Betrayal and Redemption

How does the story of thirty pieces of silver remind me of God's ability to redeem?

Ezekiel's Vision

What visions or callings has God shown me in my own season of service?

____

____

____

____

____

____

Actionable Steps

Step Into Calling
Take one step of obedience that aligns with the maturity God has cultivated in you.

Reflect on Redemption
Identify one area where God has turned betrayal or brokenness into redemption.

Serve with Joy
Engage in service not from duty but from the overflow of God's redeeming grace.

Personal Reflection

The number thirty reminds us that God appoints seasons of redemption and service. It is the number of stepping into calling with maturity and trusting Him to redeem what was lost. As you reflect, consider whether you are living in redemption and serving from that place of freedom.

Redemption is His gift; service is our response.

Am I living from the fullness of God's redemption? How will I step into my calling with maturity? What area of my life do I need to surrender so God can redeem and use it for service?

____

____

Closing Prayer: *Lord, thank You for the message of the number thirty. Teach me to live from redemption and to serve from a heart transformed by Your grace. Help me step into my calling with maturity and faith, trusting Your timing in every season. Amen.*

Chapter 31

The Number Thirty-One

Journey of Wisdom

The fear of the Lord is the beginning of wisdom, and the knowledge of the Holy One is understanding. (Proverbs 9:10, NKJV)

The number thirty-one preaches a journey of wisdom, maturity, and divine authority. Written as ל (lamed = 30) and א (aleph = 1), it unites redemption, priestly service, learning, and wisdom (lamed) with unity, beginnings, and God Himself (aleph). Together, א + ל form "El," one of the Hebrew names for God, found in titles such as Elohim, El Shaddai, and El Elyon. Thirty-one thus points directly to God's presence, authority, and the wisdom He imparts to His people.

The Scriptures tie this number to significant stories of divine fulfillment and maturity. Josiah reigned thirty-one years in Jerusalem, leading reform and restoration (2 Chronicles 34:1). Joshua defeated thirty-one kings as Israel entered the Promised Land (Joshua 12:24), marking victory through God's promises. Proverbs 31 describes the virtuous woman, a portrait of wisdom, integrity, and devotion to God in thirty-one verses. Each of these examples declares that true wisdom is lived out in maturity, victory, and faithfulness.

History also affirms this meaning. On October 31, 1517, Martin Luther nailed his 95 Theses to the church door in Wittenberg, sparking the Protestant Reformation. His courage challenged the religious and political structures of his day and restored access to grace and God's Word for all believers. That moment was a thirty-one event—wisdom applied in courage, changing the course of history.

The message of thirty-one is that wisdom is not abstract. It is the lived journey of faith, reform, and maturity, where God's presence guides, His promises sustain, and His authority is revealed.

Focus Point

If any of you lacks wisdom, let him ask of God, who gives to all liberally and without reproach, and it will be given to him. (James 1:5, NKJV)

This verse reveals thirty-one's theme: wisdom is a divine gift. It is granted to those who ask and lived out in obedience and faith.

Main Theme

Thirty-one preaches wisdom as a journey, not a destination. It represents victory, maturity, and the authority of God's presence in the life of His people.

"Thirty-one declares that wisdom is a journey of faith, victory, and maturity in God's presence."

Key Scriptures

- *The fear of the Lord is the beginning of wisdom, and the knowledge of the Holy One is understanding.* (Proverbs 9:10, NKJV)
- *Josiah was eight years old when he became king, and he reigned in Jerusalem thirty-one years.* (2 Chronicles 34:1, NKJV)
- *These are the kings of the land whom Joshua and the children of Israel conquered... thirty-one kings in all.* (Joshua 12:7,24, NKJV)

Key Points

- **Lamed + Aleph = El** Thirty-one unites redemption, service, and wisdom with God Himself, forming His name "El."

- **Josiah's Reign** Thirty-one years of leadership reveal wisdom through reform and covenant restoration.
- **Victory over Kings** Joshua's defeat of thirty-one kings testifies of God's promises fulfilled in wisdom and obedience.
- **Proverbs 31** The virtuous woman embodies wisdom, faith, and devotion lived out practically.
- **Martin Luther's 31st** October 31, 1517, marked a wisdom-driven act that reshaped history and faith.
- **Wisdom Is Maturity** Thirty-one preaches that wisdom grows through lived experience and faithful action.
- **God's Presence in Wisdom** As "El," thirty-one reminds us that wisdom comes from God's presence and authority.

Journaling Questions

Journaling about thirty-one invites us to consider where wisdom is guiding our journey. Writing about these themes helps us connect reform, maturity, and faith to God's presence in our lives. It reminds us that wisdom is not merely knowledge but lived truth.

Through reflection, readers will see that wisdom calls for action—like Josiah's reforms, Joshua's obedience, or Luther's boldness. Journaling reveals how God's presence empowers us to live wisely.

Wisdom from God

Where do I need to ask God for wisdom, trusting His promise in James 1:5?

Reform and Renewal

How does Josiah's thirty-one-year reign inspire me to restore covenant faithfulness in my life?

Victory in Obedience

What battles in my life require wisdom to achieve victory?

Proverbs 31 Example

Which trait of the virtuous woman most challenges or inspires me?

WISDOM IN ACTION

How can I apply wisdom in a practical way this week, like Luther did on October 31?

____
____
____
____
____
____

ACTIONABLE STEPS

Ask for Wisdom
Pray specifically for God's wisdom in one pressing decision this week.

Act in Obedience
Take a concrete step that applies wisdom, whether in relationships, work, or ministry.

Mark a Thirty-One Moment
Recognize a recent victory or reform in your life as part of your journey of wisdom.

PERSONAL REFLECTION

The number thirty-one teaches that wisdom is a journey of maturity, victory, and reform. It calls us to live faithfully, guided by God's presence, and to act courageously when His truth demands it.

Wisdom is not merely knowing—it is applying God's truth to every area of life.

Where do I need God's wisdom most today? How will I walk in maturity and obedience? What step of faith will I take to make wisdom my journey, not just my knowledge?

____
____
____

Closing Prayer: *Lord, thank You for the message of thirty-one. Teach me to seek wisdom as a gift from You, to live it out in maturity, and to apply it boldly in my journey of faith. May every step I take reflect Your presence and authority. Amen.*

Chapter 32

The Number Thirty-Two

A Mature Heart

Above all else, guard your heart, for everything you do flows from it. (Proverbs 4:23, NIV)

The number thirty-two preaches a mature heart—one spiritually connected to God's wisdom and love. Written as ל (lamed = 30) and ב (beit = 2), it unites maturity, redemption, and priestly service (lamed) with faithful witness and being set apart (beit). Together, ל + ב form the word *lev*, which means "heart" in Hebrew. Thirty-two thus declares that the heart, when shaped by God's wisdom and love, becomes the foundation for spiritual maturity and testimony.

Scripture confirms this meaning. The name Elohim appears thirty-two times in Genesis 1, emphasizing God's creative power and love from the beginning. Numbers 31:40 records that thirty-two persons were set apart as the Lord's tribute, symbolizing consecration and divine ownership. Luke 1:32 prophesies that Jesus will be great and inherit David's throne, and Acts 2:32 affirms His resurrection witnessed by many. These verses tie maturity, testimony, and divine love together in the theme of thirty-two.

Even history echoes this number. On March 2, 1836 (3/2), the Texas Declaration of Independence was signed. Though a secular event, it reflects the spirit of freedom that flows from hearts desiring liberty and refusing oppression. This illustrates how a mature heart, connected to God's wisdom and love, always leans toward truth, freedom, and testimony.

The message of thirty-two is this: maturity in God is not measured by age or knowledge alone but by a heart set apart, filled with wisdom, and anchored in His love.

FOCUS POINT

Set your mind on things above, not on things on the earth. (Colossians 3:2, NKJV)

This verse reminds us that a mature heart is focused on God's wisdom and eternal perspective, not earthly distractions.

MAIN THEME

Thirty-two preaches a mature heart, set apart for God's wisdom and love, strengthened by testimony, and marked by consecration.

"Thirty-two is the number of a mature heart—anchored in wisdom, consecrated in love, and set apart for God."

KEY SCRIPTURES

- *Above all else, guard your heart, for everything you do flows from it.* (Proverbs 4:23, NIV)
- *He will be great, and will be called the Son of the Highest; and the Lord God will give Him the throne of His father David.* (Luke 1:32, NKJV)
- *This Jesus God has raised up, of which we are all witnesses.* (Acts 2:32, NKJV)

KEY POINTS

- **Lev = Heart** Thirty-two forms the Hebrew word *lev*, teaching that true maturity is rooted in the heart.
- **Elohim in Genesis** God's name *Elohim* appears thirty-two times in Genesis 1, revealing love and wisdom in creation.
- **Set Apart for God** Thirty-two persons were given as the Lord's tribute in Numbers 31, symbolizing consecration.
- **Christ's Throne** Luke 1:32 points to Christ's eternal reign, a promise tied to God's love and wisdom.

- **Resurrection Witness** Acts 2:32 shows Jesus' resurrection witnessed, affirming the mature testimony of His disciples.
- **Freedom's Connection** The Texas Declaration signed on March 2nd illustrates how hearts connected to truth long for liberty.
- **Maturity Is Love** Thirty-two reminds us that spiritual maturity flows from love, not knowledge alone.

Journaling Questions

Journaling about thirty-two allows us to explore the state of our heart—whether it is maturing in God's wisdom and love or distracted by the world. Writing gives us perspective on how consecration, testimony, and freedom flow from a heart aligned with Him.

Through reflection, readers will see that a mature heart is not perfect but surrendered. Journaling helps identify areas where God is shaping our hearts for wisdom, consecration, and testimony.

Guarding My Heart

What steps can I take to guard my heart as Proverbs 4:23 commands?

____

____

____

____

____

____

Consecrated Heart

Where is God asking me to set apart my heart more fully for Him?

____

____

____

____

____

CHRIST'S REIGN

How does Luke 1:32 shape my view of Christ's rule in my life?

____

____

____

____

____

____

WITNESS OF RESURRECTION

What testimony has God given me that strengthens my faith and others'?

____

____

____

____

____

____

FREEDOM AND MATURITY

How do I see freedom as evidence of a heart maturing in God's wisdom and love?

____

____

____

____

____

____

ACTIONABLE STEPS

Guard the Heart
Set boundaries around influences that hinder wisdom and love.

Testify Boldly
Share one personal testimony this week of God's love and power in your life.

Practice Consecration
Dedicate intentional time daily to prayer and Scripture, setting apart your heart for God.

PERSONAL REFLECTION

The number thirty-two preaches maturity through the heart. It reminds us that growth in God is not about intellectual gain but about a surrendered, consecrated heart filled with His wisdom and love.

A mature heart is one that guards truth, treasures freedom, and testifies of God's power.

Am I living with a mature heart? How will I consecrate my heart more fully to God? What testimony will I share as evidence of His wisdom and love?

Closing Prayer: *Father, thank You for the message of thirty-two. Teach me to live with a mature heart, anchored in Your wisdom and love. Guard my heart from distraction, consecrate it for Your purposes, and let my life testify of Your power and truth. Amen.*

Chapter 33

The Number Thirty-Three

Spiritual Maturity

When I was a child, I spoke as a child, I understood as a child, I thought as a child; but when I became a man, I put away childish things. (1 Corinthians 13:11, NKJV)

The number thirty-three preaches spiritual maturity and the completeness of redemption. Written as ל (lamed = 30) and ג (gimel = 3), it unites wisdom, priestly service, and redemption (lamed) with perfect completion and divinity (gimel). Together, ג + ל mark God's completeness for those who are spiritually mature.

Scripture anchors this meaning with powerful examples. Jesus was crucified at the age of thirty-three, completing His earthly mission and fulfilling divine prophecy. His sacrifice was the ultimate sign of maturity, redemption, and the completion of God's plan of salvation. Similarly, King David reigned in Jerusalem for thirty-three years, a reign that reflected God's covenant promise and divine authority. Jacob's family included thirty-three descendants through Leah (Genesis 46:15), showing continuation of covenant blessing.

Even modern history affirms this number's message. In 2010, thirty-three Chilean miners were trapped underground for sixty-nine days, only to be miraculously rescued in a capsule thirty-three feet long. Psalm 33 was read by survivors, emphasizing God's mercy, redemption, and hope. This living parable preached spiritual maturity and the faithfulness of God to redeem.

The message of thirty-three is that God brings His people into spiritual maturity and fullness through redemption. It is a call to live beyond childish faith and into the maturity of trust, obedience, and completion in Christ.

Focus Point

But let patience have its perfect work, that you may be perfect and complete, lacking nothing. (James 1:4, NKJV)

This verse reflects thirty-three's meaning. Spiritual maturity is about completeness—trusting God to finish what He has started.

Main Theme

Thirty-three preaches spiritual maturity and the completeness of redemption. It reveals the fullness of God's plan worked out in His people.

"Thirty-three is the number of spiritual maturity—redemption completed and faith made whole."

Key Scriptures

- *And when they had come to the place called Calvary, there they crucified Him.* (Luke 23:33, NKJV)
- *In Hebron he reigned over Judah seven years and six months, and in Jerusalem he reigned thirty-three years over all Israel and Judah.* (2 Samuel 5:5, NKJV)
- *These were the sons of Leah, whom she bore to Jacob in Padan Aram, with his daughter Dinah. All the persons, his sons, and his daughters, were thirty-three.* (Genesis 46:15, NKJV)

Key Points

- **Lamed + Gimel** Thirty-three unites wisdom, redemption, and priestly service with completion and divinity.
- **Jesus' Crucifixion** Christ's death at thirty-three marked the completion of His redemptive mission.

- **David's Reign** David ruled in Jerusalem for thirty-three years, fulfilling God's covenant promise.
- **Jacob's Descendants** Leah's thirty-three descendants showed God's faithfulness to covenant lineage.
- **Psalm 33 in Chile** Thirty-three miners rescued in Chile became a living parable of redemption.
- **Maturity in Faith** Thirty-three calls believers beyond immaturity into mature trust in God.
- **Completeness in Christ** It preaches that redemption is finished and maturity is found in Him.

Journaling Questions

Journaling about thirty-three invites us to reflect on our own spiritual maturity. Writing reveals whether we are still clinging to childish faith or stepping into the fullness of God's redemption. It helps us see life events through the lens of God's completion.

Through reflection, readers will discover that spiritual maturity is not about perfection but about allowing redemption to shape faith, obedience, and trust. Journaling becomes a way to track growth and surrender.

Childish vs. Mature

What areas of my faith still reflect immaturity, and how can I grow into maturity?

____

____

____

____

____

____

____

Jesus' Completion

How does Christ's crucifixion at thirty-three encourage me to trust God's timing of completion?

____

____

____

____

____

____

David's Reign

What does David's thirty-three-year reign teach me about God's covenant faithfulness?

____

____

____

____

____

____

Modern Parables

How does the story of the thirty-three Chilean miners inspire my faith in God's redemption?

____

____

____

____

____

____

COMPLETENESS IN CHRIST

How do I see God finishing what He started in my life right now?

____

____

____

____

____

____

ACTIONABLE STEPS

Put Away Childish Things
Identify one immature pattern in your faith and surrender it to God.

Embrace Redemption
Meditate on Christ's completed work at the cross as the foundation of maturity.

Live in Completeness
Take a practical step of obedience that reflects trust in God's finished work.

PERSONAL REFLECTION

The number thirty-three reminds us that God brings His people to maturity through redemption. It preaches completeness, fulfillment, and the call to live in maturity. As you reflect, consider where God is asking you to grow beyond immaturity and into fullness.

Maturity is not about doing more but about trusting more deeply in His finished work.

Where am I still clinging to childish faith? How will I step into maturity in Christ? What area of my life is God completing by His redemption?

____

____

____

____

Closing Prayer: *Father, thank You for the message of thirty-three. Teach me to walk in spiritual maturity, to trust in Christ's completed work, and to live as one made whole by redemption. Let my life reflect completeness in You. Amen.*

Chapter 34

The Number Thirty-Four

Miracle Deliverance

The righteous cry out, and the Lord hears, and delivers them out of all their troubles.
(Psalm 34:17, NKJV)

The number thirty-four preaches miracle deliverance. It is tied to overcoming victory, being 17 × 2, a doubled witness of triumph. Written as ל (lamed = 30) and ד (dalet = 4), it joins maturity, wisdom, and priestly service (lamed) with humility, structure, and creation (dalet). Together, they signify the transition from learning to leadership, a journey that opens doors to divine fulfillment. Thirty-four represents acts of redemption manifesting in creation, where God intervenes in miraculous ways.

Jesus exemplifies this truth through thirty-four pre-resurrection miracles recorded in Scripture, from turning water into wine to healing Malchus' ear in Gethsemane. Each miracle was a testimony of deliverance, proving that Jesus is the ultimate leader who overcomes. The connection between 17 and 34 reinforces this: victory is not hidden but manifested, a deliverance visible to all.

Biblical patterns echo this theme. The 34th time David is mentioned is in 1 Samuel 17:45, where he declares victory over Goliath in the name of the Lord. The 34th mention of Abraham records the naming of Isaac, the child of promise (Genesis 21:3). The 34th mention of Noah records God's covenant after the flood (Genesis 9:8–18), a promise sealed with a rainbow. Jewish tradition even suggests Isaac was 34 when Sarah died, marking a turning point in covenant continuation. King Josiah, by age 34, had already begun temple reforms and national renewal. Each of these moments testifies to miracle deliverance and divine intervention.

The message of thirty-four is clear: God's people are not only promised victory—they are delivered by miracles. This number declares that His acts of redemption produce overcoming victories that transform creation itself.

FOCUS POINT

Then said David to the Philistine, "You come to me with a sword, with a spear, and with a javelin. But I come to you in the name of the Lord of hosts, the God of the armies of Israel, whom you have defied." (1 Samuel 17:45, NKJV)

This verse captures thirty-four's essence. True deliverance is not in human power but in God's miraculous intervention.

MAIN THEME

Thirty-four preaches miracle deliverance, the visible manifestation of God's overcoming power in creation.

"Thirty-four declares that God's redemption produces miracle deliverance and visible victory."

KEY SCRIPTURES

- *The righteous cry out, and the Lord hears, and delivers them out of all their troubles.* (Psalm 34:17, NKJV)
- *Then said David to the Philistine, "You come to me with a sword, with a spear, and with a javelin. But I come to you in the name of the Lord of hosts."* (1 Samuel 17:45, NKJV)
- *And Abraham called the name of his son who was born to him—whom Sarah bore to him—Isaac.* (Genesis 21:3, NKJV)

Key Points

- **Witness of Victory** Thirty-four, as 17 × 2, doubles the witness of overcoming triumph.
- **Jesus' Thirty-Four Miracles** From Cana to Gethsemane, His miracles reveal deliverance as the pattern of redemption.
- **David's Declaration** The 34th mention of David shows him defeating Goliath in God's strength.
- **Isaac Named** Abraham's 34th mention ties to Isaac's naming, a miracle child of promise.
- **Noah's Covenant** The 34th mention of Noah records God's covenant sealed by a rainbow.
- **Isaac's Turning Point** At 34, Jewish tradition says Isaac faced loss and prepared for covenant continuation.
- **Josiah's Renewal** By 34, Josiah had launched reforms, restoring the temple and reviving Judah's faith.

Journaling Questions

Journaling about thirty-four invites us to reflect on moments of deliverance in our lives. Writing helps us trace how God's miraculous hand intervened where human strength failed. It encourages us to see His redemption not just as hidden victory but as visible deliverance.

By reflecting, readers will recognize that every battle, loss, or transition can become a platform for God's miracle deliverance. Journaling highlights how His redemption transforms defeat into visible triumph.

Victory Manifested

Where has God turned hidden battles into visible victories in my life?

____

____

____

____

____

Miracle Encounters

Which miracle of Jesus most inspires me to trust Him for deliverance?

____

____

____

____

____

____

David's Boldness

How does David's declaration in 1 Samuel 17:45 challenge me to face my giants?

____

____

____

____

____

____

Covenant Promises

What covenant promises has God confirmed to me in times of trial?

____

____

____

____

____

____

TURNING POINTS

How can I see personal turning points as opportunities for miracle deliverance?

____

____

____

____

____

____

ACTIONABLE STEPS

Declare Deliverance
Speak boldly like David, declaring God's name over battles you face.

Remember Miracles
List specific times God has delivered you and share them as testimonies.

Expect Victory
Approach current challenges with expectancy, trusting God for miraculous outcomes.

PERSONAL REFLECTION

The number thirty-four reminds us that God's deliverance is not hidden—it is miraculous, visible, and undeniable. As you reflect, consider where God has already shown Himself strong and where He is calling you to expect a "miracle deliverance."

God's redemption produces victories that shape history, covenant, and creation.

Where do I need God's miracle deliverance? How will I declare His victory in my battles? What testimony will I share of His visible redemption?

____

____

____

____

Closing Prayer: *Lord, thank You for the message of thirty-four. Teach me to trust Your miracle deliverance, to declare victory in Your name, and to expect visible redemption in my life. Let my testimony bring glory to You as the God who delivers. Amen.*

Chapter 35

The Number Thirty-Five

Grace and Revelation

Let them shout for joy and be glad, who favor my righteous cause; and let them say continually, "Let the Lord be magnified, who has pleasure in the prosperity of His servant."
(Psalm 35:27, NKJV)

The number thirty-five preaches grace and revelation, leading to growth and favor from the Lord. Written as ל (lamed = 30) and ה (he = 5), it unites wisdom, maturity, and priestly service (lamed) with divine grace, revelation, and the breath of God (he). Together, thirty-five reveals that wisdom combined with grace produces spiritual growth, renewal, and the favor of God in the lives of His people.

This number surfaces in both Scripture and history as a marker of divine favor and turning points. Psalm 35 is David's prayer for deliverance, declaring God's justice and salvation. Luke 1:35 records the angel's words to Mary, revealing the miraculous conception of Christ by the Holy Spirit—a moment of divine grace and revelation shaping history forever. Proverbs 3:5 calls believers to trust in God's wisdom, not human understanding, while Titus 3:5 proclaims that salvation is not earned but given through God's mercy and renewal by the Spirit.

Even modern history echoes this theme. John F. Kennedy, the 35th president of the United States, symbolized vision and favor during a pivotal time in American history. His leadership during the space race and civil rights era revealed the weight of grace and responsibility in shaping national destiny. His untimely assassination underscored how fragile favor can seem in human hands, yet it did not erase the legacy of change his presidency represented.

The message of thirty-five is this: grace and revelation empower God's people to overcome challenges, walk in His favor, and experience renewal by His Spirit.

Focus Point

Trust in the Lord with all your heart, and lean not on your own understanding. (Proverbs 3:5, NKJV)

This verse reminds us that true grace and revelation come from God's wisdom, not from human strength or intellect.

Main Theme

Thirty-five preaches the union of wisdom and grace, producing revelation, growth, and favor from God.

"Thirty-five declares that God's grace and revelation bring spiritual growth, renewal, and favor."

Key Scriptures

- *And the angel answered and said to her, "The Holy Spirit will come upon you, and the power of the Highest will overshadow you; therefore, also, that Holy One who is to be born will be called the Son of God."* (Luke 1:35, NKJV)
- *Trust in the Lord with all your heart, and lean not on your own understanding.* (Proverbs 3:5, NKJV)
- *Not by works of righteousness which we have done, but according to His mercy He saved us, through the washing of regeneration and renewing of the Holy Spirit.* (Titus 3:5, NKJV)

Key Points

- **Wisdom and Grace Combined** Thirty-five unites wisdom (30) with grace (5), producing growth and favor.
- **Psalm 35's Prayer** David calls on God for deliverance, declaring His justice and prosperity for His servants.
- **Divine Overshadowing** Luke 1:35 reveals the miraculous grace and revelation of Christ's conception.
- **Trust in God's Wisdom** Proverbs 3:5 urges us to lean not on our understanding but on divine revelation.
- **Renewal by the Spirit** Titus 3:5 teaches that salvation and renewal come by grace, not works.
- **Historical Turning Point** The 35th U.S. president, John F. Kennedy, symbolizes the favor and responsibility of leadership in critical times.
- **Breath of God** He (5) in thirty-five reminds us of God's Spirit breathing life and revelation into His people.

Journaling Questions

Journaling about thirty-five helps us explore how God's grace and revelation have shaped our journey. Writing allows us to recognize the places where His Spirit breathed life into dead situations, offering renewal, favor, and growth. It challenges us to lean on His wisdom rather than our own understanding.

Through reflection, readers will discover that thirty-five is not just about favor received but favor stewarded. It is the call to grow spiritually, to embrace revelation as divine guidance, and to walk in the breath of God's Spirit.

Wisdom and Grace

Where have I seen God's wisdom and grace combine to bring growth in my life?

___

___

___

___

Psalm 35 Reflection

How does David's prayer for deliverance inspire me to seek God's justice and favor?

Divine Overshadowing

What area of my life needs the Holy Spirit's overshadowing presence, like Mary in Luke 1:35?

Leaning on God

What does Proverbs 3:5 reveal about how I rely on God's wisdom instead of my own?

RENEWAL BY THE SPIRIT

How have I experienced God's renewing grace as described in Titus 3:5?

ACTIONABLE STEPS

Lean on His Wisdom
Practice surrender by asking God for guidance before making key decisions.

Receive Renewal
Set aside daily moments to invite the Holy Spirit's breath into areas of weariness.

Walk in Favor
Look for one way this week to use the favor God has given you to bless others.

PERSONAL REFLECTION

The number thirty-five preaches that grace and revelation bring growth, favor, and renewal. It calls us to trust not in ourselves but in the wisdom and breath of God. As you reflect, consider how His grace has carried you and how His revelation has shaped your journey.

God's grace is not only sufficient—it multiplies wisdom, opens doors, and breathes life into every season.

Am I living in God's grace and revelation? How will I lean more fully on His wisdom? What step can I take to steward His favor in my life?

Closing Prayer: *Father, thank You for the message of thirty-five. Teach me to walk in Your grace and revelation, trusting in Your wisdom and breath of life. Renew me by Your Spirit and let my life overflow with Your favor. Amen.*

Chapter 36

The Number Thirty-Six

Divine Connection

In all your ways acknowledge Him, and He shall direct your paths. (Proverbs 3:6, NKJV)

The number thirty-six preaches divine connection—spiritually linking humanity to God. Written as ל (lamed = 30) and ו (vav = 6), it joins wisdom, maturity, and priestly service (lamed) with humanity's imperfection and shortcomings (vav). Alone, six exposes our insufficiency and rebellion, but joined with thirty, it becomes a picture of redemption—our works and weaknesses covered by God's wisdom and grace. Thirty-six reveals that even in our frailty, we are drawn into connection with Him through hidden righteousness and spiritual light.

Scripture confirms this number's meaning with powerful imagery. Proverbs 3:6 urges believers to acknowledge God in all things, finding direction in Him. Hebrews 3:6 reminds us that we are Christ's house if we remain firm in confidence and hope. John 1:36 reveals Jesus as the Lamb of God—the bridge of divine connection—and John 3:36 declares eternal life for those who believe in Him, while warning of judgment for unbelief. Together, these passages highlight thirty-six as the meeting point of human weakness and divine redemption, where true connection is found in Christ.

This number teaches that divine connection is not achieved by human effort alone but by God's grace sanctifying our lives. Thirty-six is a testimony that maturity and redemption transform human insufficiency into spiritual intimacy, lighting the path toward God's presence.

Focus Point

But Christ as a Son over His own house, whose house we are if we hold fast the confidence and the rejoicing of the hope firm to the end. (Hebrews 3:6, NKJV)

This verse captures the theme of thirty-six: divine connection comes through holding fast to Christ, who unites us to God as His dwelling place.

Main Theme

Thirty-six preaches divine connection, where human weakness meets God's wisdom, producing intimacy, redemption, and spiritual light.

"Thirty-six is the number of divine connection—where our insufficiency is redeemed into intimacy with God."

Key Scriptures

- *In all your ways acknowledge Him, and He shall direct your paths.* (Proverbs 3:6, NKJV)
- *But Christ as a Son over His own house, whose house we are if we hold fast the confidence and the rejoicing of the hope firm to the end.* (Hebrews 3:6, NKJV)
- *And looking at Jesus as He walked, he said, "Behold the Lamb of God!"* (John 1:36, NKJV)

Key Points

- **Lamed + Vav** Thirty-six combines wisdom and maturity (30) with human weakness (6), preaching redemption.
- **Acknowledging God** Proverbs 3:6 assures that divine connection directs our steps when we submit fully to Him.
- **Christ's House** Hebrews 3:6 teaches that believers, as God's house, are sustained by confidence and hope in Christ.

- **The Lamb of God** John 1:36 identifies Jesus as the Lamb, the ultimate bridge of divine connection.
- **Eternal Life or Wrath** John 3:36 divides destiny—belief brings eternal connection; unbelief brings separation.
- **Hidden Righteousness** Thirty-six signifies righteousness not in self but in God's covering presence.
- **Light of Connection** It preaches spiritual maturity that transforms human insufficiency into divine intimacy.

JOURNALING QUESTIONS

Journaling about thirty-six allows us to reflect on how God takes our shortcomings and transforms them into connection with Him. Writing helps us see that divine intimacy is not earned by perfection but received by acknowledging Him, trusting His wisdom, and holding firm to His promises.

Through these reflections, readers will recognize that their failures do not disqualify them but invite them into deeper reliance on God. Thirty-six reminds us that divine connection is sustained by Christ, not self-effort.

HUMAN WEAKNESS

Where have I seen God redeem my shortcomings into opportunities for divine connection?

____

____

____

____

____

____

____

Christ's House

What does it mean to me that I am part of Christ's house, as Hebrews 3:6 describes?

____
____
____
____
____
____

The Lamb of God

How does John 1:36—Jesus as the Lamb of God—shape my understanding of redemption?

____
____
____
____
____
____

Acknowledging Him

How can I better acknowledge God in all my ways, as Proverbs 3:6 commands?

____
____
____
____
____
____

Connection or Separation

How does John 3:36 challenge me to deepen my faith and trust in Christ?

____
____
____
____
____
____

Actionable Steps

Acknowledge Him Daily
Begin each day by inviting God's direction in every decision and step.

Hold Fast in Faith
Commit to standing firm in confidence and hope, even when faced with trials.

Live Redeemed
Recognize that divine connection is not earned by perfection but received through grace—walk each day as one connected to God.

Personal Reflection

The number thirty-six preaches that divine connection is found when our weakness is redeemed by God's wisdom and grace. It reminds us that the Lamb of God makes intimacy possible and that acknowledging Him in all things secures our steps.

As you reflect, consider whether you are striving in self-effort or resting in divine connection through Christ.

Am I truly living as one connected to God? How will I acknowledge Him in every way today? What step will I take to embrace my identity as part of Christ's house?

____
____

Closing Prayer: *Father, thank You for the message of thirty-six. Teach me to embrace divine connection, to trust in Your wisdom, and to rest in the redemption Christ provides. Let my life reflect intimacy with You, as I walk daily in the light of Your presence. Amen.*

Chapter 37

The Number Thirty-Seven

Divine Completion

Do not be wise in your own eyes; fear the Lord and depart from evil. (Proverbs 3:7, NKJV)

The number thirty-seven preaches divine completion, connection to God's holiness, and alignment with His purpose. Written as ל (lamed = 30) and ז (zayin = 7), it unites wisdom, maturity, and priestly service (lamed) with the Spirit of God and divine perfection (zayin). Seven is the number of creation and spiritual completion, reflecting the fullness of God's work and His rest. Together, thirty-seven declares that human wisdom and maturity find their fulfillment only in God's Spirit, bringing about true holiness and divine order.

This number holds profound biblical significance. The very first verse of the Bible, Genesis 1:1, contains a hidden pattern: "In the beginning God created the heavens and the earth" totals 2701 in Hebrew gematria, which equals 37 × 73. This emphasizes thirty-seven as foundational to creation and divine order. It illustrates that wisdom (73) and divine completion (37) are intertwined, showing God's perfection in both design and purpose.

Scriptural passages reinforce this meaning. Revelation 3:7 proclaims that Christ holds the key of David, opening and closing with divine authority. John 3:7 calls all believers to be born again, marking divine completion in new life. Titus 3:7 reminds us that justification by grace leads to the hope of eternal life, while Zechariah 3:7 promises authority and access to God's courts for those who walk in His ways. Together, these verses show that thirty-seven is the number of holiness, purpose, and the Spirit's perfection.

The message of thirty-seven is clear: divine completion is not achieved by human wisdom but through the Spirit of God, who brings perfection, order, and purpose into our lives.

FOCUS POINT

And to the angel of the church in Philadelphia write, "These things says He who is holy, He who is true, He who has the key of David, He who opens and no one shuts, and shuts and no one opens." (Revelation 3:7, NKJV)

This verse affirms the essence of thirty-seven: divine completion flows from God's authority, opening doors no one can shut and shutting doors no one can open.

MAIN THEME

Thirty-seven preaches divine completion, where wisdom and maturity are fulfilled by the Spirit of God, producing holiness, order, and eternal purpose.

"Thirty-seven is the number of divine completion—where God's Spirit perfects His purpose in creation and in us."

KEY SCRIPTURES

- *Do not be wise in your own eyes; fear the Lord and depart from evil.* (Proverbs 3:7, NKJV)
- *Do not marvel that I said to you, "You must be born again."* (John 3:7, NKJV)
- *That having been justified by His grace we should become heirs according to the hope of eternal life.* (Titus 3:7, NKJV)

KEY POINTS

- **Lamed + Zayin** Thirty-seven unites wisdom (30) with divine perfection and Spirit (7), symbolizing completion.
- **Genesis 1:1 Pattern** The Hebrew text totals 2701 = 37 × 73, tying creation itself to divine order and completion.
- **Revelation's Key** Revelation 3:7 points to Christ's authority as the one who governs divine order.

- **Born Again** John 3:7 teaches that divine completion is found in spiritual rebirth.
- **Grace and Hope** Titus 3:7 declares that justification by grace makes us heirs of eternal life.
- **Zechariah's Promise** Zechariah 3:7 assures divine authority and access for those who walk in God's ways.
- **Holiness Perfected** Thirty-seven preaches that human wisdom must yield to the Spirit's perfection.

Journaling Questions

Journaling about thirty-seven allows us to see where God has brought divine completion in our lives. Writing helps us acknowledge that our wisdom alone cannot achieve holiness but must be surrendered to the Spirit of God. It encourages us to identify where His Spirit has brought order, purpose, and rebirth into our journey.

Through reflection, readers will discover that divine completion is not an end point but a continual process of walking in holiness and alignment with God's Spirit. Journaling allows us to celebrate the ways God has already completed His work and trust Him for what is still being perfected.

Wisdom and Spirit

How have I seen God take my limited wisdom and complete it by His Spirit?

____

____

____

____

____

____

____

Genesis 1:1 Connection

What does the divine pattern in creation teach me about God's order in my life?

Revelation's Authority

What doors has God opened or shut in my life that confirm His divine completion?

Born Again Life

How does John 3:7 challenge me to live as one who is spiritually reborn?

Walking in Holiness

Where is God calling me to yield my wisdom for His Spirit's perfection?

____

____

____

____

____

____

Actionable Steps

Surrender Wisdom
Lay down reliance on your own understanding and invite the Spirit to perfect your ways.

Celebrate Completion
Mark moments where God has already completed His work in your life as testimonies of His faithfulness.

Walk in Purpose
Commit to daily walking in holiness, trusting that God's Spirit is guiding you into His divine plan.

Personal Reflection

The number thirty-seven reminds us that divine completion belongs to the Spirit of God. It preaches that human wisdom is insufficient without His perfection. As you reflect, ask yourself whether you are clinging to your own wisdom or surrendering to His Spirit's leading.

God completes what He begins, and His Spirit brings purpose, holiness, and order to our lives.

Am I trusting my wisdom or God's Spirit for divine completion? How will I yield to His authority in my life today? What step can I take to walk in His holiness and purpose?

Closing Prayer: *Father, thank You for the message of thirty-seven. Teach me to surrender my wisdom to Your Spirit, to walk in holiness, and to trust in Your divine completion. Perfect in me what You have begun, that my life may reveal Your purpose and glory. Amen.*

Chapter 38

The Number Thirty-Eight

Transition

And the time we took to come from Kadesh-Barnea until we crossed over the Valley of Zered was thirty-eight years, until all the generation of the men of war was consumed from the midst of the camp, just as the Lord had sworn to them. (Deuteronomy 2:14, NKJV)

The number thirty-eight preaches transition. It marks the movement from learning to renewal, from wandering to inheritance, from suffering to restoration. Written as ל (lamed = 30) and ח (chet = 8), it unites wisdom, maturity, and redemption (lamed) with new beginnings, grace, and resurrection life (chet). Together, thirty-eight signifies that while human weakness often delays promise, God uses those delays to transform hearts, prepare His people, and usher them into a new season.

Israel's story at Kadesh-Barnea is the greatest picture of this number. Though delivered from Egypt with miracles, Israel hesitated in fear rather than stepping forward in faith. That hesitation led to thirty-eight years of wandering, not simply as punishment but as transition. God waited for a generation of unbelief to pass away so that a new heart could rise. Deuteronomy 29:5 reminds us that even in the wilderness, God's provision never failed—their clothes and sandals did not wear out. His presence sustained them until they were ready to step into promise.

The healing at the pool of Bethesda (John 5:5) reinforces this truth. A man suffered for thirty-eight years until Jesus intervened with miraculous restoration. His story embodies the waiting, the longing, and the sudden transition into new life. Even the Hebrew word *kavodo* ("His glory") has a value of thirty-eight, declaring that God's glory is revealed after endurance.

The message of thirty-eight is this: transition often requires waiting, but God uses that waiting to prepare hearts for renewal. In redemption, thirty-eight preaches transformation into promise; in the flesh, it preaches delay and suffering. Yet always, it points toward God's mercy, intervention, and glory revealed.

Focus Point

I know your works. See, I have set before you an open door, and no one can shut it; for you have a little strength, have kept My word, and have not denied My name. (Revelation 3:8, NKJV)

This verse reflects thirty-eight's theme: transition is an open door from God. Even when strength is small, His Word sustains and ushers us into renewal.

Main Theme

Thirty-eight preaches transition. It is the number of waiting, suffering, and preparation, yet also of redemption, new beginnings, and God's glory revealed.

"Thirty-eight declares that God uses waiting seasons to prepare us for new beginnings and divine renewal."

Key Scriptures

- *And the time we took to come from Kadesh-Barnea until we crossed over the Valley of Zered was thirty-eight years.* (Deuteronomy 2:14, NKJV)
- *Now a certain man was there who had an infirmity thirty-eight years.* (John 5:5, NKJV)
- *Then Mary said, "Behold the maidservant of the Lord! Let it be to me according to your word."* (Luke 1:38, NKJV)

Key Points

- **Lamed + Chet** Thirty-eight combines wisdom (30) with new beginnings (8), preaching transformation through transition.

- **Israel's Waiting** Thirty-eight years of wilderness wandering prepared a new generation for promise.
- **God's Provision** Even in delay, God sustained His people—clothes and sandals did not wear out.
- **Bethesda Healing** A man's thirty-eight years of suffering ended in miraculous restoration by Christ.
- **His Glory Revealed** The Hebrew word *kavodo* (glory) equals thirty-eight, showing endurance leads to glory.
- **Open Door of Transition** Revelation 3:8 assures us that God sets the door to new beginnings before His people.
- **From Fear to Faith** Thirty-eight warns against hesitation but promises renewal when faith rises.

Journaling Questions

Journaling about thirty-eight helps us explore seasons of waiting, suffering, and transition in our lives. Writing reveals that delays are not always denials but invitations to deeper transformation. These reflections help us recognize God's provision in the wilderness and His power to bring renewal at the appointed time.

Through journaling, readers will discover that thirty-eight moments are not wasted years—they are seasons where old unbelief dies, new hearts are formed, and God's glory is revealed.

Waiting Seasons

What thirty-eight season of waiting or suffering have I walked through, and what did God teach me?

____

____

____

____

____

____

____

Israel's Lesson

How does Israel's thirty-eight years in the wilderness challenge me to trust God rather than fear?

Bethesda Healing

Where do I need Christ to speak healing and renewal into a long-standing struggle?

God's Provision

How has God sustained me in seasons of delay, like Israel's clothes and sandals not wearing out?

Open Door

What open door of transition is God setting before me right now?

____

____

____

____

____

____

Actionable Steps

Acknowledge Waiting
Identify one area where you've been waiting and reframe it as God's preparation, not abandonment.

Look for Provision
Journal three ways God has sustained you in the wilderness season.

Step Forward in Faith
Take one practical step toward the open door God is setting before you, trusting His timing.

Personal Reflection

The number thirty-eight preaches that transition is part of God's redemptive process. What feels like delay is often preparation. His presence sustains us in wilderness years, and His Spirit renews us in due season.

As you reflect, ask whether you are hesitating in fear like Israel or stepping forward in faith like the healed man at Bethesda.

Am I embracing my season of transition as God's preparation? How will I trust His provision while waiting? What step of faith will I take toward renewal today?

____

____

Closing Prayer: *Father, thank You for the message of thirty-eight. Teach me to see waiting as preparation, suffering as transition, and endurance as the pathway to Your glory. Lead me into new beginnings and help me step forward in faith. Amen.*

Chapter 39

The Number Thirty-Nine

Godly Judgment

And even now the ax is laid to the root of the trees. Therefore, every tree which does not bear good fruit is cut down and thrown into the fire. (Luke 3:9, NKJV)

The number thirty-nine preaches godly judgment. Written as ל (lamed = 30) and ט (tet = 9), it joins wisdom, maturity, and priestly service (lamed) with divine judgment and its twofold outcomes (tet). Nine represents both sides of God's judgment: life, in the form of fruit-bearing and spiritual progress, or death, in the form of finality and removal. Together, thirty-nine declares that wisdom leads to refinement, godly discipline, and ultimately, the production of good works.

In Scripture, the number 39 is tied to mercy in the midst of judgment. Deuteronomy 25:3 limits punishment to forty lashes, but Jewish tradition capped it at thirty-nine to ensure the command was not exceeded. Paul affirmed this practice in 2 Corinthians 11:24, saying he received "forty lashes minus one" five times. Jesus Himself bore the thirty-nine lashes before His crucifixion, a picture of judgment placed upon Him so that grace and life might flow to us.

Thirty-nine also ties to the unity of God. The phrase *YHWH Echad* ("The Lord is One") in Deuteronomy 6:4 has a numerical value of 39, declaring His oneness and sovereign rule in judgment. Scriptures reinforce this meaning: Ephesians 3:9 speaks of hidden wisdom in Christ; Titus 3:9 warns against disputes unworthy of God's people; Psalm 9:3 proclaims enemies perishing in His presence. Mark 1:39 records Jesus casting out demons, a demonstration of judgment over evil.

The message of thirty-nine is this: godly judgment is never arbitrary. In the redeemed, it refines, purifies, and bears fruit. In the unredeemed, it brings finality and separation. Either way, it reveals God's wisdom, justice, and oneness.

Focus Point

Hear, O Israel: The Lord our God, the Lord is one! (Deuteronomy 6:4, NKJV)

This verse captures thirty-nine's theme. Judgment flows from the oneness of God—His unified authority to refine, correct, and bring finality.

Main Theme

Thirty-nine preaches godly judgment. It is the number of discipline, mercy, and refinement that leads to either fruitful life or final separation.

"Thirty-nine declares that God's judgment refines the redeemed and exposes the unfruitful."

Key Scriptures

- *And even now the ax is laid to the root of the trees. Therefore, every tree which does not bear good fruit is cut down and thrown into the fire.* (Luke 3:9, NKJV)
- *From the Jews five times I received forty stripes minus one.* (2 Corinthians 11:24, NKJV)
- *Hear, O Israel: The Lord our God, the Lord is one!* (Deuteronomy 6:4, NKJV)

Key Points

- **Lamed + Tet** Thirty-nine combines wisdom (30) with divine judgment (9), producing refinement and good works.
- **Mercy in Judgment** Thirty-nine lashes marked the limit of discipline—enough for correction, restrained by mercy.

- **Jesus' Scourging** Christ bore thirty-nine lashes, taking judgment upon Himself to redeem us.
- **Paul's Testimony** Paul endured lashes, showing godly discipline produces perseverance and witness.
- **Unity of God** *YHWH Echad* equals thirty-nine, connecting judgment to God's oneness and authority.
- **Fruit and Fire** Luke 3:9 warns that fruitless trees face removal, underscoring judgment's purpose.
- **Authority Over Evil** Mark 1:39 shows Jesus casting out demons, exercising godly judgment over darkness.

Journaling Questions

Journaling about thirty-nine invites us to consider how God's judgment works in our lives. Writing helps us reflect on the areas where His discipline is refining us and where fruit is being produced. It reminds us that judgment in the redeemed is not condemnation but correction leading to life.

Through reflection, readers will see that godly judgment is always purposeful: to refine His people, to cut off fruitlessness, and to reveal His oneness. Journaling helps us recognize His discipline as a sign of His love.

Discipline and Mercy

How have I experienced God's discipline as both firm and merciful, like the thirty-nine lashes?

____

____

____

____

____

____

____

Fruitfulness Check

What fruit is growing in my life, and where is God calling me to greater growth?

Christ's Judgment

How does Jesus bearing the thirty-nine lashes shape my view of judgment and mercy?

Unity of God

What does Deuteronomy 6:4 teach me about God's oneness in judgment and authority?

REFINEMENT PROCESS

Where do I sense God pruning or refining me to prepare for greater fruitfulness?

____

____

____

____

____

____

ACTIONABLE STEPS

Welcome Refinement
Invite God to reveal areas of unfruitfulness in your life and surrender them to Him.

Bear Fruit
Choose one tangible way to grow in good works this week, reflecting His wisdom.

Remember His Mercy
Meditate on Christ's thirty-nine lashes and thank Him for bearing judgment in your place.

PERSONAL REFLECTION

The number thirty-nine preaches godly judgment. It calls us to recognize that judgment in the redeemed is discipline that produces fruit, while judgment in the unredeemed is finality. Either way, it reveals the oneness of God and His perfect justice.

As you reflect, consider whether you are welcoming His discipline as a sign of His love and yielding fruit in your walk with Him.

Am I bearing the fruit of redemption or resisting the refining hand of God? How will I respond to His discipline with trust? What fruit will I choose to cultivate through obedience this week?

____

____

Closing Prayer: *Father, thank You for the message of thirty-nine. Refine me through Your godly judgment. Prune away unfruitfulness, strengthen me in wisdom, and let my life bear the fruit of good works. I thank You that Christ bore judgment on my behalf, and I choose to walk in Your mercy. Amen.*

Chapter 40

Section B:

Larger Numbers – Forty – Trial, Probation

Then Jesus was led up by the Spirit into the wilderness to be tempted by the devil. And when He had fasted forty days and forty nights, afterward He was hungry. (Matthew 4:1–2, NKJV)

The number forty preaches trial and probation. It is the number most associated with testing and the refining of character. The dictionary defines probation as "the act of testing," "the trial of conduct and character," and "a period of evaluation." This definition mirrors how Scripture repeatedly uses forty as the appointed span of testing—whether for individuals, nations, or creation itself.

Forty days of rain in Genesis 7 tested the world under judgment, leading to a new beginning through Noah and the ark. Israel's wilderness experience lasted forty years, a period of refining and preparation for entering the Promised Land. Jesus Himself was tempted by Satan for forty days in the wilderness, proving His faithfulness as the spotless Son of God. Moses' life also testifies of forty in cycles: forty years as a prince in Egypt, forty years as a shepherd in Midian, and forty years leading Israel through the wilderness. Each season marked a time of preparation, trial, and transition into new assignment.

This number is not about punishment but about purpose. Forty reveals that testing seasons are designed to prepare God's people for greater responsibility and victory. What feels like delay or hardship is probation—a proving ground where character is formed, faith is strengthened, and obedience is solidified.

The message of forty is clear: trials are temporary, but their results are eternal. Probation is not about disqualification but preparation for what God has promised.

Focus Point

And you shall remember that the Lord your God led you all the way these forty years in the wilderness, to humble you and test you, to know what was in your heart, whether you would keep His commandments or not. (Deuteronomy 8:2, NKJV)

This verse explains forty's purpose: to test hearts, reveal obedience, and prepare God's people for promise.

Main Theme

Forty preaches trial and probation, declaring that seasons of testing are God's way of refining character and preparing His people for promise.

"Forty is the number of trial and probation—where testing forms character for future promise."

Key Scriptures

- *And the rain was on the earth forty days and forty nights.* (Genesis 7:12, NKJV)
- *Your sons shall be shepherds in the wilderness forty years, and bear the brunt of your infidelity, until your carcasses are consumed in the wilderness.* (Numbers 14:33, NKJV)
- *Then Jesus was led up by the Spirit into the wilderness... And when He had fasted forty days and forty nights, afterward He was hungry.* (Matthew 4:1–2, NKJV)

Key Points

- **Defined by Trial** Forty is consistently used in Scripture to mark seasons of testing and probation.
- **Flood of Forty Days** Genesis 7 records forty days and nights of rain, a trial for the whole earth.

- **Israel's Wilderness** Israel endured forty years in the desert, a time of refining before entering promise.
- **Jesus' Temptation** Christ was tested forty days in the wilderness, proving His obedience and faithfulness.
- **Moses' Life Cycles** Moses lived three distinct periods of forty years, each preparing him for greater purpose.
- **Not Punishment but Purpose** Forty shows that trials are meant to prepare, not destroy.
- **Temporary but Transformative** Every forty-season ends with transition into something new.

Journaling Questions

Journaling about forty allows us to reflect on our own testing seasons. Writing helps us see where God has been refining our hearts, teaching us obedience, and shaping us for promise. It gives us perspective that trials are not endless but purposeful.

Through reflection, readers will recognize that probation seasons prepare them for greater fruitfulness. Journaling shifts our view of hardship from discouragement to anticipation of what God is building in us.

Season of Testing

What forty-season of trial or probation have I walked through, and what did I learn from it?

____

____

____

____

____

____

____

Refining Purpose

How does Israel's forty years in the wilderness help me view my own delays differently?

Jesus' Example

What does Jesus' forty days of temptation teach me about endurance and faithfulness?

Moses' Cycles

How does Moses' life of three forty-year seasons encourage me about God's timing?

Promise Ahead

Where is God using trial now to prepare me for future promise?

____
____
____
____
____
____

Actionable Steps

Reframe Trials
See your current testing as God's probation, refining you for purpose.

Learn in the Wilderness
Commit to learning the lessons of your trial instead of resisting them.

Prepare for Promise
Take one step of obedience today that reflects readiness for what God is preparing.

Personal Reflection

The number forty preaches that trials are not wasted—they are preparation for promise. Seasons of probation reveal what is in our hearts, shape our character, and strengthen our faith.

As you reflect, ask whether you are resisting or embracing the refining hand of God in your forty-season.

Am I willing to see my trials as preparation instead of punishment? How will I let testing shape my character? What promise might God be preparing me to step into after this season?

____
____
____
____

Closing Prayer: *Father, thank You for the message of forty. Teach me to see trials as purposeful probation, refining my character and preparing me for promise. Strengthen me to endure testing with faith, and let me emerge ready to walk into all You have planned. Amen.*

Chapter 41

The Number Fifty

Jubilee

And you shall consecrate the fiftieth year, and proclaim liberty throughout all the land to all its inhabitants; it shall be a Jubilee for you; and each of you shall return to his possession, and each of you shall return to his family. (Leviticus 25:10, NKJV)

The number fifty preaches Jubilee—freedom, restoration, and the outpouring of the Holy Spirit. Jubilee is the time when what was lost or taken is returned, debts are canceled, and liberty is proclaimed. It is the number of release and renewal, pointing to God's heart of redemption for His people.

Biblically, the fiftieth year was declared as Jubilee, where land returned to original owners and families were restored. Spiritually, this pointed to a deeper fulfillment in Christ, who came to set captives free. Fifty is also the number tied to Pentecost: fifty days after Passover, the Holy Spirit was poured out upon the disciples, empowering the Church with boldness and divine purpose. Thus, fifty is inseparably linked to the freedom of the Spirit and the restoration of God's people.

This number is more than a calendar marker—it is a prophetic declaration. Jubilee teaches that God does not forget what was lost. He restores inheritance, heals brokenness, and breathes new life through His Spirit. In seasons where we feel bound, fifty proclaims liberty. Where we've suffered loss, it announces restoration. Where we've been powerless, it ushers in empowerment through the Holy Spirit.

The message of fifty is this: in Christ, Jubilee is not only an event every fifty years but a continual reality. Through the Spirit, we live in a perpetual season of freedom and restoration.

FOCUS POINT

Now the Lord is the Spirit; and where the Spirit of the Lord is, there is liberty. (2 Corinthians 3:17, NKJV)

This verse encapsulates Jubilee's heart: true liberty comes only from God's Spirit.

MAIN THEME

Fifty preaches Jubilee, the restoration of what was lost and the liberty of the Spirit.

"Fifty declares freedom, restoration, and the power of the Spirit poured out for God's people."

KEY SCRIPTURES

- *And you shall consecrate the fiftieth year, and proclaim liberty throughout all the land to all its inhabitants.* (Leviticus 25:10, NKJV)
- *When the Day of Pentecost had fully come, they were all with one accord in one place.* (Acts 2:1, NKJV)
- *The Spirit of the Lord is upon Me, because He has anointed Me to preach the gospel to the poor; He has sent Me to heal the brokenhearted, to proclaim liberty to the captives and recovery of sight to the blind, to set at liberty those who are oppressed.* (Luke 4:18, NKJV)

KEY POINTS

- **Year of Jubilee** The fiftieth year restored land and families, proclaiming liberty across Israel.
- **Spirit Poured Out** Pentecost, fifty days after Passover, marked the outpouring of the Spirit on the Church.
- **Freedom in Christ** Jubilee is fulfilled in Jesus, who proclaims liberty and healing to the broken.

- **Restoration Promised** What was lost or stolen, God restores through His covenant of grace.
- **Debt Released** Jubilee canceled debts, a prophetic picture of Christ canceling sin's debt for us.
- **Spirit of Liberty** Where the Spirit of the Lord is, there is freedom—an eternal Jubilee.
- **Hope of Renewal** Fifty preaches hope, reminding us that God always brings restoration after loss.

Journaling Questions

Journaling about fifty allows us to reflect on where we need God's restoration. Writing helps us identify areas of loss, bondage, or brokenness, and see how the Spirit is calling us into liberty. It shifts our perspective from despair to expectation of renewal.

Through reflection, readers will recognize that Jubilee is not distant but present in Christ. The Spirit empowers us to walk in freedom now, proclaiming liberty to others and living restored lives.

Areas of Loss

What area of my life needs God's Jubilee restoration right now?

____
____
____
____
____

Debt Released

How has Christ canceled the debt of sin in my life, and how does that change my outlook?

____
____
____
____

Spirit of Liberty

Where am I experiencing the liberty of the Spirit today?

____

____

____

____

____

____

Proclaiming Freedom

How can I proclaim Jubilee—freedom and restoration—to someone else this week?

____

____

____

____

____

____

Living Restored

What step can I take to live as though God has already restored what was lost?

____

____

____

____

____

____

Actionable Steps

Embrace Freedom
Declare liberty over areas of bondage in your life, trusting the Spirit's power.

Seek Restoration
Invite God to restore what was lost or broken, aligning with His covenant promise.

Walk in Spirit
Live daily in dependence on the Holy Spirit, embracing Jubilee as a lifestyle.

Personal Reflection

The number fifty preaches that in Christ, Jubilee is our reality. What was lost can be restored, what was bound can be freed, and what was powerless can be empowered. His Spirit guarantees liberty, not just once every fifty years, but every day.

As you reflect, consider where you need to step into Jubilee and how you can proclaim liberty to others.

Am I living as though Jubilee is now? How will I embrace the liberty of the Spirit? What step will I take toward restoration today?

Closing Prayer: *Father, thank You for the message of fifty. Teach me to live in Jubilee, to walk in Your liberty, and to trust in Your Spirit's power to restore what was lost. May my life proclaim freedom to others, reflecting the hope of Your covenant. Amen.*

Chapter 42

The Number Sixty-Six

A Witness to the Flesh

Search the Scriptures, for in them you think you have eternal life; and these are they which testify of Me. (John 5:39, NKJV)

The number sixty-six preaches a witness to the flesh. Six is the number of man, and when doubled, it becomes a testimony—often a testimony against human pride and weakness. Together, sixty-six highlights the call for man to humble himself under the authority of God's Word and live as a true witness.

Sixty-six is inseparably tied to the Scriptures, as there are sixty-six books in the Bible. The Word itself is God's faithful witness to humanity, testifying of Christ. Remarkably, key words like "rule" and "crown" each appear sixty-six times in Scripture, emphasizing that God's Word is meant to govern and crown our lives. Luke 4:4 reminds us that man does not live by bread alone but by every word of God, and the sixty-six books of the Bible are that living bread.

The number has also surfaced prophetically in culture. U.S. Route 66, once called "The Mother Road," symbolized America's backbone but has largely faded from the mainstream. Its decline mirrors the waning influence of the Bible in American life. Likewise, the 1990 trial of Zsa Zsa Gabor at age sixty-six was a striking picture to the author: the church in America, spoiled and rebellious, was being told to "act its age" and bear true witness to the world. Sixty-six reminds us that without humility, the flesh resists God's authority—but with submission, it becomes a powerful witness to His truth.

The message of sixty-six is this: humanity must reckon with the testimony of the flesh, either humbling itself under God's Word or standing condemned by its own witness.

Focus Point

It is written, "Man shall not live by bread alone, but by every word of God." (Luke 4:4, NKJV)

This verse affirms that the sixty-six books of the Bible are the sustenance of life, testifying of Christ and calling man beyond the weakness of flesh.

Main Theme

Sixty-six preaches a witness to the flesh, calling man to humble himself under the authority of the Word of God.

"Sixty-six declares that humanity must bear true witness—humbled under God's Word rather than ruled by the flesh."

Key Scriptures

- *Search the Scriptures, for in them you think you have eternal life; and these are they which testify of Me.* (John 5:39, NKJV)
- *Hear, O Israel: The Lord our God, the Lord is one!* (Deuteronomy 6:4, NKJV)
- *It is written, "Man shall not live by bread alone, but by every word of God."* (Luke 4:4, NKJV)

Key Points

- **Six Doubled** When six is doubled into sixty-six, it becomes a testimony—often exposing the flesh.
- **Sixty-Six Books** The Bible's sixty-six books stand as God's witness, testifying of Christ.
- **Rule and Crown** Both words appear sixty-six times in Scripture, symbolizing authority and glory through the Word.
- **Cultural Mirror** Route 66 fading from prominence parallels the Bible's diminished role in culture.

- **Prophetic Parable** Zsa Zsa Gabor's trial at sixty-six pictured the church being told to bear true witness.
- **Authority of the Word** Sixty-six points to the need for God's Word to govern and guide human life.
- **Witness of Flesh** Sixty-six reminds us that our lives testify either to submission or rebellion against God.

Journaling Questions

Journaling about sixty-six invites us to reflect on how our lives are acting as witnesses. Writing helps us ask whether our testimony reflects submission to God's Word or pride of the flesh. It helps us examine cultural parallels and challenges us to live as true witnesses.

Through reflection, readers will realize that their lives are testimonies—either in alignment with God's Word or in resistance to it. Sixty-six calls us to choose humility and obedience as our witness.

Witness of My Life

What does my life currently testify about my relationship with God's Word?

____

____

____

____

____

____

Authority of Scripture

How are the sixty-six books of the Bible ruling and guiding my daily choices?

____

____

____

____

____

Cultural Decline

What does the decline of Route 66 symbolize to me about our culture's relationship to Scripture?

Personal Rebellion

Where am I tempted to "slap the law in the face" like Gabor, resisting God's authority?

True Witness

How can I bear a faithful witness of Christ to the world around me?

Actionable Steps

Submit to Scripture
Commit to letting God's Word—not fleshly desires—rule your decisions this week.

Guard Your Testimony
Be mindful that your actions are always a witness, either for or against Christ.

Act Your Age
Mature spiritually by embracing humility and responsibility as God's witness in the world.

Personal Reflection

The number sixty-six preaches that our lives are testimonies, for better or worse. The sixty-six books of Scripture testify of Christ, and our response to them reveals whether we are witnesses of truth or of fleshly rebellion.

As you reflect, consider whether your witness aligns with the Word or resists it.

Am I living as a true witness of Christ? How will I submit to the authority of the Word today? What testimony will my life bear before the world?

Closing Prayer: *Father, thank You for the message of sixty-six. Teach me to submit to Your Word, to humble my flesh, and to live as a faithful witness to Your truth. May my life reflect the authority of Scripture and point others to Christ. Amen.*

Chapter 43

The Number One Hundred Twenty

Testing Is Finished, and God Shows Up!

These all continued with one accord in prayer and supplication, with the women and Mary the mother of Jesus, and with His brothers... altogether the number of names was about a hundred and twenty. (Acts 1:14–15, NKJV)

The number one hundred twenty preaches the completion of testing and the moment when God shows up. It is the number of transition into a new phase of destiny, the graduation from trial into fulfillment. When one hundred twenty appears in Scripture, it signals the end of a long preparation and the beginning of a powerful move of God.

Consider Noah. He built the ark for one hundred twenty years, faithfully obeying God through ridicule and waiting. At the appointed time, God showed up, filling the ark with animals and shutting the door Himself. Moses also lived in cycles of forty: forty years as a prince in Egypt, forty years as a shepherd in Midian, and forty years leading Israel through the wilderness. At age one hundred twenty, he died, and Israel entered the Promised Land under Joshua's leadership. Testing was finished, and promise had come.

In the New Testament, one hundred twenty again signals divine arrival. In the upper room at Pentecost, one hundred twenty disciples gathered in prayer. Then God showed up—the Holy Spirit descended with power, birthing the Church. The testing and waiting ended, and the new covenant era began. One hundred twenty marks not just the end of a season, but the dramatic intervention of God to launch something greater.

The message of one hundred twenty is this: when testing is complete, God's presence arrives to move His people forward. It assures us that waiting is not wasted—there is a divine moment when God shows up, bringing promise, power, and breakthrough.

FOCUS POINT

And suddenly there came a sound from heaven, as of a rushing mighty wind, and it filled the whole house where they were sitting. (Acts 2:2, NKJV)

This verse captures the essence of one hundred twenty: after testing, God suddenly appears with undeniable power.

MAIN THEME

One hundred twenty preaches the end of testing and the arrival of God's presence, launching His people into destiny.

"One hundred twenty declares that when testing is finished, God shows up with power and promise."

KEY SCRIPTURES

- It took Noah 120 years to build the ark; then God showed up and shut the door. (Paraphrased from Genesis 6:3, 7:16, NKJV)
- *So Moses the servant of the Lord died there in the land of Moab... Moses was one hundred and twenty years old when he died.* (Deuteronomy 34:5, 7, NKJV)
- *...Altogether the number of names was about one hundred and twenty.* (Acts 1:15, NKJV)

KEY POINTS

- **End of Testing** One hundred twenty marks the completion of trial and the beginning of fulfillment.
- **Noah's Obedience** Noah built for one hundred twenty years before God Himself shut the ark's door.
- **Moses' Lifespan** Moses lived to one hundred twenty, completing his leadership before Israel's entry into promise.

- **Upper Room Unity** One hundred twenty disciples gathered in prayer before the Spirit descended.
- **God's Intervention** This number signals the dramatic moment when God steps into history.
- **Transition to Promise** Testing seasons give way to fulfillment marked by God's presence.
- **Power and Breakthrough** One hundred twenty ushers in new beginnings empowered by God.

Journaling Questions

Journaling about one hundred twenty allows us to reflect on long seasons of testing in our own lives. Writing helps us recognize where God has been preparing us, even when His arrival seemed delayed. It gives us hope that His presence will come suddenly and decisively.

Through reflection, readers will see that testing seasons are not endless—they lead to the moment when God shows up. One hundred twenty shifts our perspective to expect His intervention at the appointed time.

Seasons of Testing

Where have I experienced a long period of waiting or testing that God is now preparing to complete?

____

____

____

____

____

____

____

NOAH'S OBEDIENCE

How does Noah's perseverance for one hundred twenty years challenge my own faithfulness?

MOSES' LIFE

What can I learn from Moses' completion of his life and leadership at one hundred twenty?

UPPER ROOM EXPECTANCY

How does the gathering of one hundred twenty disciples encourage me to remain in prayer and unity while waiting?

Sudden Breakthrough

Where am I expecting God to suddenly "show up" in my life with power and promise?

Actionable Steps

Stay Faithful in Waiting
Commit to perseverance in prayer, even when the wait is long.

Prepare for His Arrival
Like Noah and the disciples, live ready for the moment God shows up.

Expect Breakthrough
Choose to view your testing season as preparation for sudden divine intervention.

Personal Reflection

The number one hundred twenty preaches that testing seasons end when God arrives. His presence brings transition, promise, and breakthrough. What looks like long waiting is preparation for sudden intervention.

As you reflect, ask whether you are living in expectancy, ready for the moment when testing is complete and God shows up.

Am I remaining faithful in my season of testing? How will I prepare for God's sudden arrival? What breakthrough am I expecting Him to bring?

Closing Prayer: *Father, thank You for the message of one hundred twenty. Teach me to endure testing with faith, to wait with expectancy, and to prepare my heart for the moment You show up. Let my life reflect perseverance, readiness, and the joy of Your sudden arrival. Amen.*

Chapter 44

The Number One Hundred Fifty-Three

The Sons of God

Simon Peter went up, and drew the net to land full of great fishes, an hundred and fifty and three: and for all there were so many, yet was not the net broken. (John 21:11, KJV)

The number one hundred fifty-three preaches sonship and the gathering of God's children. The Greek phrase *"sons of God"* (*οἱ υἱοὶ τοῦ θεοῦ*) has a gematria value of 153, directly linking this number to the identity of God's redeemed people. It surfaces dramatically in John 21:11, when the disciples—after a fruitless night—obey Jesus' instruction and catch 153 fish. The catch is not random; it is prophetic, symbolizing the great ingathering of God's children into His Kingdom.

This number also carries significance in biblical symbolism. Early Christians in Rome used the *Vesica Piscis*, or "vessel of the fish," as a sacred sign of Christ and His people. The shape's ratio of 265:153 is called the "measure of the fish," a hidden mathematical witness to the gospel. In it, two circles—representing God and man—overlap to form the fish symbol, a picture of divine union. Thus, 153 represents not only the sons of God but also their union with Christ.

Theologians have also seen a connection between the 153 fish in John 21 and Ezekiel's vision of the river of life in Ezekiel 47. The river flows into the Dead Sea, transforming it from death to life and filling it with multitudes of fish. This prophetic imagery reveals God's heart to bring life, healing, and multiplication to the nations. Jesus confirmed this when He called His disciples "fishers of men" (Matthew 4:19–20). The number 153 therefore points to redemption, transformation, and the eternal identity of God's people as His sons and daughters.

The message of 153 is this: God is gathering His children. The sons of God are called, redeemed, and multiplied in Christ, bearing witness to His life-giving power.

Focus Point

And looking at Jesus as He walked, he said, "Behold the Lamb of God!" (John 1:36, NKJV)

This verse reminds us that the gathering of the sons of God is centered in Christ, the Lamb who redeems and unites His people.

Main Theme

One hundred fifty-three preaches the identity and gathering of God's sons into His Kingdom.

"One hundred fifty-three declares that God is gathering His children into union with Christ."

Key Scriptures

- *Simon Peter went up, and drew the net to land full of great fishes, an hundred and fifty and three.* (John 21:11, KJV)
- *Follow Me, and I will make you fishers of men.* (Matthew 4:19, NKJV)
- *And it shall be that every living thing that moves, wherever the rivers go, will live. There will be a very great multitude of fish, because these waters go there.* (Ezekiel 47:9, NKJV)

Key Points

- **Sons of God** The Greek phrase has a gematria value of 153, linking the number to identity in Christ.
- **Prophetic Catch** The 153 fish in John 21 symbolize the redeemed gathered into God's Kingdom.
- **Vesica Piscis** The ancient Christian fish symbol, with a 265:153 ratio, testifies of divine union.

- **River of Life** Ezekiel 47's vision of multitudes of fish parallels the ingathering of the redeemed.
- **Identity in Christ** 153 reminds believers of their place as sons and daughters of God.
- **Fishers of Men** Jesus called His disciples to bring in the harvest of souls, fulfilled in the 153 catch.
- **Life from Death** Like the Dead Sea transformed in Ezekiel's vision, God brings life through His sons.

Journaling Questions

Journaling about 153 encourages us to reflect on our identity as sons and daughters of God. Writing helps us consider how God is gathering us into His Kingdom and how we can join in His mission to "fish for men." It shows us that 153 is not only symbolic but deeply personal—it is about belonging, identity, and purpose.

Through reflection, readers will discover that being a son of God means living in union with Christ and joining His work of redemption. It is a call to live as part of the great ingathering, testifying of His transforming power.

Identity in Christ

How does knowing I am a son or daughter of God shape the way I live daily?

Prophetic Catch

What does the story of the 153 fish teach me about God's heart for gathering souls?

Union with Christ

How does the symbol of the Vesica Piscis deepen my understanding of life in Him?

River of Life

Where have I seen God transform a place of death into a place of life?

Mission to Fish

How am I joining Jesus in His call to be a "fisher of men"?

Actionable Steps

Live as His Child
Walk daily in the confidence of being God's beloved son or daughter.

Join the Mission
Actively participate in sharing the gospel, helping gather the sons of God.

Testify of Transformation
Share a personal story of how Christ has brought life where there was once death.

Personal Reflection

The number one hundred fifty-three preaches that God is gathering His children. It reminds us that we are sons of God, called into union with Christ and sent to bring others into His Kingdom.

As you reflect, ask whether you are living in the fullness of that identity and actively joining the harvest.

Am I living as a true son or daughter of God? How will I join Christ in gathering others? What does it mean for me to be part of the prophetic catch of 153?

Closing Prayer: *Father, thank You for the message of one hundred fifty-three. Thank You that I am Your child, redeemed and gathered into Your Kingdom. Teach me to live in union with Christ and to join Your mission of gathering souls into life. Amen.*

Chapter 45

Section C:

The Numbers Agree

It is the glory of God to conceal a matter, but the glory of kings is to search out a matter.
(Proverbs 25:2, NKJV)

The numbers agree. That is the testimony of Scripture. God uses numbers as prophetic markers, weaving them into His Word in ways that reveal His character, His order, and His purposes. This section begins with a call for balance—avoiding both extremes of superstition and the equally dangerous error of excessive moderation. Too often, believers resist diving deeper into the numeric treasures of the Bible out of fear of being lumped in with New Age philosophies or fringe extremes. But the author reminds us that pursuing the revelation of numbers is not about mystical mantras—it is about discovering God's order in creation and aligning ourselves with His truth.

A personal reflection highlights how many Christians are content to sip teaspoons of God's vastness when He invites us into the depth of the ocean. Excessive moderation, like lukewarmness in the Laodicean church, keeps us from truly seeing the richness of His Word. Instead of shying away from numeric revelation, we are invited to handle it with maturity—embracing what glorifies God while steering clear of distortion.

The author stresses that the misuse of numbers by others does not invalidate their biblical significance. Just as people can misuse any gift of God, so too can they misuse prophetic understanding. But mature believers are called to walk in wisdom and discernment, finding the balance of mercy and truth (Proverbs 3:3). The key is to remain close to Jesus, ensuring that every numeric insight points us back to Him.

The message of this section is clear: when studied with reverence and responsibility, the numbers in Scripture agree with one another, bearing witness to the God of order, truth, and revelation.

Focus Point

For God is not the author of confusion but of peace, as in all the churches of the saints. (1 Corinthians 14:33, NKJV)

This verse reminds us that numeric revelation is not chaos or superstition but an expression of God's order.

Main Theme

The numbers agree, testifying to God's order and revelation when studied with wisdom and balance.

"The numbers agree because the God of order has written His testimony into creation and His Word."

Key Scriptures

- *It is the glory of God to conceal a matter, but the glory of kings is to search out a matter.* (Proverbs 25:2, NKJV)
- *Let not mercy and truth forsake you; bind them around your neck, write them on the tablet of your heart.* (Proverbs 3:3, NKJV)
- *For God is not the author of confusion but of peace, as in all the churches of the saints.* (1 Corinthians 14:33, NKJV)

Key Points

- **Balance in Study** The use of numbers in Scripture must be approached with maturity, avoiding both extremism and excessive moderation.

- **Not Superstition** Biblical numbers are not mystical chants but prophetic markers revealing God's order.
- **Ocean vs. Teaspoon** God invites us to the depth of His revelation, not to be content with tiny sips.
- **Misuse Doesn't Negate Truth** Just because some misuse numbers doesn't mean believers should ignore them.
- **Mercy and Truth** Wisdom in biblical numbers requires balance—holding both mercy and truth together.
- **Stay Close to Jesus** All numeric revelation must lead us back to Christ as the center.
- **Numbers Agree** When rightly understood, numbers harmonize with one another and with God's Word.

JOURNALING QUESTIONS

Journaling about this section invites us to consider our approach to biblical revelation. Are we excessively moderate, afraid to seek deeper meaning, or are we willing to pursue maturity in wisdom? Writing helps us reflect on our own fears or hesitations and challenges us to embrace the treasures God has hidden in His Word.

Through reflection, readers will discover that numbers are not meant to confuse but to clarify God's voice. They testify to His order, His purposes, and His presence in creation. Journaling about this truth helps us grow in confidence that the numbers truly do agree.

BALANCE IN STUDY

Have I avoided deeper study of numbers out of fear of extremes?

____

____

____

____

____

____

____

God's Invitation

Where am I sipping a teaspoon when God is offering me the ocean of His truth?

Mercy and Truth

How can I practice the balance of mercy and truth in my study of God's Word?

Close to Jesus

How will I ensure that every numeric insight points me back to Christ?

Agreement of Numbers

Where have I seen numbers in Scripture agree to reinforce a single truth of God?

Actionable Steps

Reject Fear of Extremes
Refuse to let misuse by others keep you from pursuing God's revelation.

Seek Depth, Not Moderation
Go beyond surface-level understanding—study numbers as prophetic markers.

Stay Rooted in Christ
Always measure numeric insights by whether they glorify Jesus.

Personal Reflection

This section preaches that the numbers agree. God has woven His testimony into creation and Scripture, and we are invited to search it out. But it must be done with maturity, humility, and balance—holding mercy and truth, staying close to Christ, and refusing both superstition and excessive moderation.

As you reflect, ask yourself whether you are resisting God's deeper revelations or embracing them as part of His glory.

Am I willing to trust that the numbers agree? How will I study with balance and maturity? What step will I take to embrace the fullness of God's numeric revelation?

Closing Prayer: *Father, thank You for the message of the numbers agreeing. Teach me to handle Your revelation with balance, to embrace mercy and truth, and to stay close to Jesus. Let every number I study testify of Your order, Your wisdom, and Your glory. Amen.*

Chapter 46

I Am Statements

Jesus said to them, "Most assuredly, I say to you, before Abraham was, I AM."
(John 8:58, NKJV)

In the Gospel of John, Jesus gives seven declarations beginning with the divine words, "I AM." These statements are not simply poetic metaphors—they are revelations of His identity, His mission, and His divine connection to the eternal God. Each statement is layered with meaning, rooted in the Old Testament revelation of God as *YHWH*—"I AM WHO I AM" (Exodus 3:14).

Through gematria, the numerical values of these declarations align with biblical truths, amplifying their prophetic weight. For example, when Jesus said, "I AM the Bread of Life" (John 6:35), the gematria value 3248 reduces to 17, the number for overcoming victory. Likewise, "I AM the Light of the World" (John 8:12) carries the value 2691, reducing to 18, representing abundant life. These patterns reveal that every "I AM" statement is not just a declaration—it is a prophetic equation of who He is and what He does.

The hidden numeric harmony confirms that Jesus' words were more than teachings; they were divine revelations of His nature as Messiah, Savior, and Son of God. The bread sustains, the light reveals, the door grants access, the shepherd guides, the resurrection conquers death, the way leads to the Father, and the vine unites us to God. Together, they present a complete picture of Christ's ministry and eternal purpose.

This section challenges us to see that every "I AM" statement is also an invitation. They are not only descriptions of Christ but doorways into deeper relationship with Him. To embrace the "I AM" is to accept Him fully as the source of life, truth, and eternal connection to the Father.

Focus Point

I am the bread of life. He who comes to Me shall never hunger, and he who believes in Me shall never thirst. (John 6:35, NKJV)

This verse shows that Jesus is more than provision; He is the source of eternal sustenance for body, soul, and spirit.

Main Theme

The "I AM" statements reveal Jesus' divine identity and mission, confirmed by both Scripture and hidden numerical patterns.

"Every 'I AM' is both a revelation of Christ and an invitation to abide in Him."

Key Scriptures

- *I am the light of the world. He who follows Me shall not walk in darkness, but have the light of life.* (John 8:12, NKJV)
- *I am the door. If anyone enters by Me, he will be saved, and will go in and out and find pasture.* (John 10:9, NKJV)
- *I am the good shepherd. The good shepherd gives His life for the sheep.* (John 10:11, NKJV)

Key Points

- **Bread of Life** Jesus provides spiritual sustenance that leads to overcoming victory.
- **Light of the World** He shines divine illumination that brings abundant life.
- **The Door** He grants access to salvation and the Kingdom of God.
- **The Good Shepherd** He guides, protects, and lays down His life for His people.

- **The Resurrection and the Life** He conquers death and gives eternal life.
- **The Way, Truth, and Life** He is the only path to the Father, the source of truth, and the giver of eternal life.
- **The True Vine** He connects us to God, uniting us with the source of all life and growth.

Journaling Questions

Journaling on the "I AM" statements helps us explore how Jesus' words apply personally to our walk. Writing out reflections allows us to see Him as sustainer, guide, and redeemer in our daily struggles and victories. These statements move us from knowing about Jesus to experiencing Him in intimate relationship.

Through reflection, readers will see that every declaration of Christ is both truth and invitation. By journaling, we place ourselves inside the promises He offers: provision, light, protection, resurrection, and eternal union. This practice draws us closer to His heart.

Sustenance in Christ

How has Jesus been my Bread of Life in times of need?

____

____

____

____

____

____

Walking in Light

Where is He calling me to step out of darkness into His light?

____

____

____

____

____

Access Through Him

What doors has Jesus opened that I could not open myself?

Guidance of the Shepherd

How is the Good Shepherd guiding me today?

Union with the Vine

What does abiding in Christ look like in my daily life?

Actionable Steps

Receive His Provision
Turn to Christ daily as your source of strength and sustenance.

Follow His Light
Commit to walking in His truth, rejecting darkness and deception.

Abide in the Vine
Intentionally remain connected to Him through prayer, worship, and obedience.

Personal Reflection

The "I AM" statements remind us that Jesus is more than teacher—He is God revealed in flesh. Each declaration is a lifeline, extending His nature into our reality. They are promises we can cling to and doorways into deeper intimacy with Him.

As you reflect, consider how these truths can reshape your relationship with Christ and bring new life to your faith.

Am I living as though Jesus is my Bread, my Light, my Door, my Shepherd, my Resurrection, my Way, my Vine? How will I step into the invitation of each "I AM"? Which declaration of Christ is He asking me to embrace most fully today?

Closing Prayer: *Lord Jesus, thank You for revealing Yourself as the great I AM. Teach me to live in Your light, to rest in Your provision, and to abide in You as my vine. May each "I AM" You spoke become truth alive in me, shaping how I walk with You daily. Amen.*

Chapter 47

We've Got Their Numbers

But the very hairs of your head are all numbered. Do not fear therefore; you are of more value than many sparrows. (Luke 12:7, NKJV)

This section emphasizes that God is a God of order, precision, and intentionality—even down to the smallest details of creation. Numbers are not random accidents in Scripture or in life. They are divine fingerprints, showing that the Lord not only sees the big picture but also the smallest components of it. The title itself, *We've Got Their Numbers*, reflects this truth: everything and everyone is accounted for in God's design.

Divine patterns in Scripture testify that God is not chaotic but perfectly structured. From the days of creation to the genealogies, from temple measurements to prophetic timelines, numbers reinforce that the Bible is a supernatural book authored by a supernatural God. Just as He counts the stars and calls them by name, He also numbers His people and assures them that their lives are woven into His eternal plan.

The misuse of numbers in worldly superstition or occultism should never cause believers to shy away from the real revelation of God's design through numbers.. Instead, it should deepen our awe of God's sovereignty. In Him, numbers reveal destiny, covenant, and identity. When Scripture tells us even the hairs of our head are numbered, it is a declaration of God's intimate care and precision in our lives.

The message of this section is clear: the numbers are not only known by God—they testify of Him. They reveal that nothing is overlooked, and that His design for creation and for our lives is both deliberate and glorious.

Focus Point

He counts the number of the stars; He calls them all by name. (Psalm 147:4, NKJV)

This verse confirms that God is the master of both the vast and the detailed, numbering the stars as well as the hairs on our heads.

Main Theme

God's numbers reveal His order, sovereignty, and intentional care for creation and His people.

"We've got their numbers because God has had them all along—every star, every hair, every detail accounted for."

Key Scriptures

- *But the very hairs of your head are all numbered. Do not fear therefore; you are of more value than many sparrows.* (Luke 12:7, NKJV)
- *He counts the number of the stars; He calls them all by name.* (Psalm 147:4, NKJV)
- *For God is not the author of confusion but of peace, as in all the churches of the saints.* (1 Corinthians 14:33, NKJV)

Key Points

- **God's Precision** Numbers in Scripture testify to God's exactness and sovereignty.
- **Every Detail Matters** Even the hairs of our heads are numbered, showing His intimate care.
- **Biblical Order** From creation to prophecy, numbers reveal divine structure.
- **No Chaos in God** Numbers demonstrate that God is not random but purposeful.
- **Stars and Sparrows** God's numbering encompasses both the vast and the minute.
- **Reject Superstition** Numbers in Scripture are revelation, not occult mysticism.
- **Assurance of Care** If God counts every detail, He will surely care for our lives and futures.

Journaling Questions

Journaling about this section helps us consider how deeply God is involved in the details of our lives. Writing allows us to shift our perspective from randomness to providence, from fear to trust. It leads us to recognize that what feels insignificant to us is still numbered by God.

Through reflection, readers will realize that nothing escapes God's attention. Journaling allows us to align our trust with His sovereignty, understanding that every detail has been written into His eternal plan.

God's Precision

How does it comfort me to know that even the smallest details of my life are numbered by God?

____

____

____

____

____

____

____

Personal Assurance

Where have I seen God's intentional care in my circumstances?

____

____

____

____

____

____

Rejecting Superstition

How can I distinguish between biblical revelation and worldly misuse of numbers?

____

____

____

____

____

____

Stars and Sparrows

What does it mean to me personally that God numbers both the stars and the hairs on my head?

____

____

____

____

____

____

Living with Trust

How should the truth of God's precise numbering affect the way I face uncertainty?

____

____

____

____

____

____

Actionable Steps

Trust His Order
When life feels chaotic, remind yourself that God has already numbered the details.

Live Without Fear
Because you are valued and counted, you can walk in confidence, not anxiety.

Honor His Precision
Study Scripture with fresh appreciation for the intentionality of God's numeric patterns.

Personal Reflection

This section preaches that God has every number accounted for. He knows the stars in the heavens and the hairs on our heads. Nothing is random, nothing is overlooked, and nothing is beyond His sovereign care.

As you reflect, ask whether you are living as though your life is truly counted and valued in His eternal plan.

Do I trust God's numbering in the details of my life? How can I rest in His order instead of fearing chaos? What step will I take today to walk in confidence that I am counted and cared for by Him?

Closing Prayer: *Father, thank You for numbering the stars, the hairs of my head, and every detail of my life. Teach me to rest in Your sovereignty and to trust in Your order. Let me live with confidence that I am known, counted, and loved by You. Amen.*

Chapter 48

Section D:

Multiplying Effects

For precept must be upon precept, precept upon precept, line upon line, line upon line, here a little, there a little. (Isaiah 28:10, NKJV)

Repetition is one of God's greatest teaching tools. Just as children master their sight words through the steady rhythm of flashcards, so too does our Father patiently repeat lessons until they are written on our hearts. At first, repetition feels simple or even redundant, but over time, it transforms into instant recognition, producing confidence and clarity in what once seemed unfamiliar.

In the same way, God uses numbers to mark His messages in our lives. He repeats them, weaving them into our daily experiences, until suddenly we notice the pattern and realize He has been speaking all along. These numeric repetitions are not random coincidences; they are divine flashcards, reminders of His promises and invitations to trust Him.

The multiplying effects of numbers are designed to strengthen our understanding and deepen our faith. When we repeatedly encounter the same number in Scripture, in prayer, or in daily life, it is a call to lean in and discern what the Lord is emphasizing. Just as the disciples needed to hear Jesus teach the same truths in different ways, we also need the reinforcement of repetition until revelation sinks deep into our spirits.

The message of this section is clear: repetition is not wasted. God uses it as a multiplying effect, pressing His truths into our hearts until they become second nature, guiding us with confidence and reminding us that His Word is alive and personal.

Focus Point

For whatever things were written before were written for our learning, that we through the patience and comfort of the Scriptures might have hope. (Romans 15:4, NKJV)

This verse highlights the patience of God in teaching us—through repetition, Scripture, and numeric patterns that multiply meaning.

Main Theme

God uses repetition and numbers as divine flashcards to reinforce truth and multiply understanding.

"Repetition is God's way of pressing eternal truths into our hearts until they transform us."

Key Scriptures

- *For precept must be upon precept, precept upon precept, line upon line, line upon line, here a little, there a little.* (Isaiah 28:10, NKJV)
- *For whatever things were written before were written for our learning, that we through the patience and comfort of the Scriptures might have hope.* (Romans 15:4, NKJV)
- *Finally, my brethren, rejoice in the Lord. For me to write the same things to you is not tedious, but for you it is safe.* (Philippians 3:1, NKJV)

Key Points

- **Repetition as Teaching** God patiently repeats truth until it becomes part of our spiritual reflex.
- **Divine Flashcards** Numbers often serve as reminders, strategically placed in our lives by God.

- **Multiplying Understanding** Repeated patterns multiply meaning, reinforcing lessons we might otherwise miss.
- **Not Random** Numeric repetition is intentional, a sign of God's personal communication.
- **From Confusion to Clarity** Repetition turns what was once unfamiliar into instant recognition.
- **Patience of God** The Lord's persistence reflects His love, much like a parent teaching a child.
- **Living Revelation** Repeated numbers remind us that Scripture is alive and speaks directly to us.

JOURNALING QUESTIONS

Journaling about multiplying effects invites us to track repeated numbers and themes in our spiritual lives. Writing these down allows us to recognize patterns we might otherwise dismiss as coincidence. Reflection reveals that God is patiently reinforcing His truth until it becomes part of our very nature.

Through journaling, readers will realize that the multiplying effects of repetition are meant to anchor us in God's promises. What may seem repetitive is actually the Spirit carving His Word deeper into our hearts.

RECOGNIZING REPETITION

What repeated numbers or themes has God been showing me lately?

____

____

____

____

____

____

____

Divine Flashcards

How might God be using numeric repetition to capture my attention?

____
____
____
____
____
____

Personal Lessons

Which lessons in my life has God patiently repeated until I finally understood?

____
____
____
____
____
____

Multiplying Faith

How does repetition help strengthen my trust in God's promises?

____
____
____
____
____
____

Scripture Reinforcement

What biblical truths has God reinforced through repeated encounters with His Word?

____

____

____

____

____

____

Actionable Steps

Track the Patterns
Keep a journal of repeated numbers or themes and prayerfully seek their meaning.

Embrace the Lesson
Instead of dismissing repetition, see it as God's way of pressing truth into your spirit.

Respond with Obedience
Act on the lessons God is repeating, allowing them to shape your daily walk.

Personal Reflection

The multiplying effects remind us that God is patient and persistent in teaching us. Repetition is not redundancy—it is reinforcement, multiplying understanding until His truth becomes our second nature.

As you reflect, consider where God has been repeating Himself in your life and how you will respond.

Am I paying attention to the patterns God is repeating? How will I embrace repetition as His way of teaching me? What step will I take to act on the lessons He keeps showing me?

____

____

____

Closing Prayer: *Father, thank You for the multiplying effects of repetition. Open my eyes to the patterns You are showing me through numbers and Scripture. Help me to embrace Your lessons with patience, allowing them to sink deep into my heart and guide my steps. Amen.*

Chapter 49

Triplicates

For God may speak in one way, or in another, yet man does not perceive it. (Job 33:14, NKJV)

When God really wants to get our attention, He repeats Himself. Numbers appearing in triplicate—such as 111, 222, or 666—are one of His ways of pressing a message deeper into our hearts. Just as Job reminds us, when we fail to perceive what God is saying the first time, He patiently repeats until we do.

Many believers find themselves repeatedly noticing these "triplicate" numbers. The author notes that the most frequent inquiries he receives are about 222 and 111. These repetitions are not random accidents but invitations to pay attention. When God highlights a number over and over again, He is urging us to stop, pray, and discern the lesson attached to it.

In Scripture, when numbers appear in triplicate, they point to the fullness or completion of that number's meaning. If the number one represents unity, then 111 represents complete or perfect unity. That is why 111 is associated with Jehovah God, the fullness of divine unity. Conversely, 666 is the fullness of man's rebellion against God. Each set of triplicate numbers carries a weight that magnifies its core message.

The lesson of triplicates is this: God is persistent. He will repeat Himself in love until we perceive, discern, and respond. Repetition is His mercy, not His annoyance. These repeating numbers serve as divine highlighters, reminding us that His voice is consistent, His messages are deliberate, and His heart is for us to understand.

Focus Point

By the mouth of two or three witnesses every word shall be established. (2 Corinthians 13:1, NKJV)

Triplicate numbers serve as witnesses, confirming and reinforcing what God is speaking.

Main Theme

Triplicate numbers emphasize the completeness and certainty of God's message.

"When God repeats, He confirms—triplicates highlight the fullness of His truth."

Key Scriptures

- *For God may speak in one way, or in another, yet man does not perceive it.* (Job 33:14, NKJV)
- *By the mouth of two or three witnesses every word shall be established.* (2 Corinthians 13:1, NKJV)
- *Holy, holy, holy is the Lord of hosts; the whole earth is full of His glory!* (Isaiah 6:3, NKJV)

Key Points

- **God Repeats to Teach** Triplicates show God's persistence in making sure His people understand.
- **Numbers That Capture Attention** 111 and 222 are often noticed because they represent unity and covenant.
- **Fullness of Meaning** When a number is tripled, it emphasizes totality and completeness.
- **111 and Unity** This number speaks of divine unity, representing Jehovah God.
- **666 and Rebellion** The fullness of man's opposition to God is revealed in this infamous triplicate.

- **Not Coincidence** Repeated numbers are intentional, calling us to seek the Lord's meaning.
- **Divine Witness** Triplicates function as confirmation that God is establishing His word.

Journaling Questions

Journaling about triplicates encourages us to track when God highlights repeating numbers in our lives. Writing them down helps us look for patterns and discern what the Spirit may be saying. Over time, we see His persistence and His faithfulness to confirm His word.

Through journaling, readers will discover that triplicates are not coincidences but invitations. They point to God's desire for us to grasp His truth in fullness, drawing us closer to Him in understanding and obedience.

Recognizing Patterns

What triplicate numbers have I noticed repeatedly, and how have I responded?

____
____
____
____
____
____
____

Unity in 111

What does it mean to me that 111 symbolizes divine unity?

____
____
____
____
____
____

Covenant in 222

How might 222 be reminding me of God's covenant promises?

____

____

____

____

____

____

Warning in 666

How does the fullness of rebellion in 666 challenge me to stay aligned with God?

____

____

____

____

____

____

Responding to Repetition

How can I be more attentive when God repeats something in my life?

____

____

____

____

____

____

Actionable Steps

Track and Pray
Write down repeating numbers you see and ask God what He is speaking.

Test by Scripture
Always align numeric insights with the Word of God for confirmation.

Act on the Message
When a triplicate confirms God's word, obey and apply it immediately.

Personal Reflection

Triplicates remind us that God is a patient Teacher. He will repeat Himself until His children truly understand. Repeated numbers are not coincidences; they are confirmations. They call us into deeper attention, inviting us to embrace the fullness of His truth.

As you reflect, consider how God has been repeating Himself to you and what response He is waiting for.

Am I listening when God repeats Himself? How will I seek His meaning in the numbers I see? What step will I take to obey when His confirmation comes in triplicate?

Closing Prayer: *Father, thank You for repeating Your truth until I perceive it. Open my eyes to see the patterns You highlight in my life. Teach me to discern triplicates as Your confirmation, and help me to respond with obedience and faith. Amen.*

Chapter 50

111

The Presence of God

For in Him dwells all the fullness of the Godhead bodily. (Colossians 2:9, NKJV)

The number 111 preaches the Presence of God. Jesus is *The One*, the Chosen One, the Anointed One, the Messiah. When He manifests as 111, it signifies the fullness of His presence as the triune God—Father, Son, and Holy Spirit—revealed in unity. In Heaven, Jesus is called *The One*, and Scripture confirms this title through passages that declare His singular, divine identity.

Revelation 4:8 records the living beings around God's throne crying out, *"Holy, holy, holy is the Lord God, the Almighty—the one who always was, who is, and who is still to come."* John the Baptist, too, sent messengers to ask, *"Are you the one who is to come, or should we expect someone else?"* (Luke 7:19–20). Over and over, Scripture confirms Jesus as *The One*. This unity and completeness is captured in the triplicate 111.

Biblically, 111 is connected to key truths and divine titles. The possessive form of Jehovah —"the Lord's"—appears 111 times in the Bible. Words and phrases like *Wonderful*, *The Most High*, *House*, and *The Root of Jesse* carry the numerical value of 111. Multiples of 111 align with profound truths: 111 × 9 = The Lord (Luke 1:43), 111 × 12 = The Child Jesus (Luke 2:27). These patterns reinforce that 111 is inseparably tied to Christ's identity and presence.

The author shares personal testimony of repeatedly encountering 111 in daily life, interpreting it as a reminder of God's nearness and blessing. Deuteronomy 1:11 promises a thousand-fold blessing, and Joshua 1:11 calls God's people to prepare to enter their inheritance. Scriptures marked with "1:11"—like Nehemiah 1:11, Jeremiah 1:11, Mark 1:11, Acts 1:11, and Romans 1:11—speak of answered prayer, prophetic vision, divine affirmation, angelic messages, and spiritual gifts. Together, they emphasize that 111 signals the awareness of God's presence, His prophetic voice, and His call to courage and multiplication.

The message of 111 is this: when you see it, God is reminding you that He is present, that He is speaking, and that He desires to multiply blessing, impart gifts, and draw you deeper into His divine unity.

Focus Point

Hear, O Israel: The Lord our God, the Lord is one! You shall love the Lord your God with all your heart, with all your soul, and with all your strength. (Deuteronomy 6:4–5, NKJV)

This passage affirms that 111 points to the divine unity of God's presence.

Main Theme

111 reveals the fullness of God's presence—Jesus as *The One,* manifesting in unity and blessing.

"111 is the Presence of God—reminding us that Jesus is The One, and He is here."

Key Scriptures

- *For in Him dwells all the fullness of the Godhead bodily.* (Colossians 2:9, NKJV)
- *Then a voice came from heaven, "You are My beloved Son, in whom I am well pleased."* (Mark 1:11, NKJV)
- *Saying, "I am the Alpha and the Omega, the First and the Last, and, What you see, write in a book and send it to the seven churches which are in Asia..."* (Revelation 1:11, NKJV)

Key Points

- **The One** Jesus is "The One," confirmed in Heaven and on earth as Messiah and Savior.

- **Unity in Triplicate** 111 magnifies divine unity—the fullness of the Trinity in perfect harmony.
- **Prophetic Titles** 111 aligns with words like *Wonderful*, *The Most High*, *House*, and *Root of Jesse*.
- **Multiples of 111** Numerical patterns (111 × 9, 111 × 12, etc.) highlight Christ's identity and mission.
- **Scripture Witness** Verses marked "1:11" often emphasize blessing, vision, prayer, and divine affirmation.
- **Personal Presence** Seeing 111 repeatedly is a sign of God's nearness and His desire to bless and multiply.
- **Courage and Inheritance** 111 calls believers to step into promises, trusting God's presence to lead the way.

Journaling Questions

Journaling about 111 helps us discern how God is manifesting His presence in our lives. Writing down the times we encounter this number can build awareness of His nearness and open us to prophetic insight. It shifts our mindset from chance encounters to divine reminders that God is speaking.

Through journaling, readers will come to see 111 as a divine signal—a call to courage, blessing, and attentiveness. It is a reminder that God is not only present but actively guiding, affirming, and multiplying His promises in our lives.

Awareness of Presence

When have I sensed God's presence while noticing 111?

UNITY OF GOD

How does 111 remind me of the fullness of the Trinity in my daily walk?

PROPHETIC CONFIRMATION

Which "1:11" Scriptures speak most powerfully to my current season?

MULTIPLICATION OF BLESSING

Where might God be calling me to expect increase and breakthrough connected to 111?

Responding to His Voice

How will I act on the reminders of God's presence when I encounter 111?

____
____
____
____
____
____

Actionable Steps

Pay Attention
Be alert to moments when 111 appears, seeing them as invitations to pray and listen.

Claim His Promises
Stand on Deuteronomy 1:11, asking God to multiply blessing in your life.

Step Into Courage
Like Joshua 1:11, prepare to enter your inheritance with faith and boldness.

Personal Reflection

111 is more than a number—it is a declaration that Jesus is *The One*. It reminds us that God is present, speaking, affirming, and multiplying His promises. When 111 appears, it is a call to awareness, to courage, and to deeper intimacy with the One who is all in all.

As you reflect, consider how God is using 111 to capture your attention and lead you into His fullness.

Am I noticing when God speaks through 111? How will I respond to His presence in this season? What step of courage and faith will I take, knowing that The One is with me?

____
____
____

Closing Prayer: *Father, thank You for reminding me through 111 that You are present and faithful. Teach me to recognize Your nearness in the ordinary and extraordinary moments. Multiply Your blessings in my life and give me courage to walk into my inheritance with confidence in You. Amen.*

Chapter 51

222

Complete Witness

This man came for a witness, to bear witness of the Light, that all through him might believe.
(John 1:7, NKJV)

The number 222 points to God's message of a complete witness. Just as John the Baptist was sent to testify of Jesus, 222 becomes a numerical marker of testimony, confirmation, and unity in divine truth. It emphasizes that God is persistent in confirming His voice, ensuring that His people do not miss what He is saying.

The gematria of "John the Baptist" equals 2220, highlighting him as the perfect and complete witness to Christ. This aligns with John 1:6–8, which says John was not the Light but was sent to bear witness of the Light. In the same way, when believers encounter 222 repeatedly, it is often God's way of pointing them back to the testimony of Christ.

222 also reveals layers of prophetic depth in Scripture. Acts 2:22 uniquely contains the words "miracles, wonders, and signs" together, confirming God's witness through power. Genesis 2:22 shows the intimacy of creation in marriage, while Deuteronomy 22:22 highlights the seriousness of covenant fidelity. Together, they reveal how 222 connects to intimacy, covenant, and purity.

History also confirms 222 as a prophetic marker. On February 22, 1906, William J. Seymour arrived in Los Angeles, leading to the Azusa Street Revival, one of the greatest outpourings of the Holy Spirit in American history. Even the birth of America ties to 222 through dates and numerical patterns, underscoring God's hand in history.

Scripture after Scripture reinforces the power of 222: Joshua 2:22 speaks of God hiding His people from their enemies, 2 Kings 2:22 records the healing of waters, and Daniel 2:22

reveals deep and secret things. Ephesians 2:22 emphasizes the believer's place in the body of Christ, while James 2:22 shows that faith is made perfect through works. Again and again, 222 ties to witness, revelation, and intimacy with God.

The message of 222 is clear: it is God's assurance that He is speaking, confirming, and calling His people to a deeper place of intimacy, revelation, and faith. It is a reminder that His miracles, wonders, and signs bear witness to His glory and that we are called to respond in faithfulness as His complete witnesses in the earth.

Focus Point

Men of Israel, hear these words: Jesus of Nazareth, a Man attested by God to you by miracles, wonders, and signs which God did through Him in your midst, as you yourselves also know. (Acts 2:22, NKJV)

Main Theme

222 represents the complete witness—God's confirmation through testimony, intimacy, miracles, and prophetic signs.

"222 reminds us that God is persistent in His witness—through His Word, His Spirit, and His people."

Key Scriptures

- *Then the rib which the Lord God had taken from man He made into a woman, and He brought her to the man.* (Genesis 2:22, NKJV)
- *So the water remains healed to this day, according to the word of Elisha which he spoke.* (2 Kings 2:22, NKJV)
- *He reveals deep and secret things; He knows what is in the darkness, and light dwells with Him.* (Daniel 2:22, NKJV)

Key Points

- **Witness of the Light** John the Baptist's life and ministry show 222 as a complete testimony of Christ.
- **Miracles, Wonders, and Signs** Acts 2:22 confirms that 222 connects with God's supernatural witness.
- **Covenant Intimacy** Genesis 2:22 and Deuteronomy 22:22 show 222's tie to covenant relationships.
- **Prophetic Patterns** History and revival, including Azusa Street, reveal 222 as a marker of God's timing.
- **Protection and Guidance** Verses like Joshua 2:22 and Matthew 2:22 emphasize God's protection and direction.
- **Revelation of Secrets** Daniel 2:22 reveals 222 as a number tied to divine mysteries and light.
- **Faith Completed** James 2:22 teaches that faith matures through works—evidence of complete witness.

Journaling Questions

When 222 shows up in your life, God may be speaking of covenant, witness, or a season of deeper revelation. Journaling these encounters helps believers discern God's confirmation. By writing down when and where you encounter 222, you can connect the dots to moments of His leading, protection, or call to intimacy.

222 is not random. It's God's way of saying, *"I am confirming my Word to you. Pay attention."* Whether through miracles, historical timing, or personal encounters, 222 challenges believers to be faithful witnesses to His presence and power.

Witness to the Light

How can I, like John the Baptist, bear witness to the Light of Christ today?

____

____

____

____

Supernatural Confirmation

Where has God confirmed His Word to me with signs, miracles, or wonders?

____
____
____
____
____
____

Covenant Intimacy

What does Genesis 2:22 reveal to me about intimacy with God and others?

____
____
____
____
____
____

Historical Reminders

What revivals or moves of God inspire me to expect more of His Spirit?

____
____
____
____
____
____

Faith in Action

How is God calling me to bring my faith to maturity through works?

____
____
____
____
____
____

Actionable Steps

Acknowledge His Witness
Recognize the ways God confirms His Word through people, signs, and Scripture.

Guard Covenant
Commit to integrity in your relationships as a testimony of God's presence.

Seek Revelation
Pray for God to reveal "deep and secret things" (Daniel 2:22) and write them down.

Personal Reflection

222 is a number of assurance. It says, *"I am with you, I am confirming my Word, and I am calling you to be a witness of My Light."* From John the Baptist to Acts 2:22, God's message through 222 is consistent: He uses repetition and testimony to draw us closer to Him.

When you see 222, let it remind you that God is faithful in covenant, clear in His witness, and calling you to live as a testimony of His presence in a dark world.

Take a moment to recall a time when God reassured you through Scripture, prayer, or circumstance — *how did that strengthen your faith? How am I living as a witness of God's light in my current environment? Do I trust God's timing and covenant faithfulness when things feel uncertain?*

Closing Prayer: *Lord, thank You for the witness of 222. Teach me to recognize Your confirming voice, to embrace covenant intimacy with You, and to walk as a faithful witness of Your Light. Let my life testify of Your presence, Your miracles, and Your love. Amen.*

Chapter 52

333

Urgent Need

Call to Me, and I will answer you, and show you great and mighty things, which you do not know. (Jeremiah 33:3, NKJV)

When I see 3:33 on the clock, it always draws my attention back to God's invitation in Jeremiah 33:3. It's a call to urgency, to cry out in prayer, and to expect an answer. Numbers often speak prophetically, and 333 is one of the clearest signals that God is calling us to lift our voices and seek Him for direction, revelation, or deliverance.

Focus Point

Sing to Him a new song; play skillfully with a shout of joy. (Psalm 33:3, NKJV)

This verse reminds us that 333 is not a quiet prompting but a loud invitation to engage God with passion. Just as a distress signal in Morse code (... --- ...) repeats three dots, three dashes, and three dots, God uses the repetition of three to awaken us, alert us, and call us into active pursuit of Him.

Main Theme

333 represents an urgent cry for divine intervention—a number that points to prayer, deliver-

ance, revelation, and God's covenant promises. It carries both the urgency of need and the assurance that when we call, He will respond with wisdom, direction, and protection.

"333 reminds us that when life is urgent, God's mercy and revelation are even greater."

KEY SCRIPTURES

- *Call to Me, and I will answer you, and show you great and mighty things, which you do not know.* (Jeremiah 33:3, NKJV)
- *And when this comes to pass—surely it will come—then they will know that a prophet has been among them.* (Ezekiel 33:33, NKJV)
- *Bring Me a three-year-old heifer, a three-year-old female goat, a three-year-old ram...* (Genesis 15:9, NKJV)

KEY POINTS

- **An Urgent Cry** Jeremiah 33:3 reveals 333 as a call to pray urgently, expecting God's answer.
- **Inheritance of the Promise** Exodus 33:3 connects 333 to Israel's journey into the Promised Land, symbolizing inheritance and destiny.
- **Judgment and Mercy** David's three choices in 1 Chronicles 21 show that 333 can reveal God's discipline but also His great mercy.
- **Prophetic Assurance** Ezekiel 33:33 ties 333 to the confirmation that God's word through His prophets is true.
- **Family Redefined** Mark 3:33 shows 333 as Jesus' reminder that obedience to God marks true spiritual family.
- **Deliverance and Refuge** The three sets of cities of refuge in Deuteronomy 19 show 333 as God's provision of safety and protection.
- **Creation and Groundedness** The Hebrew word *sadeh* (field) appears 333 times, connecting 333 with God's creation, provision, and covenant blessing in the land.

Journaling Questions

333 is a reminder that prayer is not optional when we face urgent need—it is the pathway to revelation and deliverance. Journaling helps capture the cries of the heart that often come in these moments. By writing down what you're urgently asking God for, you leave a record of both your desperation and God's faithful answers.

Reflection on 333 also shows us that God is deeply involved in our inheritance and identity. Just as Israel was called into the Promised Land, 333 reminds us that He has promises prepared for us. Our role is to respond with faith, urgency, and obedience, knowing that His mercies are greater than our failures.

Calling Out

What urgent need am I crying out to God for right now?

Inheritance

What promises of God am I still waiting to step into, and how is He preparing me for them?

Mercy in Judgment

Where have I seen God's mercy in the midst of correction or discipline?

Prophetic Assurance

What prophetic word has God confirmed to me recently, and how am I responding to it?

Family of Faith

How can I live out my identity as part of Christ's true family through obedience?

Actionable Steps

Pray with Urgency
Set aside time to pray aloud, calling on God with intentional passion, as Jeremiah 33:3 instructs.

Document God's Answers
Keep a journal of 333 moments—times when God confirms His presence, answers prayers, or directs your steps.

Step Into Promise
Take one practical step this week toward walking in the inheritance God has promised you, even if it seems small.

Personal Reflection

333 is not just a number on the clock—it is a divine alarm, alerting us to press into God's presence with urgency. It reminds us that when life feels overwhelming, God is not silent but inviting us into dialogue. He calls us to cry out, to listen, and to step into the inheritance He has already prepared.

God's mercy, revelation, and protection are always greater than the urgency of our need. The question is whether we will respond or ignore His repeated call.

Am I willing to cry out to Him in desperation? Am I ready to trust Him with my inheritance? Am I listening for His urgent voice in the numbers and patterns He places before me?

Closing Prayer: *Father, thank You for the urgency of 333 that calls me to cry out to You. Thank You that You hear and answer, revealing great and unsearchable things. Help me to trust You in times of distress, to step into the promises You've given me, and to recognize the mercy in Your judgments. Teach me to live as part of Your true family, obedient and faithful to Your will. In Jesus' name, Amen.*

Chapter 53

444

Complete Creation

And to the angel of the church in Philadelphia write, "These things says He who is holy, He who is true, He who has the key of David, He who opens and no one shuts, and shuts and no one opens."
(Revelation 3:7, NKJV)

When I tune my guitar to a standard frequency, it's typically set to 440 Hz. That's not the way it's always been; that actually changed during the French Revolution. Before that shift, the standard was 444, and I don't think that was accidental. Every song you hear on the radio now is tuned to 440—Nashville even has the "440 Loop." But that's not what King David tuned everything to. David, the psalmist and worship leader, established a standard that aligned worship with Heaven's sound.

The key of David is a remarkable mystery. It's connected to the throne of David and to supernatural access—doors that open and doors that close. I want you to think about that: access to what God wants you to have, and closure against what shouldn't reach you. The favor of the Lord upon you is demonstrated by the doors He opens for you, and the protection of the Lord is demonstrated by the doors He shuts. David's key is about both—holy access and holy boundaries.

This isn't just a theory; Scripture spells it out. Jesus holds the Key of David—He opens and no one can shut, and He shuts and no one can open (Revelation 3:7–10). Ezekiel saw four living creatures with four faces and four wings—heavenly order stamped with fours (Ezekiel 1:5–6). Strong's 444 (*anthropos*) reminds us that "man shall not live by bread alone, but by every word" (Matthew 4:4). Even the prophets' books total 4,440 verses, and when grace is introduced, it sums to 888—the gematria of the name Jesus. Heaven's frequency, Heaven's order, Heaven's access—this is the Key of David.

So let me challenge you: Which doors has Jesus been trying to shut that you keep propping open? Which doors has He set before you that you're afraid to walk through? Will you let Him tune your life to Heaven's frequency instead of the world's distortion? The Key of David is in His hand—agree with His opening and His closing, and step into divine order and complete creation.

Focus Point

Man shall not live by bread alone, but by every word that proceeds from the mouth of God. (Matthew 4:4, NKJV)

This verse reveals 444 as a reminder that our true life comes only from God's Word. It aligns with the "Key of David," a symbol of supernatural access, authority, and divine order, where God opens the right doors and closes those that lead to destruction.

Main Theme

444 represents complete creation, supernatural access, and divine order. It is tied to the "Key of David," which unlocks the frequency of Heaven, establishing worship, intimacy, and authority. It also serves as a reminder that God's standards do not change, and His timing brings about fulfillment in both personal and global events.

"444 is the sound and key of Heaven, the reminder that God opens and closes doors to align us with His divine order."

Key Scriptures

- *I know your works. See, I have set before you an open door, and no one can shut it; for you have a little strength, have kept My word, and have not denied My name.* (Revelation 3:8, NKJV)

- *Also from within it came the likeness of four living creatures. And this was their appearance: they had the likeness of a man. Each one had four faces, and each one had four wings.* (Ezekiel 1:5–6, NKJV)
- *The fool has said in his heart, "There is no God." They are corrupt, and have done abominable iniquity; there is none who does good.* (Psalm 53:1, NKJV)

Key Points

- **The Key of David** 444 signifies supernatural access—doors opened to God's purposes and closed against the enemy's schemes.
- **Heaven's Frequency** David established 444 Hz as the tuning for worship, symbolizing the pure sound of Heaven.
- **Divine Order** Ezekiel's vision of four creatures with four faces and four wings reflects 444 as God's structure and completeness.
- **Man's Dependence on God** Strong's Concordance 444 points to *anthropos* (man), reminding us that life is sustained by God's Word alone.
- **Historical Witness** The 444-day Iran Hostage Crisis and the fall of the Berlin Wall marked God's hand in history, stamping 444 on world events.
- **Judgment and Covenant** The gematria of "Damascus" as 444 connects the number to God's dealings with nations and His covenant faithfulness.
- **Creation Fulfilled** From the 4,440 verses in the prophets to chapters with 44 verses, 444 points to the completion of God's creation and His perfect timing.

Journaling Questions

444 challenges us to pay attention to divine doors of opportunity. When you see 444 repeatedly, it's often God's reminder that He is the One opening and shutting doors in your life. Journaling these encounters will help you identify when He has granted you access to new seasons, relationships, or callings.

This number also urges believers to embrace worship as warfare. Just as David tuned his instruments to Heaven's sound, 444 invites us to align our lives, prayers, and songs with God's eternal frequency. True freedom and breakthrough come when we let Him set the standard.

Supernatural Access

What doors is God opening or closing in my life right now?

Frequency of Worship

How can I align my worship with Heaven's standard, both in spirit and in truth?

Historical Lessons

How has God revealed His order and timing in world events that inspire my faith?

Dependence on the Word

Am I living by bread alone, or by every word that comes from God's mouth?

____

____

____

____

____

____

Divine Order

Where do I need to allow God to bring structure and completion in my life?

____

____

____

____

____

____

Actionable Steps

Embrace God's Doors
Pray daily for discernment to recognize the doors God is opening and courage to walk through them.

Align Worship with Heaven
Commit to a lifestyle of worship, not just songs, that brings your heart into Heaven's rhythm.

Record His Timing
Journal encounters with 444 and note how God uses them to align your steps with His divine order.

Personal Reflection

444 reminds us that we are part of God's complete creation, aligned with His eternal order. Just as David carried the key of worship and intimacy, we too are invited into supernatural access. God's authority determines which doors open and which remain closed, ensuring that His perfect will prevails.

In seasons of uncertainty, 444 assures us that God's frequency is never distorted. His Word is steady, His covenant unbroken, and His timing flawless. This number is both a call to worship and a reassurance that creation is complete in Him.

Am I willing to let God set the frequency of my life? Am I ready to trust His doors of opportunity and closed pathways? Am I aligned with the sound of Heaven that brings divine order into chaos?

Closing Prayer: *Lord, thank You for the assurance of 444. Thank You that You hold the Key of David, opening doors no one can shut and shutting those that are not for me. Align my life to the frequency of Heaven so that my worship becomes warfare and my walk reflects Your order. Let me live by every word that proceeds from Your mouth, trusting that Your divine timing will always bring me into fulfillment. In Jesus' name, Amen.*

Chapter 54

555

Complete Grace

My grace is sufficient for you, for My strength is made perfect in weakness.
(2 Corinthians 12:9, NKJV)

When I think of the number 555, I remember times when I felt completely overwhelmed, moments when I had no strength left to keep pushing. It was in those seasons that God reminded me of His grace—always more than enough, always perfectly timed, and always greater than my weakness. Grace has a way of showing up right when we've run out of options.

The number 5 represents grace, favor, and God's ability to supply what we cannot. Seeing it multiplied as 555 is God's way of saying His grace is complete and abundant. It's the divine reassurance that whatever you are walking through, His hand is covering you, His breath is sustaining you, and His favor is opening doors you could never earn.

Throughout Scripture, grace is seen in patterns of five. The five books of the Torah, the fivefold ministry gifts in the New Testament, the five loaves that fed thousands—all remind us that God provides in ways that surpass our natural ability. 555 is the prophetic picture of grace multiplied to completion, wrapping our lives in mercy and empowerment.

So let me ask you this: When you see 555, do you believe God is reminding you that His grace is already sufficient? Are you willing to lay down striving and trust His supernatural supply? Will you allow grace to become not just a safety net but the very power that propels you forward?

Focus Point

But God, who is rich in mercy, because of His great love with which He loved us, even when we were dead in trespasses, made us alive together with Christ (by grace you have been saved). (Ephesians 2:4–5, NKJV)

Grace is more than unmerited favor—it is the power of God working in us and through us. 555 speaks of the fullness of this grace, reminding us that we live, move, and thrive only because of His mercy.

Main Theme

555 represents complete grace—God's all-sufficient favor, power, and provision poured out in fullness. It is a reminder that no matter the weakness, His grace abounds even more. Grace is not only for salvation but also for living, overcoming, and fulfilling our divine purpose.

"555 is the multiplied assurance that God's grace will always be enough."

Key Scriptures

- *And of His fullness we have all received, and grace for grace.* (John 1:16, NKJV)
- *For if by the one man's offense death reigned through the one, much more those who receive abundance of grace and of the gift of righteousness will reign in life through the One, Jesus Christ.* (Romans 5:17, NKJV)
- *The Lord make His face shine upon you, and be gracious to you.* (Numbers 6:25, NKJV)

Key Points

- **Grace Multiplied** Five symbolizes grace, but 555 emphasizes its fullness and abundance, reminding us that His provision never runs out.
- **Sufficient in Weakness** 2 Corinthians 12:9 shows that grace becomes most visible where we feel least capable.

- **Overflowing Favor** Romans 5:17 reveals that abundance of grace empowers us to reign in life through Jesus Christ.
- **Unmerited Gift** Grace is not earned; it is given freely, ensuring that we cannot boast in our own strength.
- **Covering and Protection** Grace not only saves but also shields us, as seen in the blessing of Numbers 6:25.
- **Empowerment to Reign** Grace equips believers to step into authority and victory, not merely survive hardship.
- **Grace Upon Grace** John 1:16 reminds us that God layers grace upon grace, always enough for the season we are in.

Journaling Questions

555 is God's signature over our lives that His grace is not partial but complete. Journaling when and where you see this number will help you connect how God is speaking about His provision in your journey. Each sighting may be a reminder to stop striving, to lean into His strength, and to acknowledge that He alone sustains you.

Reflection on 555 pushes us to see grace as more than forgiveness—it is empowerment. It transforms challenges into testimonies and equips us to face trials with confidence. Journaling on grace invites us to record stories of God's sufficiency, helping us remember in the future what He has already done.

Grace Multiplied

Where have I seen God's grace multiply in my life when I had no strength left?

Weakness and Strength

What weakness is God asking me to surrender so His strength can be perfected in me?

Unmerited Favor

Am I relying on my performance, or am I resting in the gift of grace?

Grace as Empowerment

How can I use the grace God has given me to serve and bless others?

Grace for Today

What new measure of grace do I need to believe God for in this season?

____

____

____

____

____

____

Actionable Steps

Rest in His Sufficiency
Choose one area of striving in your life and intentionally lay it before God, trusting His grace to be enough.

Record Grace Encounters
Keep a grace journal where you track daily moments of God's provision, protection, or favor.

Extend Grace to Others
Demonstrate the fullness of grace by forgiving or showing kindness to someone who may not deserve it.

Personal Reflection

555 is Heaven's reminder that grace is not scarce—it is complete. God's grace carries us when we cannot walk, empowers us when we feel incapable, and multiplies beyond our ability to imagine. This number is God's declaration that His sufficiency covers every area of our lives.

Grace calls us not only to rest but to reign. To trust that our identity, provision, and destiny are rooted not in our performance but in Christ's finished work. When you see 555, hear the whisper of the Spirit saying, "My grace is enough for you today."

Am I truly leaning into God's grace? Am I allowing His strength to shine through my weakness? Am I willing to live as someone who reflects His multiplied grace to the world?

***Closing Prayer:** Lord, thank You for the multiplied grace of 555. Thank You that Your grace is sufficient, covering my weakness and empowering me to live in victory. Help me to rest in Your provision, to extend grace to others, and to walk with confidence in the abundance of Your love. May my life be a testimony that Your grace is always enough. In Jesus' name, Amen.*

Chapter 55

666

Complete Flesh

Here is wisdom. Let him who has understanding calculate the number of the beast, for it is the number of a man: His number is 666. (Revelation 13:18, NKJV)

I remember the first time I truly studied Revelation 13:18 and saw the number 666. It struck me as more than just a frightening symbol—it was the very picture of humanity apart from God. Flesh without Spirit, man without God, life without hope. The weight of that realization was sobering, and it reminded me how easy it is for people to drift into living as though God does not exist.

The number six throughout Scripture points to man. When repeated three times as 666, it becomes the ultimate expression of man-centered life—flesh in its fullness, apart from God's presence. Just as the mark of the beast represents total rebellion, 666 calls attention to what happens when humanity relies only on its own strength, its own systems, and its own pride.

Examples of this number echo through Scripture and history. Solomon's wealth was marked with 666 talents of gold (1 Kings 10:14). John 6:66 describes many disciples walking away from Jesus. Even Goliath bore the mark in his height, armor, and weapons. Each moment reveals how 666 is stamped on pride, rebellion, betrayal, and systems that oppose God.

So let me ask you: Have you recognized the areas in your life where flesh tries to take over? Where pride and self-reliance want to silence faith? 666 is not just about the end times—it is a warning today. Will you choose Spirit over flesh? God over man? Eternal life over temporary power?

FOCUS POINT

But these, like natural brute beasts made to be caught and destroyed, speak evil of the things they do not understand, and will utterly perish in their own corruption. (2 Peter 2:12, NKJV)

This verse reflects the essence of 666—living like a beast, driven by flesh and corruption, without knowledge of God.

MAIN THEME

666 represents the complete flesh—man at his fullest without God. It is the symbol of rebellion, pride, and the systems of this world in opposition to God's Kingdom. While 7 represents completion in God, 6 represents falling short; multiplied three times, it becomes total separation and deception.

"666 is the mark of flesh in its fullness, reminding us that life apart from God leads only to destruction."

KEY SCRIPTURES

- *But these speak evil of whatever they do not know; and whatever they know naturally, like brute beasts, in these things they corrupt themselves.* (Jude 1:10, NKJV)
- *From that time many of His disciples went back and walked with Him no more.* (John 6:66, NKJV)
- *And the weight of gold that came to Solomon yearly was six hundred and sixty-six talents of gold.* (1 Kings 10:14, NKJV)

KEY POINTS

- **Mark of the Beast** Revelation 13:18 identifies 666 as the number of man—complete flesh apart from God.
- **Beast Nature** 2 Peter 2:12 and Jude 1:10 describe fleshly people as brute beasts, revealing the animalistic state of man without God.

- **Stamped in History** Events like the Great Fire of London in 1666 and Islamic conquests in AD 666 bear witness to destruction tied to this number.
- **Solomon's Wealth** 1 Kings 10:14 shows Solomon's 666 talents of gold, highlighting how wealth can mark both greatness and the dangers of excess.
- **Mass Rejection** John 6:66 records the greatest exodus of disciples from Jesus, stamped with 666 as ultimate rebellion.
- **Human Systems** 666 reflects false religion, corrupt government, and worldly economics—the threefold system of man in opposition to God.
- **Spirit vs. Flesh** The choice between 7 (Spirit and completion in God) and 6 (flesh without God) is before us daily.

Journaling Questions

When 666 appears, it is a warning against living by flesh rather than Spirit. Journaling about encounters with 666 can reveal where God is urging us to surrender pride, greed, or rebellion. It's not always about the "end times"—it's often about today's choices between living by the Spirit or the flesh.

Reflection on 666 helps us see the deception of worldly systems. Politics, economics, and even religious traditions can drift into being man-centered rather than God-centered. Journaling on these moments challenges us to ask: Am I aligning my life with the Spirit of God, or with the systems of flesh?

Flesh vs. Spirit

Where do I see the pull of the flesh in my own life, and how can I surrender it to God?

____

____

____

____

____

____

____

Warning Signs

Have I noticed patterns where God is warning me to avoid pride, greed, or rebellion?

Systems of the World

In what ways have I placed too much trust in human systems instead of God's Kingdom?

Mass Rejection

What does John 6:66 teach me about staying faithful when others walk away?

Victory over Flesh

How can I practically choose the Spirit over flesh in my daily walk?

____

____

____

____

____

____

Actionable Steps

Reject the Flesh
Identify one area of your life where you've been led by self or pride and bring it under God's authority.

Stay Alert
Pay attention to when you see 666—it may be God's way of reminding you to stay Spirit-led.

Cling to the Spirit
Commit daily to prayer and Scripture reading, letting God's Word guide you over the voices of the world.

Personal Reflection

666 is not just an apocalyptic number—it is the mark of flesh, pride, and rebellion in every age. From Solomon's wealth to John's account of betrayal, it shows us the danger of life without God. But for believers, it is not a cause of fear. It is a call to vigilance, to choose the Spirit over the flesh.

The systems of this world—religion, government, and economy—may be stamped with 666, but God's Kingdom is stamped with His Spirit. Seeing 666 reminds us that even in a world of deception, His Spirit empowers us to live above the flesh.

Am I living Spirit-led or flesh-driven? Am I recognizing God's warnings when He shows me the futility of pride? Am I willing to reject the mark of the flesh and embrace the seal of His Spirit?

Closing Prayer: *Lord, thank You for opening my eyes to the warning of 666. Teach me to walk by the Spirit and not by the flesh. Help me to reject pride, rebellion, and the systems of this world, and to live in the freedom of Your truth. Seal me with Your Spirit and keep me faithful, even when the world turns away. In Jesus' name, Amen.*

Chapter 56

777

Complete Perfection of Spirit

But in the days when the seventh angel is about to sound his trumpet, the mystery of God will be accomplished, just as He announced to His servants the prophets. (Revelation 10:7, NIV)

Perfection has always been one of humanity's deepest longings. We chase it in beauty, in work, in relationships, and even in religion. Yet every earthly attempt falls short, leaving us empty and striving for more. The number 777 is God's way of showing us that true perfection cannot be found in man—it can only be found in Him. It is His stamp of spiritual completion, His divine "finished work."

Throughout Scripture, sevens echo the fullness of God's design. Creation itself was built upon the rhythm of seven days, and the Sabbath became a sign of rest and completion in Him. When seven is repeated three times—777—it points directly to the perfection of Father, Son, and Holy Spirit in complete unity. Where 666 shouts of man's imperfection and rebellion, 777 declares heaven's wholeness and Spirit-filled life.

Biblical examples reinforce this truth. Lamech lived exactly 777 years, symbolizing a life marked by God's divine number of completeness. In the fall of Jericho, seven priests blew seven trumpets on the seventh day, a prophetic act tied to spiritual breakthrough. Revelation's three mentions of the seventh angel reveal the unfolding of God's mystery, the establishment of His Kingdom, and the final declaration, "It is finished." Each layer of Scripture confirms that 777 points to the perfect completion of God's Spirit at work.

When we see 777, it is not a coincidence—it is an invitation. God is calling us to align ourselves with His Spirit and step into the wholeness only He can give. It is a reminder that perfection is not about human effort but about surrendering fully to the triune God who completes us. The perfection of 777 is not future only—it is available now, in the Spirit-filled life of every believer.

Focus Point

The kingdom of the world has become the kingdom of our Lord and of His Messiah, and He will reign for ever and ever. (Revelation 11:15, NIV)

777 points to the reign of Christ and the eternal perfection of His Kingdom.

Main Theme

777 represents the complete perfection of Spirit—the fullness of the Father, Son, and Holy Spirit in unity, victory, and eternal reign.

"777 is heaven's declaration that God's Spirit completes what man never can."

Key Scriptures

- *So all the days of Lamech were seven hundred and seventy-seven years; and he died.* (Genesis 5:31, NKJV)
- *And seven priests shall bear seven trumpets of rams' horns before the ark. But the seventh day you shall march around the city seven times, and the priests shall blow the trumpets.* (Joshua 6:4, NKJV)
- *The seventh angel poured out his bowl into the air. And a mighty shout came from the throne and in the Temple, saying, "It is finished!"* (Revelation 16:17, NLT)

Key Points

- **Lamech's Life** Lamech lived 777 years, symbolizing divine completion in a man's lifetime.
- **Victory at Jericho** The seven priests, seven trumpets, and seven marches on the seventh day reveal God's perfection in bringing supernatural breakthrough.
- **Revelation 777** The seventh angel appears three times, marking the completion of

God's mystery, the announcement of His Kingdom, and the final declaration of fulfillment.

- **Perfect Trinity** 777 reflects the perfection of Father, Son, and Holy Spirit—the fullness of divine unity.
- **Contrast to 666** Where 666 represents fallen flesh, 777 demonstrates completion through God's Spirit.
- **Finished Work of Christ** Jesus declared, "It is finished," bringing us into the fullness of 777 completion.
- **Invitation to Wholeness** When we see 777, it is God reminding us that His Spirit alone perfects and completes us.

Journaling Questions

When you see 777, pause and recognize that it is not random—it is a message from heaven. God is reminding you that His Spirit is working to bring you into completion. Journaling about 777 encounters can help you notice areas where God is calling you into greater wholeness, surrender, or breakthrough.

This number is not just about the end of the story—it's about how we live today. 777 challenges us to let go of striving in the flesh and rest in the Spirit's perfection. Instead of trying to perfect ourselves, we are called to yield to the One who makes us whole.

Wholeness in Spirit

Where am I striving in my own strength instead of relying on the Spirit's perfection?

___

___

___

___

___

___

___

Breakthrough at Jericho

What walls in my life need to fall through obedience to God's perfect plan?

____
____
____
____
____
____

Revelation's 777

How does the promise of God's finished work encourage me in seasons of waiting?

____
____
____
____
____
____

Contrast with 666

Where do I see the tug-of-war between the flesh (666) and the Spirit (777) in my own life?

____
____
____
____
____
____

Living Complete

What practical step can I take to walk in Spirit-led completeness today?

____

____

____

____

____

____

Actionable Steps

Rest in His Perfection
Choose one area of life where you've been striving and intentionally surrender it to God's Spirit.

Stand in Victory
Like Israel at Jericho, obey God in small steps and trust Him for supernatural breakthrough.

Align with Heaven
Whenever you see 777, take it as a personal reminder to live in Spirit-led completeness.

Personal Reflection

The number 777 is a reminder that perfection does not come from man but from God. It is heaven's way of declaring that the Father, Son, and Spirit are at work to bring us into wholeness. While the world is marked by 666—the perfection of flesh—those who belong to Christ are invited into 777, the perfection of Spirit.

When I see 777, I take it as a reminder to stop striving and start trusting. It tells me that God's Spirit is already working, already perfecting, already completing His plan in me. It reminds me that wholeness is not something I achieve, but something I receive.

How might I release my need to strive and instead rest in the perfection of God's Spirit already at work within me? In what ways have I seen the Father, Son, and Spirit bringing whole-

ness to areas of my life that once felt incomplete? What would it look like today to receive, rather than achieve, the wholeness God freely offers through His Spirit?

Closing Prayer: *Father, thank You for the reminder of 777—that You are perfect, complete, and whole. Teach me to rest in the finished work of Christ and to live by the power of the Holy Spirit. Help me to trust that You are completing what You began in me, and to walk in the fullness of Your Spirit. In Jesus' name, Amen.*

Chapter 57

888

Jesus

Behold, I make all things new. And He said unto me, Write: for these words are true and faithful.
(Revelation 21:5, NKJV)

When we speak of the number 888, we are speaking directly of the name of Jesus in the Greek language. This is no accident. In the Bible, 8 represents new beginnings, resurrection, and eternal life. When it is repeated three times—888—it points directly and perfectly to Jesus Christ, the One who conquered sin, death, and the grave, and who brings complete and eternal renewal.

The gematria of the Greek name *Iēsous* (Ἰησοῦς) adds up exactly to 888. This astonishing mathematical precision is not coincidence but divine design. It declares to us that Jesus is the embodiment of perfection, completion, and eternal new beginnings. He is the Alpha and Omega, the First and the Last, and the sum of all things. While 666 represents man's rebellion, 888 reveals heaven's ultimate answer—Jesus Himself.

Eight is significant throughout Scripture. Circumcision, the covenant sign given to Israel, was performed on the eighth day. Jesus rose from the dead on the first day of the week, which is spiritually the "eighth day," marking the dawn of a new creation. Elijah performed eight miracles, while his successor Elisha received a double portion and performed sixteen—together, a perfect reflection of the power of 888.

When we see 888, God is preaching a sermon of hope. He is reminding us that no matter how broken, defeated, or lost we may feel, in Christ we have a new beginning. Just as America's birth year, 1776, points to 888 multiplied, history itself bears witness to God's numerical fingerprint pointing back to His Son. Jesus is the complete new beginning for every nation, every generation, and every person who calls upon His name.

FOCUS POINT

Search the Scriptures, for in them you think you have eternal life; and these are they which testify of Me. (John 5:39, NKJV)

888 reminds us that all Scripture, all history, and even numbers themselves testify of Jesus Christ.

MAIN THEME

888 represents Jesus, the Perfect New Beginning—the Alpha and the Omega, the Bringer of eternal life and the One who makes all things new.

"888 is heaven's proclamation: Jesus is the beginning of every new creation."

KEY SCRIPTURES

- *I am the Alpha and the Omega, the Beginning and the End, the First and the Last.* (Revelation 22:13, NKJV)
- *She bore a male Child who was to rule all nations with a rod of iron. And her Child was caught up to God and His throne.* (Revelation 12:5, NKJV)
- *For whoever calls on the name of the Lord shall be saved."* (Romans 10:13, NKJV)

KEY POINTS

- **Gematria of Jesus** The name of Jesus in Greek equals 888, showing divine precision and prophetic meaning.
- **Number of New Beginnings** Eight represents resurrection and new creation, fulfilled perfectly in Christ.

- **Historical Witness** America's birth year (1776 = 888 x 2) and other historical events carry God's witness of 888.
- **Biblical Declarations** Phrases like *"The salvation of our God"* and *"Immanuel"* equal 888, testifying of Jesus.
- **Resurrection Power** Jesus rose on the "eighth day," securing eternal life for all who believe.
- **Prophetic Fulfillment** From Daniel and his friends to Ezekiel's temple with eight steps, 888 echoes through the Word.
- **Living Witness** Even today, 888 is stamped into culture—toll-free numbers, translations, and global witness point back to Jesus.

Journaling Questions

When you see 888, God is reminding you of the endless new beginning you have in Christ. It's not a number of chance—it's His fingerprint. Journaling these moments can help you trace how God is leading you into seasons of renewal, resurrection, and deeper intimacy with Him.

This number is a call to live in the reality of Christ's finished work. Instead of staying bound by the failures of yesterday, 888 declares that today is a new day in Him. Jesus is not just part of your story—He is the beginning, the middle, and the end of it.

New Beginnings

What area of my life is God inviting me to surrender so He can make it new?

____

____

____

____

____

____

____

Resurrection Power

Where have I experienced the "eighth day" resurrection power of Jesus in my journey?

Scriptural Witness

How does seeing 888 confirm John 5:39—that all Scripture testifies of Jesus?

Historical Reminder

What moves of God in history remind me that He is still writing new beginnings today?

Personal Witness

How can I live daily as a testimony that Jesus is the One who makes all things new?

____

____

____

____

____

____

Actionable Steps

Call Upon His Name
Declare Romans 10:13—call on Jesus (888) and invite Him to renew every area of your life.

Step Into Resurrection
Celebrate the "eighth day" by starting new habits that align your life with Christ's Spirit.

Be a Witness
Share your testimony of how Jesus has made you new—someone else's life may depend on it.

Personal Reflection

The number 888 proclaims the reality that Jesus is the complete and perfect new beginning. While 666 marks the flesh and imperfection, 888 declares eternal life through Christ. It is a number that sings of resurrection, hope, and transformation. Every time I see 888, I hear the Lord say, "I am making all things new."

In my own life, I've seen this truth time and time again—moments where despair gave way to hope, where loss gave way to restoration, and where death gave way to life. 888 is not just a number; it is a reminder that Jesus is alive, reigning, and renewing. He is the Alpha, the Omega, and the everlasting new beginning for all who believe.

Where do I need to invite Jesus to bring new life and renewal in my current season? How have I experienced His resurrection power turning despair into hope? What does it mean for me today to live as someone made new in Christ?

Closing Prayer: *Lord Jesus, thank You that You are the Alpha and the Omega, the perfect new beginning. Thank You that through Your resurrection, I have eternal life. Teach me to live in the power of 888—resting in Your Spirit, walking in newness of life, and proclaiming to the world that You make all things new. Amen.*

Chapter 58

999

Divine Order

But the fruit of the Spirit is love, joy, peace, longsuffering, kindness, goodness, faithfulness, gentleness, self-control. Against such there is no law. (Galatians 5:22–23, NKJV)

The number 999 is a prophetic symbol of divine order and spiritual maturity. If 666 represents the fullness of flesh and rebellion, 999 stands as its mirror opposite—God's perfection prevailing over chaos, His Spirit triumphing over the world's corruption. To see 999 is to be reminded that the Kingdom of God is advancing toward completion, where every gift, fruit, and administration of the Spirit comes into alignment.

Nine is the number of finality and fullness in the Bible. Jesus gave up His spirit at the ninth hour, completing His earthly mission. The nine fruits of the Spirit mark the evidence of a mature Christian walk. The nine spiritual gifts Paul lists in 1 Corinthians 12 display the dynamic workings of the Spirit for building the Church. And the seven Spirits of God before the throne (Revelation 1:4), together with the Father and the Son, complete the heavenly witness. Triple nines—999—represent this fullness multiplied, the perfection of maturity carried into every realm of life.

Yet 999 also comes with a warning. Strong's Concordance links it in Hebrew (biynah) to discernment and in Greek (bothunos) to a pit or ditch. Just as God is calling His people into alignment, discernment, and maturity, the enemy is always seeking to trip us up through blindness and immaturity. If 999 appears repeatedly in your life, it may be a call to sharpen your vision, to avoid hidden pitfalls, and to step into the Spirit's fullness.

Ultimately, 999 proclaims the victory of Christ and the maturity of His Bride. It is a divine invitation to move past childish ways, to bear fruit in every good work, and to live in the order of heaven on earth. It reminds us that God's plan is not chaos but completion, not disorder but divine structure, not immaturity but full maturity in Christ Jesus.

Focus Point

Jesus died at the ninth hour, and in doing so, He brought the completion of redemption and the fullness of God's plan for mankind. (paraphrase from Mark 15:34)

Main Theme

999 represents divine order, maturity, and completion in the Spirit. It is God's signal that His people are being called into alignment, bearing fruit, and walking in wisdom to avoid the pitfalls of spiritual blindness.

"999 is heaven's invitation to live in order, maturity, and the fullness of God's Spirit."

Key Scriptures

- *For to one is given the word of wisdom through the Spirit, to another the word of knowledge through the same Spirit...* (1 Corinthians 12:8–10, NKJV)
- *Grace to you and peace from Him who is and who was and who is to come, and from the seven Spirits who are before His throne.* (Revelation 1:4, NKJV)
- *Blessed be the name of God forever and ever, for wisdom and might are His. And He changes the times and the seasons; He removes kings and raises up kings; He gives wisdom to the wise and knowledge to those who have understanding [biynah].* (Daniel 2:20–21, NKJV)

Key Points

- **Fruit of the Spirit** The first nine of 999 calls us to bear all nine fruits of the Spirit, evidencing maturity.
- **Gifts of the Spirit** The second nine represents the nine gifts of the Spirit given for service and edification of the Church.

- **Heavenly Witness** The third nine points to the heavenly order: the Father, Son, and seven Spirits before the throne.
- **Discernment** Strong's #H999—biynah—reminds us of the need for discernment to recognize God's timing and order.
- **Avoiding Pitfalls** Strong's #G999—bothunos—warns against spiritual blindness that leads to falling into hidden pits.
- **Victory over Flesh** 999 is the divine reversal of 666, pointing to triumph over the flesh and victory in the Spirit.
- **Season of Completion** 999 signals a closing of one chapter and the beginning of a new one in divine order.

Journaling Questions

When you see 999, it may be God's way of urging you toward maturity, reminding you that He is aligning your life with His order. Write down the areas where He is calling you to bear more fruit, exercise discernment, or embrace spiritual gifts for service. Seeing 999 is a divine nudge to step into your next level of spiritual growth.

At the same time, be aware of pitfalls. Just as 999 is linked with maturity and order, its Greek meaning warns against blind spots. Reflect on where you might be spiritually blind or ignoring God's voice. In those places, ask for His Spirit to open your eyes, steady your path, and lead you into wisdom.

Fruit of Maturity

Which of the nine fruits of the Spirit is God calling me to cultivate more deeply right now?

____

____

____

____

____

____

____

Spiritual Gifts

How am I using the gifts of the Spirit to serve and strengthen the body of Christ?

Discernment

Where do I need greater wisdom and discernment to recognize God's timing and direction?

Avoiding Blindness

Am I ignoring any spiritual warnings or blind spots that could lead me into a pit?

Completion

What chapter in my life might God be bringing to completion to usher me into His new season?

____
____
____
____
____
____

Actionable Steps

Cultivate Fruit
Daily practice one fruit of the Spirit in a tangible way (kindness, patience, gentleness, etc.).

Activate Gifts
Pray and ask the Holy Spirit to reveal and activate the gifts He has placed within you for service.

Seek Discernment
Spend focused time in prayer asking God for biynah—understanding and insight for your current season.

Personal Reflection

999 is heaven's way of saying that God is bringing things into divine order. It is not just a number but a prophetic declaration: fruitfulness, gifting, and heavenly authority working together in perfect maturity. Where 666 represents man's rebellion and immaturity, 999 reveals Christ's victory, completion, and the fullness of His Spirit operating in His people.

Every time I see 999, I hear God whispering: "I am aligning you. I am bringing you into maturity. Do not fear what is ending, for I am completing it to make way for something greater." It is both an encouragement and a call to responsibility—to walk worthy of His Spirit, to bear fruit, and to live in discernment.

Where might God be bringing divine order or alignment in my life right now? How is He calling me to grow in maturity and fruitfulness through His Spirit? What endings in my life might actually be God's way of making room for something greater?

Closing Prayer: *Lord, thank You for the gift of divine order. Thank You that 999 is a reminder that You are bringing my life into alignment with Your Spirit. Teach me to bear fruit, to use my gifts for Your glory, and to walk in discernment so I avoid the pitfalls of blindness. Let my life be marked by maturity, victory, and Your perfect order. Amen.*

Chapter 59

God's Time 11:11

But after the three-and-a-half days the breath of life from God entered them, and they stood on their feet, and great fear fell on those who saw them. (Revelation 11:11, NKJV)

Few numbers capture as much attention today as 11:11. People often notice it on clocks, receipts, or even in dreams, and they wonder if it carries a deeper meaning. Biblically and prophetically, the number 11 points to transition, paradox, or disorder. When doubled, as 11:11, it becomes an emphatic signal, almost as if God Himself is highlighting it with flashing lights to ensure we don't miss the message.

The paradox of 11:11 is that it can speak of either chaos or the rise of heroes. On one side, it may represent disorder, instability, or judgment—being "not quite 12," and therefore falling short of divine order. On the other side, when redeemed, it is the call to rise, to become a hero in faith who steps out of instability into destiny. God uses the tension of this paradox to call His people to maturity and courage.

History confirms this prophetic pattern. On 11/11/1833, when Reverend Daniel Parker brought his church to Texas, a meteor shower filled the skies with over 70,000 falling stars. To the settlers, it felt like the heavens themselves were declaring God's presence in their journey of faith. Was it a sign of judgment or a celebration of obedience? In the paradox, God made His presence undeniable, reminding them that He would be with them in hardship, tragedy, and triumph.

Spiritually, seeing 11:11 often serves as a wake-up call. Just as John 11:11 records Jesus declaring that Lazarus would rise from his sleep, 11:11 can signify resurrection, renewal, or spiritual awakening. It is God's way of telling His people: "Pay attention. A transition is at hand. You can rise above the chaos and step into your testimony."

Focus Point

11:11 is God's reminder that even in chaos, He is calling heroes to rise and awaken into their destiny.

Main Theme

11:11 represents the prophetic paradox: heroes rising or disorder prevailing. It is a number of transition, spiritual awakening, and God's intervention in times of instability.

"11:11 is God's exclamation mark—wake up, rise up, and step into your testimony."

Key Scriptures

- *But the land you are crossing the Jordan to take possession of is a land of mountains and valleys that drinks rain from heaven.* (Deuteronomy 11:11, NIV)
- *Our friend Lazarus sleeps, but I go that I may wake him up.* (John 11:11, NKJV)
- *But after the three-and-a-half days the breath of life from God entered them, and they stood on their feet, and great fear fell on those who saw them.* (Revelation 11:11, NKJV)

Key Points

- **Prophetic Paradox** The number 11 represents both chaos and the rise of heroes.
- **Wake-Up Call** John 11:11 ties 11:11 to spiritual awakening and resurrection.
- **Crossing Over** Deuteronomy 11:11 highlights transition from wandering to promise.
- **Testimony After Trial** Revelation 11:11 shows God's breath reviving the two witnesses after opposition.
- **Historical Marker** The meteor shower of 1833 on 11/11 confirmed God's presence to early Texas settlers.

- **Disorder at Babel** Genesis 11 illustrates how human pride brought scattering and disorder.
- **Heroic Rising** When redeemed, 11:11 signals a call to courage and to rise up out of instability.

Journaling Questions

If you keep seeing 11:11, God may be calling you into a new season of transition. Like Lazarus, you may be asleep spiritually, but the Lord is speaking resurrection over your life. Write down the areas where you sense Him urging you to awaken or rise up. He may be calling you into leadership, testimony, or courage in the face of instability.

At the same time, be aware that 11:11 can also warn of disorder. Examine your life for areas of compromise, confusion, or delay. God may be highlighting that unless you rise in faith, chaos could prevail. The key is to respond by leaning into Him, seeking clarity in prayer, and stepping into obedience.

Wake-Up Call

What area of my life might God be calling me to "wake up" and rise into?

____

____

____

____

____

____

Crossing Over

Where am I transitioning from one season to another, and how is God leading me?

____

____

____

____

____

Facing Chaos

Are there areas of instability or disorder in my life that God is asking me to confront?

Hero Rising

What step of faith could I take today that reflects courage and obedience?

Testimony

How is God preparing me to be a witness in this season of transition?

Actionable Steps

Seek Awakening
Pray daily for God to breathe fresh life into areas that feel asleep or stagnant.

Confront Disorder
Identify one place of instability in your life and bring it under God's order.

Step Into Transition
Journal and declare where you sense God calling you to cross into new territory.

Personal Reflection

11:11 is not a coincidence—it is God's divine exclamation point. It says, "I am here in your instability. I am calling you to rise." It is both a warning and an invitation, urging us to leave behind confusion and step into order, courage, and testimony. Just as Daniel Parker's congregation saw the heavens blaze with falling stars on 11/11, so too does God remind us that He is with us in every step of transition.

Every time you see 11:11, remember: this is God's time. It is a call to awaken, to rise, and to step boldly into the season He has prepared for you.

Where in my life is God inviting me to rise above confusion and step into His divine order? How can I respond with courage and faith when I sense God calling me into a new season? What signs or moments has God used recently to remind me that He is present in my transitions?

Closing Prayer: *Father, thank You that You speak through times and seasons. When I see 11:11, let it awaken me to Your voice and remind me that You are present in both order and transition. Raise me up as a hero of faith, and keep me aligned with Your Spirit in times of change. In Jesus' name, Amen.*

Chapter 60

Section E:

Prophetic from a Rearview Mirror

This is what was spoken by the prophet Joel: "And it shall come to pass in the last days, says God, that I will pour out of My Spirit on all flesh..." (Acts 2:16–17, NKJV)

When we think about prophecy, our minds often go straight to the future. We imagine predictions about what is to come and how God will intervene in the days ahead. Yet, prophecy in its biblical form is much more layered than just foresight. One of its most overlooked dimensions is hindsight—seeing God's voice revealed in the events of the past. This is what I call prophecy from a "rearview mirror."

Just as a driver uses a rearview mirror to understand where they've come from and how it shapes their next move, believers can look at history to discern what God has already been preaching through world events. Scripture demonstrates this principle clearly. On the day of Pentecost, Peter stood up and declared, "This is that which was spoken by the prophet Joel." He connected what was unfolding in his present moment to a prophecy spoken 700 years earlier. This was not new foresight—it was hindsight revelation that gave present meaning and direction.

Many Christians do not think of hindsight as prophetic, yet it is one of the most powerful tools for discernment. When we look back, we can see patterns, numbers, and events that were not clear in the moment but are unmistakable now. These patterns become testimonies of God's sovereignty, lessons for our present faith, and guideposts for our future walk. Hindsight doesn't diminish prophecy; it strengthens it by showing us that God has always been speaking —even when we didn't recognize it.

When you begin to approach life with this mindset, everything becomes prophetic. The headlines, the anniversaries, the tragedies, and the victories—each one can become a sermon preached by God through numbers, patterns, and timing. This is why I wrote *Numbers That Prophesy*: to help believers recognize that what God has already done in the past is still preaching today. Once we learn to see through this lens, we are better equipped to partner with the Holy Spirit in discerning His voice in our own circumstances and in the unfolding story of history.

Focus Point

Prophecy is not only about foresight but also about hindsight—recognizing God's voice in past events so we can discern His hand in the present and trust Him for the future.

Main Theme

God often speaks "from the rearview mirror," teaching us through past events. When we connect historical events, personal history, and biblical insight, we discover that His prophetic voice is woven into everything around us.

"Jesus is pursuing you—now it's time to define your relationship with Him."

Key Points

- **Hindsight Is Prophetic** Biblical prophecy often explains present events by connecting them to past revelations.
- **Peter's Example** Acts 2 shows how the early church used hindsight to recognize Joel's prophecy fulfilled.
- **Numbers That Preach** Patterns, dates, and historical events often carry divine sermons that reveal God's hand.
- **History Speaks** Events like Lincoln's assassination or the Titanic carry prophetic lessons for our times.
- **Personal Rearview** God also speaks through the history of our families, our journeys, and our testimonies.
- **Modern Application** By asking, "What is God saying through this?" we discern His voice in both common and epic events.

- **Past, Present, Future Connected** All time is prophetic. God's voice bridges what was, what is, and what is yet to come.

Journaling Questions

Take time to look back at your own history. What were the key events—both victories and struggles—that shaped your journey? Instead of viewing them only as circumstances, ask God what He was saying to you through those seasons. Was there a prophetic lesson in the timing, the number of years, or even the dates involved? Journaling these insights helps you trace God's fingerprints on your life.

Also, look at the larger history around you. National events, cultural shifts, and even global crises are opportunities to ask, "Lord, what are You speaking through this?" If Peter could look at Pentecost and declare, "This is that," then we too can learn to identify how God's voice echoes through both history and our present reality.

Personal History

What events in my life, when I look back, reveal God's hand and voice more clearly?

____

____

____

____

____

____

____

Biblical Example

How does Peter's use of hindsight prophecy in Acts 2 inspire me to read my own life this way?

____

____

____

____

____

NUMBERS THAT PREACH

Have I noticed numbers, dates, or anniversaries repeating in ways that might carry a message?

____

____

____

____

____

____

HISTORICAL EVENTS

What major world events have shaped my perspective of God's sovereignty?

____

____

____

____

____

____

PROPHETIC PARTNERSHIP

How can I better partner with the Holy Spirit to interpret the "rearview mirror" of my life and history?

____

____

____

____

____

____

ACTIONABLE STEPS

Reflect on the Past
Take one past event in your life and ask God to reveal what He was saying through it.

Study Historical Patterns
Pick a historical event that interests you and examine it through the prophetic lens of numbers and Scripture.

Write Your Own "This Is That"
Record a testimony where you now see God's hand in hindsight.

PERSONAL REFLECTION

Prophecy from a rearview mirror reminds us that nothing is wasted in God's Kingdom. Every event, whether joyful or painful, carries a prophetic lesson. Looking back allows us to see how He has always been speaking, always been present, and always been guiding us toward His purposes.

When you look into the rearview mirror of your own life or of history, may you find the courage to say, like Peter, "This is that." And may hindsight revelation empower you to walk forward in faith, knowing the same God who spoke in the past is still speaking today.

What past experiences might hold prophetic lessons I've overlooked? How has God's presence been evident in moments that once felt confusing or painful? In what ways can hindsight strengthen my faith for what God is doing now?

____

____

____

____

____

____

____

____

____

Closing Prayer: *Lord, thank You that You speak not only about the future but also through the past. Open my eyes to see the prophetic lessons hidden in my own history and in the history of nations. Teach me to discern Your voice in hindsight, and help me to partner with You as I step into the future. In Jesus' name, Amen.*

Chapter 61

A Prophetic Landing for All Mankind

Knowing this, that our old man was crucified with Him, that the body of sin might be done away with, that we should no longer be slaves of sin. (Romans 6:6, NKJV)

The Apollo 11 mission is remembered by the world as one of humanity's greatest achievements, but in the language of Heaven, it also preaches a prophetic message. Numbers, names, and circumstances stitched into this event reveal that God was speaking far more than the story of science. He was unveiling a parable of mankind's struggle with fear, sin, and death, and His divine provision for overcoming them through Christ.

On July 20, 1969, when the Eagle landed on the moon, the entire world watched. Yet hidden beneath the fanfare of history was a sermon about the weakness of flesh and the strength of redemption. From the repetition of sixes to the names of the astronauts, the hand of God was weaving a pattern that points back to the Cross. The very fact that Armstrong's words—"one small step for man, one giant leap for mankind"—came out imperfectly is no accident. In that omission of "a," the Holy Spirit stamped a reference to Romans 6:6, tying the moment to the crucifixion of the "old man."

Fear was everywhere in that mission—fuel nearly gone, dust feared as quicksand, and isolation pressing down. Yet courage carried the astronauts forward. That's the prophetic paradox: the fragility of flesh beside the sustaining strength of God. Even the dust collected from the moon spoke back to Genesis 2:7, reminding the world that man was formed from dust, destined to return to dust, yet redeemed through the breath of God.

This landing wasn't just about outer space—it was about inner space. It was a message to every believer that even in the places where humanity seems to triumph, God is still speaking.

He calls us not to glory in the strength of flesh but to embrace the victory of the Spirit. Just as Armstrong, Aldrin, and Collins bore witness through their roles, so we are called to bear witness to the greater truth: that in Christ, sin and death have been overcome, and mankind's true destiny is found in Him.

Focus Point

The Apollo 11 moon landing stands as a prophetic parable: mankind's frailty marked by the number six, yet redeemed through the crucifixion of the old man and the victory of Christ.

Main Theme

God's fingerprints are woven into history. The Apollo 11 landing shows us that what looked like a scientific milestone was also a divine message: mankind is weak in flesh, but through Christ, victory is certain.

Key Points

- **The Power of Six** From phone numbers to measurements, the mission bore the stamp of six, reminding us of mankind's frailty.
- **Romans 6:6 Connection** Armstrong's imperfect statement highlighted the crucifixion of the "old man" in Christ.
- **Prophetic Names** Armstrong ("strength"), Aldrin ("song of glory"), and Collins ("victory") mirrored Exodus 15:2.
- **Communion on the Moon** Aldrin's act declared Christ's death and resurrection beyond earth's boundaries.
- **Dust and Frailty** The fear of lunar dust recalled man's creation from dust and God's power to redeem.
- **Heroic Faith** The mission risked collapse, yet by courage, it became a testimony of divine orchestration.
- **Tranquility Base** The landing site prophetically pointed to the peace of God available in Christ.

Journaling Questions

The Apollo 11 story calls us to see our own lives as prophetic parables. Where do we face "dust" —frailty, fear, or uncertainty? God speaks even through our weaknesses, pointing us back to the Cross. Just as the astronauts had to trust their training and their mission, we must trust God's Word and Spirit to carry us through dangerous terrain.

Write down the "six" patterns in your life—the struggles with flesh, the limitations of your strength—and then match them with Romans 6:6. See how God is crucifying the old man and raising you to walk in victory. Let every weakness remind you that Christ's strength is greater, and every step you take in faith is one giant leap toward His eternal purpose.

Patterns of Six

Where do I see the weakness of flesh showing up repeatedly in my life?

____

____

____

____

____

____

____

Romans 6:6 Truth

How does the crucifixion of the "old man" give me hope for transformation?

____

____

____

____

____

____

Prophetic Parallels

What names, dates, or details in my story might carry hidden messages from God?

____

____

____

____

____

____

Dust and Frailty

What fears or weaknesses feel like "dust" that God wants to redeem?

____

____

____

____

____

____

Heroic Faith

Where is God calling me to rise courageously in the face of risk or uncertainty?

____

____

____

____

____

____

Actionable Steps

Recognize the Signs
Pay attention to repeated numbers or events in your life that may carry God's prophetic message.

Crucify the Old Man
Identify one area of flesh you need to surrender fully to Christ today.

Walk in Courage
Step out in faith in one area where fear has been holding you back.

Personal Reflection

The Apollo 11 landing reminds us that God preaches through history. What the world saw as a scientific triumph was also a prophetic sermon about flesh, fear, and faith. The same God who stamped sixes all over that mission is speaking to us today, pointing us back to the victory of Romans 6:6.

Every small step of faith we take is a giant leap toward God's purpose for our lives. In the end, it's not about mankind's achievements but about Christ's finished work. He is our strength, our song, and our victory.

How does seeing God's hand in history strengthen my faith in His work today? What "small step" of faith might God be asking me to take right now? How can I shift my focus from human achievement to Christ's finished work in my daily life?

Closing Prayer: *Lord, thank You for speaking through history and even through mankind's greatest achievements. Teach me to recognize the patterns, the numbers, and the prophetic messages You are weaving into my life. Help me to crucify the old man, overcome fear, and live fully in the victory of Christ. In Jesus' name, Amen.*

Chapter 62

The End Is Near:

The Story of Noah

But as the days of Noah were, so also will the coming of the Son of Man be.
(Matthew 24:37, NKJV)

The story of Noah is not just an account of an ancient flood—it is a prophetic blueprint that reveals how God works in cycles of judgment, grace, and restoration. Each number embedded in this story preaches a sermon, calling us to recognize that divine order is not random but intentional. From generations to cubits, from days to years, every measurement and timeline carries spiritual weight.

Noah's placement as the tenth generation from Adam was no coincidence. Ten represents divine order, and at this exact point in human history, God chose to reset creation. The corruption of the earth had reached its peak, but Noah found grace in God's eyes. This grace was not abstract—it was measured, defined, and woven into the structure of the ark, the timing of the flood, and the covenant God made afterward.

For 120 years, Noah built the ark and preached righteousness, yet no one listened. Numbers marked the preparation: seven pairs of clean animals, seven pairs of birds, and a seven-day warning before the first drop of rain fell. Judgment itself was also marked by numbers: 40 days and nights of rain, a number symbolizing testing and purification, and the 600th year of Noah's life, showing mankind's imperfection multiplied to fullness.

The story closes with hope. Eight souls were saved in the ark, and the ark rested on the 17th day of the seventh month—numbers signifying new beginnings and ultimate victory. But disorder crept back through Ham's dishonor, foreshadowing the chaos of sin that persists in every generation. Jesus Himself warned that the days before His return would look just like the days of Noah. The story is more than history—it is prophecy for our present time.

Focus Point

The story of Noah reveals God's use of numbers as markers of judgment, grace, and new beginnings, calling us to recognize His order in the midst of chaos.

Main Theme

Noah's flood is both a warning and a promise. It warns us of judgment against sin but also promises that God preserves the righteous, sets things in divine order, and brings forth new beginnings.

Key Points

- **The Tenth Generation** Noah stood as the 10th from Adam, a sign of divine order being fulfilled.
- **777 Completion** Lamech's 777 years symbolized perfection reached before judgment fell.
- **120 Years of Grace** God gave mankind time to repent before the floodwaters came.
- **Sevenfold Preservation** Seven pairs of clean animals and birds marked divine provision.
- **Forty Days of Testing** Rain for 40 days revealed purification and transition.
- **600th Year** Noah's age showed the fullness of mankind's imperfection.
- **Eight Souls Saved** New beginnings came through Noah's family, the remnant preserved.

Journaling Questions

The story of Noah is more than a Sunday school lesson. It is a mirror for our generation. Just as people ignored divine warnings then, many ignore them now. But God's timeline is not hidden —His numbers speak. From cycles of grace to signs of coming judgment, His order is consistent.

Reflect on how God's numbers are unfolding in your life. Where do you see periods of testing? Where do you notice completion, fullness, or new beginnings? Like Noah, we are called to walk in obedience even when the world mocks us. The ark is a picture of Christ, and just as Noah entered for salvation, so must we remain in Him as the storms of our generation rise.

Divine Order

Where do I see God bringing order in my personal story?

Grace in Waiting

How has God extended seasons of warning or preparation to me?

Numbers That Preach

Which numbers in Noah's story speak most powerfully to my current season?

Faithful Obedience

Am I willing to obey God even if no one else around me does?

____
____
____
____
____
____

End-Times Warning

How do Jesus' words about Noah's day challenge me to live differently today?

____
____
____
____
____
____

Actionable Steps

Walk in Obedience
Like Noah, choose obedience even when it's unpopular or misunderstood.

Recognize the Numbers
Pay attention to repeated numbers or patterns in your life as reminders of God's voice.

Prepare Spiritually
Set aside time to "build your ark"—strengthening faith, family, and prayer life in preparation for trials.

Personal Reflection

The story of Noah isn't just about ancient judgment; it is about present warnings and eternal hope. God has always marked His actions with numbers that preach. Whether it's 40 days of rain or eight people saved, every detail reveals His order. The ark was salvation then, and Christ is salvation now.

The flood teaches us that while God's judgment is real, His mercy is greater. He gives us time, He gives us warning, and He gives us a way out. Just as Noah walked in obedience, we too are called to walk in righteousness. The end is near—but for those who are in Christ, the end is not destruction but the beginning of new life.

How is God inviting me to walk in obedience and righteousness like Noah in my current season? What "warnings" or gentle nudges from God might I need to take more seriously? In what ways have I experienced God's mercy providing a way out or a new beginning?

Closing Prayer: *Father, thank You for the story of Noah that reminds me of Your justice, mercy, and divine order. Help me to recognize the signs of the times and to live in obedience, preparing my heart and my home for Your return. May I walk faithfully, even when the world does not understand. In Jesus' name, Amen.*

Chapter 63

USA:

In God We Trust

Proclaim liberty throughout all the land to all its inhabitants. (Leviticus 25:10, NKJV)

The founding of the United States was not just a political revolution—it was a prophetic act woven into the fabric of God's plan. On July 2, 1776, Congress voted for independence, and within days the Declaration of Independence was signed, read publicly, and sealed with the ringing of the Liberty Bell. What might seem like only historical details carry prophetic weight when seen through the lens of Scripture and numbers.

The Liberty Bell itself bears the inscription from Leviticus 25:10, declaring liberty to all the inhabitants of the land. This was no accident; it was a divine declaration echoing through time. The birth of America was marked by covenantal language, sacrifice, and reliance upon divine providence. The signers knew they were pledging their lives, fortunes, and sacred honor for something far greater than themselves.

It is significant that out of 56 signers, 27 were ministers, and together they wrote 27 grievances against the King of England. This numerical mirroring testifies to the prophetic symmetry of their cause. Their actions parallel Martin Luther's theses on the Wittenberg door centuries earlier, declaring irreconcilable differences with corruption and birthing a movement of reformation.

Even the year 1776 carries divine meaning. At first glance, it seems less than perfect compared to 1777. Yet when viewed through the lens of biblical numbers, 1776 reveals itself as prophetic perfection. Two is the number of faithful witness, and 888 is the number of Jesus. Multiply them together—2 x 888—and you arrive at 1776. America was birthed as a witness to Christ, a prophetic testimony to liberty rooted in Him.

Focus Point

The United States was founded not only on principles of freedom but also as a prophetic witness to Jesus Christ, with every detail marked by numbers that preach liberty and divine order.

Main Theme

God's fingerprints are all over America's founding. From the Liberty Bell's inscription to the numbers hidden within 1776, the birth of the United States testifies to divine purpose and prophetic significance.

Key Points

- **The Liberty Bell** Inscribed with Leviticus 25:10, it rang as a prophetic declaration of freedom.
- **Fifty-Six Signers** Fifty-six brave men pledged lives, fortunes, and sacred honor—half of them preachers.
- **The Power of 27** Twenty-seven ministers signed, and 27 grievances were listed, mirroring divine justice.
- **Two Faithful Witnesses** The number two marked America's witness, reflected even in Adams and Jefferson dying 50 years later on July 4.
- **1776 as Prophecy** Two (faithful witness) multiplied by 888 (Jesus) equals 1776, marking America's divine birth.
- **The Jubilee Connection** Fifty years later, the deaths of Adams and Jefferson fulfilled the Liberty Bell's Jubilee inscription.
- **A Witness Nation** America was founded as a testimony to Jesus Christ, called to proclaim liberty in His name.

Journaling Questions

America's birth was not merely political—it was prophetic. Every number, every act, and every word spoken echoed God's purposes. The Liberty Bell declared liberty in alignment with Scripture. The signers willingly embraced suffering for the sake of freedom, a shadow of the sacrifice of Christ Himself. Even the deaths of Adams and Jefferson on the 50th anniversary underscored that God's hand was marking this nation with Jubilee.

This story challenges us to consider whether we still carry that prophetic witness. Are we still proclaiming liberty rooted in Christ, or have we drifted into disorder? Just as God used 1776 to establish a nation as His witness, He continues to use numbers, events, and patterns to call His people back to Himself. The same God who orchestrated America's founding is speaking today, urging us to embrace His purpose.

Liberty Bell

How does Leviticus 25:10 inspire me to proclaim freedom in Christ today?

____
____
____
____
____

Sacrifice of the Founders

Am I willing to pledge my life, fortune, and honor for the sake of God's Kingdom?

____
____
____
____
____

Prophetic Numbers

What do I learn about God's character by studying the significance of 1776?

____
____
____
____
____

Faithful Witness

How can I serve as a faithful witness to Jesus in my generation?

National Calling

Do I believe America still has a prophetic destiny, and how can I partner with it?

Actionable Steps

Proclaim Liberty
Speak freedom into your life and the lives of others, rooted in Christ's redemption.

Study the Patterns
Pay attention to numbers and events that repeat in your life—they may carry prophetic meaning.

Be a Witness
Like the two faithful witnesses, live in a way that testifies boldly of Jesus.

Personal Reflection

The story of 1776 is a story of divine design. God was not late, nor did He miss the moment. The year, the numbers, the men, and even their sacrifices were aligned with His prophetic plan. America's birth certificate was signed in ink and sealed with blood, but it was also signed in heaven with the number of Jesus, 888, multiplied by witness.

As we reflect on this history, we see not just a nation's foundation but a call to remain faithful. Just as the Liberty Bell's inscription declared liberty across the land, so too must we proclaim the freedom found in Christ. America's story is ultimately His story, and He invites us to continue carrying it forward.

How can I view the events of history—like 1776—as part of God's greater redemptive story? In what ways am I called to proclaim and live out the true freedom found in Christ? How can I honor the sacrifices of the past by remaining faithful to God's purpose today?

Closing Prayer: *Lord, we thank You for the gift of liberty and the courage of those who declared it in 1776. Keep us mindful that true freedom comes only through Jesus Christ. May our nation return to its first love, and may our lives proclaim liberty in Your name. In Jesus' name, Amen.*

Chapter 64

God Alone:

The Attempted Assassination of President Trump

My soul, wait silently for God alone, for my expectation is from Him.
(Psalm 62:5, NKJV)

On July 13, 2024, in Butler, Pennsylvania, President Donald Trump faced gunfire during a campaign rally. The bullet clipped his ear, and in that terrifying moment, no one knew whether he would rise again. When he stood up, blood dripping from his face, he lifted his fist and declared, "Fight, fight, fight." The world watched as he went from the hospital straight to Milwaukee, Wisconsin, attending the convention as planned. It was a moment that was extraordinary, not just politically, but prophetically.

This event was more than history unfolding; it carried a divine message. In the midst of chaos and danger, the words *God Alone* rang out as President Trump declared that only God had prevented the unthinkable. It wasn't about politics or personalities—it was about the prophetic voice of the Lord speaking through the headlines of our time.

Looking deeper, the people, names, and even locations connected to the event became symbols of spiritual truth. Trump, whose name means "trumpet call," stood as a type of America. Crooks, the shooter, represented criminality and the spirit of lawlessness. Cheatle, the name of the head of the Secret Service, bore its own weight of meaning. The rally location in Butler, Pennsylvania, tied to biblical dreamers and builders, was no accident. God was showing His fingerprints in every detail.

This chapter presses us to see what God is declaring: that only He can preserve, protect, and redeem. The question we must ask ourselves is this: when the unthinkable comes close, will we place our trust in politics, culture, or ourselves—or will we wait silently for *God Alone*?

FOCUS POINT

Put on the whole armor of God, that you may be able to stand against the wiles of the devil. (Ephesians 6:11, NKJV)

This verse embodies the prophetic truth of the event. President Trump stood in the face of death, blood marking his ear as though consecrated. The church, too, must stand in the evil day, not through human strength but clothed in the armor of God. It is a call to consecration, courage, and conviction, showing that when darkness presses in, we must rise in loyalty to God alone.

MAIN THEME

This chapter reveals that God is speaking through modern events, calling His people to consecration, courage, and faithfulness. The attempted assassination of President Trump was not only a physical event but a prophetic message, highlighting the frailty of flesh and the sovereignty of God. From the numbers tied to locations and times, to the names of those involved, each detail pointed back to the Lord's hand. The overarching message is clear: our hope cannot rest in men, governments, or ideologies. Our expectation must be in God alone.

"When all else fails, God Alone stands—our protector, our consecrator, and our hope."

KEY SCRIPTURES

- *Were they ashamed when they had committed abomination? No! They were not at all ashamed; nor did they know how to blush. Therefore they shall fall among those who fall; at the time I punish them, they shall be cast down, says the Lord.* (Jeremiah 6:15, NKJV)
- *Backbiters, haters of God, violent, proud, boasters, inventors of evil things, disobedient to parents.* (Romans 1:30, NKJV)
- *Enter by the narrow gate; for wide is the gate and broad is the way that leads to destruction, and there are many who go in by it.* (Matthew 7:13, NKJV)

Key Points

- **God Alone Preserves** The bullet that clipped Trump's ear was not fatal. His survival points to divine intervention and the truth that only God alone sustains and protects.
- **Names That Prophesy** The names involved—Trump (trumpet), Crooks (criminals), and Cheatle (protection)—were prophetic types, carrying messages beyond the individuals themselves.
- **Locations with Meaning** From Butler, Pennsylvania, tied to biblical figures like Joseph's butler and Nehemiah, to the fairgrounds at 625 Evans City Road, God stamped His word onto the very geography of the event.
- **Blood on the Ear—Consecration** The blood that marked Trump's ear echoes Exodus and Leviticus, where priests were consecrated with blood on their ears. It was a prophetic call for the church to be consecrated to God.
- **Armor for the Evil Day** The timing of 6:11 p.m. points directly to Ephesians 6:11, showing that God is commanding His people to stand firm in His armor during dark times.
- **A Call to Get Off Script** At the moment of the shooting, Trump turned his head off script. This is a prophetic word to the church: our old scripts won't work. It's time to turn toward God.
- **Faith over Fear** The event calls us to reject intimidation and fear, choosing instead to stand boldly as consecrated witnesses of Jesus Christ, awaiting His return.

Journaling Questions

Journaling about this chapter allows you to process how God is speaking through modern events. By writing your thoughts, you align with the truth that God alone is sovereign. This reflection helps you see that headlines are not random—they carry messages that call us to consecration, boldness, and faith. Recording your insights allows you to recognize patterns of God's hand at work in your life and in the world.

Through journaling, you may discover areas where fear has tried to silence your voice, or places where God is calling you to step off your old script and turn toward Him. This practice can reveal prophetic patterns in your own story, helping you trust more deeply in His protection and promises.

Trusting God Alone

Where am I relying on human strength instead of trusting God alone?

Hearing the Prophetic Message

How do I discern God's voice in the midst of modern events and headlines?

Consecration and Commitment

What areas of my life need to be consecrated fully to God's purposes?

STANDING IN THE EVIL DAY

How can I put on the armor of God daily to withstand the challenges of this time?

____

____

____

____

____

____

LIVING OFF SCRIPT

What "script" in my life is God asking me to turn away from so I can follow Him more fully?

____

____

____

____

____

____

ACTIONABLE STEPS

Consecrate Your Ear to God
Like the priests of old, dedicate your hearing to the Lord. Commit to filtering out voices of fear, doubt, and compromise, and open your ear to the voice of the Spirit.

Stand in the Armor
Daily put on the full armor of God through prayer and Scripture, preparing your heart and mind to resist the enemy's schemes in the evil day.

Get Off Script
Break free from routines or cultural scripts that no longer serve God's purpose. Seek the Spirit's fresh leading in your decisions, actions, and relationships.

PERSONAL REFLECTION

This chapter invites you to reflect deeply on whether you truly believe God alone is your protector. Just as Trump's ear was marked by blood, are there places in your life where God is calling you to be consecrated? Are there fears, habits, or compromises that He is asking you to lay down?

The call to live consecrated and bold is not easy, but it is essential. Following Christ means leaving behind intimidation, fear, and reliance on human systems. It requires daily surrender, courage, and an openness to walk off the script of the world and into the story God is writing.

Will you consecrate your ear to God's voice? Will you stand armored and faithful in the evil day? Will you resolve to live "off script," trusting God Alone to be your strength and expectation?

Closing Prayer: *Lord, I consecrate my ear to hear Your voice alone. Teach me to trust You fully, to stand armored in Your strength, and to walk boldly off script into Your will. My expectation is in You alone. Amen.*

Chapter 65

Section F:

Marked as God's

Then God blessed the seventh day and sanctified it, because in it He rested from all His work which God had created and made. (Genesis 2:3, NKJV)

In the very beginning, God established a rhythm that still speaks to us today. He created the heavens and the earth in six days, and on the seventh, He rested. This wasn't rest from weariness—it was the divine act of completion. The seventh day was marked, sanctified, and blessed, forever standing as God's declaration that His work is perfect, intentional, and whole.

From Genesis to Revelation, the number seven appears like a golden thread, weaving together stories, judgments, promises, and visions. Each appearance isn't random; it carries the weight of God's holy signature. The seventh day, the seven spirits, the seven churches, the seven seals, trumpets, and bowls—all proclaim one message: God's plans are perfect and His order cannot be undone.

When we study the patterns of seven, we see the consistency of God's nature. The fullness of His Spirit, the complete evaluation of His Church, and the just outpouring of His judgments all carry the unmistakable seal of His sovereignty. It is His reminder that He leaves nothing half-finished, and that His purposes always come to their appointed end.

So, when you encounter the number seven in Scripture, pause and take note. It is God whispering through the text: *"This is Mine. This is whole. This is holy."* The question is, will we lean in and allow that truth to shape how we trust His timing and rest in His perfect completion?

Focus Point

And from the throne proceeded lightnings, thunderings, and voices. Seven lamps of fire were burning before the throne, which are the seven Spirits of God. (Revelation 4:5, NKJV)

This verse highlights the perfection and completeness of the Holy Spirit, described as seven spirits not because He is divided, but because He is whole. It reveals the fullness of God's Spirit—wisdom, understanding, counsel, might, knowledge, and the fear of the Lord. This completeness assures us that the Spirit lacks nothing in leading, comforting, and empowering us.

Main Theme

The number seven throughout Scripture represents God's fingerprint of completion, perfection, and holiness. It is His divine marker on creation, His people, His Spirit, and even His judgments. From the rest on the seventh day of Creation, to the fullness of the Spirit before His throne, to the sevenfold messages to the churches, and the cycles of seven judgments in Revelation, the message is clear: God is sovereign, and His plans are complete.

"Seven is God's holy signature—marking His work as finished, whole, and perfectly complete."

Key Scriptures

- *And on the seventh day God ended His work which He had done, and He rested on the seventh day from all His work which He had done.* (Genesis 2:2, NKJV)
- *The Spirit of the Lord shall rest upon Him, the Spirit of wisdom and understanding, the Spirit of counsel and might, the Spirit of knowledge and of the fear of the Lord.* (Isaiah 11:2, NKJV)
- *He who has an ear, let him hear what the Spirit says to the churches.* (Revelation 2:7, NKJV)

Key Points

- **Seven in Creation** The seventh day in Genesis marked completion, blessing, and holiness. It set a rhythm of work and rest as a divine order for life.
- **Seven Spirits of God** Revelation 4:5 and Isaiah 11:2 reveal the Spirit's fullness through seven attributes, showing His perfect guidance and power.
- **Seven Churches** In Revelation 2–3, Jesus addresses seven churches, representing the full spectrum of spiritual health, from faithfulness to lukewarmness.
- **Seven Seals of Destiny** The scroll with seven seals in Revelation demonstrates God's perfect plan unfolding through judgment and redemption.
- **Seven Trumpets of Warning** Each trumpet blast calls for repentance, reminding us of God's mercy even in His judgments.
- **Seven Bowls of Completion** The final judgments poured out from seven bowls reveal God's justice as perfect and complete, leaving nothing unfinished.
- **Seven as God's Signature** Wherever seven appears in Scripture, it carries His seal of holiness, reminding us that He is intentional, sovereign, and faithful to finish His work.

Journaling Questions

Journaling through this chapter allows you to slow down and notice the divine patterns God weaves throughout His Word. Writing out your reflections will help you see how the number seven points to God's perfection and completion—not just in Scripture, but in your life as well.

Through this journaling, you may recognize areas where you need to trust God's timing more fully. You may also see how He is already writing completion into your story. Reflection helps you embrace His sovereignty, silencing anxiety about unfinished things, and resting in the truth that God always finishes what He begins.

Seeing God's Signature

Where have I seen the "fingerprint of God" marking completion in my own life?

____
____
____
____
____
____
____

Resting in His Timing

Am I willing to trust God's timing as perfect, even when it doesn't align with mine?

____
____
____
____
____
____

Hearing the Spirit's Fullness

How can I invite the fullness of the Holy Spirit to operate in my daily decisions and relationships?

____
____
____
____
____
____

Learning from the Churches

Which of the seven church conditions from Revelation do I most identify with right now?

____
____
____
____
____
____

Trusting His Completion

What area of my life feels unfinished, and how can I surrender it to God's perfect plan?

____
____
____
____
____
____

Actionable Steps

Honor the Rhythm of Rest
Practice intentional rest as an act of faith, trusting God to complete what you cannot in your own strength.

Seek the Spirit's Full Counsel
Ask the Holy Spirit daily to fill you with wisdom, understanding, counsel, might, knowledge, and reverence.

Recognize God's Signature
Pay attention to patterns of completion in your life. Celebrate them as signs that God is working and finishing what He started.

Personal Reflection

This chapter draws us into the beauty of God's order. Just as He rested on the seventh day, He invites us to trust His rhythm and mark of completion in our lives. Where we feel unfinished, He is still at work. Where we feel scattered, His Spirit is whole.

The call is to rest, to lean in, and to trust the God who marks His Word and His world with seven. He is not random. His plans are intentional, and His order is unshakable. Will we step into that trust and allow His peace to guard our hearts?

Will I trust God to finish the work He started in me? Will I rest in His perfection instead of striving in my own strength? Will I pause when I see His holy signature and respond with worship?

Closing Prayer: *Father, thank You for marking Your Word and my life with the seal of completion. Teach me to rest in Your timing, to rely on the fullness of Your Spirit, and to trust that You will finish what You have begun. I choose to see Your holy signature in every detail. Amen.*

Chapter 66

The Seven Spirits of God

And from the throne proceeded lightnings, thunderings, and voices. Seven lamps of fire were burning before the throne, which are the seven Spirits of God.
(Revelation 4:5, NKJV)

In the last book of the Bible, the Holy Spirit introduces Himself with breathtaking clarity: grace and peace flow to us not only from Him who is, who was, and who is to come, and from Jesus Christ, but also "from the seven Spirits who are before His throne." This is not a casual greeting—it is a divine unveiling. Sixty-five books have led to this climactic moment, and here the Lord underlines what He does not want us to miss.

We are comfortable with the Father and with Jesus the Son; yet the question arises: who are the seven Spirits—and why are they named in the same breath as the Eternal and the Faithful Witness? Seven is the number God uses to mark what is wholly His. The seven Spirits do not describe seven different beings, but the sevenfold, perfect expression of the one Holy Spirit.

Isaiah prophesied this fullness resting upon the Messiah: the Spirit of the Lord; Wisdom; Understanding; Counsel; Might; Knowledge; and the Fear of the Lord (Isaiah 11:1–2). This is the Spirit who thunders, the lamps who burn, the voice who speaks—sometimes in roaring power, sometimes in a whisper that becomes a rhema word and changes everything.

Have you learned to recognize His one voice in its sevenfold expression—authority, strategy, revelation, direction, power, truth, and holy awe—or have you settled for hearing only one tone when God is offering the fullness of His sound?

Focus Point

Grace to you and peace from Him who is and who was and who is to come, and from the seven Spirits who are before His throne, and from Jesus Christ, the faithful witness... (Revelation 1:4–5a, NKJV)

The opening line of Revelation sets the order: grace and peace stream to us from the Eternal Father, the sevenfold Spirit, and Jesus Christ. This is Trinitarian wholeness on display—one God, perfectly revealed. The Spirit's sevenfold nature is not division but completion; He lacks nothing in leading, comforting, empowering, correcting, and consecrating the people of God.

Main Theme

The seven Spirits of God reveal the perfect fullness of the Holy Spirit: one voice expressed in seven dimensions—Lordship, Wisdom, Understanding, Counsel, Might, Knowledge, and the Fear of the Lord. His voice breaks, builds, guides, cleanses, strengthens, enlightens, and consecrates. Sometimes He thunders, sometimes He whispers a rhema word that ignites faith (Romans 10:17), but always He manifests the love of the Father and the way of Jesus. To walk in the Spirit is to welcome His sevenfold work in every area of life.

"One Spirit. Seven flames. Perfect fullness for imperfect people."

Key Scriptures

- *There shall come forth a Rod from the stem of Jesse, and a Branch shall grow out of his roots. The Spirit of the Lord shall rest upon Him, the Spirit of wisdom and understanding, the Spirit of counsel and might, the Spirit of knowledge and of the fear of the Lord.* (Isaiah 11:1–2, NKJV)
- *And from the throne proceeded lightnings, thunderings, and voices. Seven lamps of fire were burning before the throne, which are the seven Spirits of God.* (Revelation 4:5, NKJV)
- *So then faith comes by hearing, and hearing by the word [rhema] of God.* (Romans 10:17, NKJV)

Key Points

- **One Spirit, Sevenfold Fullness** Revelation and Isaiah agree: the Holy Spirit is one, yet revealed in seven perfect expressions—God's signature of completion upon His own presence and work.
- **The Voice of the Lord (Spirit of the Lord)** His voice establishes Lordship and demands obedience; the same voice that spoke creation still speaks identity, adoption, and nearness over us (1 Corinthians 3:16; Romans 8:15).
- **Divine Strategy (Spirit of Wisdom)** From His mouth come wisdom and understanding; heaven's wisdom is pure, peaceable, and practical, guiding us to love rightly and choose righteously.
- **Revelation Understanding (Spirit of Understanding)** He brings us into agreement with the will of God, turning logos into living rhema and aligning our hearts with Jesus' "not My will, but Yours be done."
- **Guiding Counsel (Spirit of Counsel)** "This is the way, walk in it." His counsel corrects, comforts, and directs, leading us step by step through valleys and crossroads.
- **Miracle Power (Spirit of Might)** His voice breaks strongholds and stills storms; He empowers fearless, sacrificial love and holy endurance beyond human strength.
- **Truth Illumined (Spirit of Knowledge)** He sanctifies by truth and rescues us from destruction through revelation knowledge that interprets our story by God's story.
- **Holy Awe (Spirit of the Fear of the Lord)** He stirs deep reverence and wonder, grounding us in humility before God's majesty. This holy fear draws us into purity and teaches us to delight in obedience to His will.

Journaling Questions

Journaling helps you recognize the sevenfold sound of the Spirit in your everyday life. Record where you've sensed His Lordship correcting you, His Wisdom guiding a decision, His Understanding opening Scripture, His Counsel directing your path, His Might strengthening your weakness, His Knowledge clarifying truth, and His Fear of the Lord deepening your awe. As you write, note the difference between general truths you know and the rhema moments that met you personally and shifted your heart.

As you answer the questions below, expect the Holy Spirit to personalize His voice. He loves to turn pages into pathways and doctrines into daily bread. Many believers discover patterns: a season of Counsel during transition, a surge of Might in hardship, or a fresh Fear of the Lord that cleanses motives. Your journal becomes an altar of remembrance—proof that the seven lamps burn for you.

Hearing His One Voice

Where have I recently sensed the Holy Spirit speaking with unusual clarity—was it authority, wisdom, understanding, counsel, might, knowledge, or holy awe?

____

____

____

____

____

____

From Logos to Rhema

Which Scripture has "leapt off the page" to me lately, and how did that rhema word produce faith or obedience?

____

____

____

____

____

Welcoming His Wisdom

In what decision do I need heaven's wisdom that is pure, peaceable, and full of mercy?

____

____

____

____

Strength in Weakness

Where do I need the Spirit of Might to empower courageous, sacrificial love beyond my natural capacity?

____

____

____

____

____

____

Walking in Holy Awe

What would change today if the Fear of the Lord governed my words, my work, and my private life?

____

____

____

____

____

____

Actionable Steps

Receive His Lordship Daily
Begin each day by intentionally yielding your mind, motives, and schedule to the Spirit of the Lord. Pray, "Not my will, but Yours," and invite His adoption to silence fear and orphan thinking.

Practice Rhema Listening

Set a short, daily window to read Scripture slowly and ask, "Holy Spirit, highlight Your word to me." Write the phrase that stands out, and respond with one concrete act of obedience that same day.

Walk the Sevenfold Way

Choose one expression (Wisdom, Understanding, Counsel, Might, Knowledge, Fear of the Lord) to practice this week. For example, "Counsel": seek godly input and obey the nudge; "Might": pray bold prayers and serve beyond comfort; "Fear of the Lord": refuse a small compromise.

PERSONAL REFLECTION

Beloved, the Spirit who hovered over chaos now hovers over your life with seven burning lamps. He is not sparse with you; He is complete. Where you feel scattered, He is whole. Where you feel unsure, He is wise. Where you feel weak, He is mighty. Let Him be who He is—fully.

Surrender is not defeat; it is alignment. Invite His counsel into your next step, His knowledge into your confusion, His fear into your motivations. Ask for a fresh rhema that kindles faith and steadies your path. The same voice that shook Sinai still whispers to your heart and says, "Walk with Me."

Will you welcome the Spirit's Lordship without reserve? Will you posture your heart to hear a fresh rhema and obey? Will you live this week under the seven flames—wise, understanding, guided, powerful, truthful, and reverent?

Closing Prayer: *Holy Spirit, sevenfold and holy, I welcome Your fullness. Rest upon me with Your Lordship, fill me with Your wisdom and understanding, guide me with Your counsel, strengthen me with Your might, enlighten me with Your knowledge, and anchor me in the fear of the Lord. Let Your one voice be my daily bread. Amen.*

Chapter 67

Seven Churches

He who overcomes, I will make him a pillar in the temple of My God, and he shall go out no more. I will write on him the name of My God and the name of the city of My God, the New Jerusalem, which comes down out of heaven from My God. And I will write on him My new name.
(Revelation 3:12, NKJV)

In the Revelation of Jesus Christ, the risen Lord dictates messages to seven specific churches and commands John to write what he sees and send it to them—Ephesus, Smyrna, Pergamum, Thyatira, Sardis, Philadelphia, and Laodicea. He holds seven stars in His hand—the angels of the churches—and walks among seven lampstands. Heaven is speaking to earth in a language stamped with sevens, the number of divine completeness.

These seven letters are not random notes to ancient congregations; they form a prophetic panorama and a spiritual mirror. Each church receives a word that exposes its condition, calls for repentance or perseverance, and offers a promise "to him who overcomes." Together they show the full spectrum of church life—from first love to lukewarmness, from suffering to steadfast brotherly love.

Within this tapestry, numerical patterns and meanings emerge—sevens marking completeness, name-values (gematria) hinting at identity, and even a rise-and-fall arc that highlights Philadelphia as a peak of faithfulness. The stars in His hand, the promises to overcomers, the warnings to the complacent—all reveal a God who governs history and hearts with holy order.

So I ask you: where do you find yourself in these seven? Busy yet drifting from first love, crushed yet faithful, compromised, persevering, renewed yet incomplete, walking through an open door, or lukewarm and self-reliant? The same Jesus still speaks—"He who has an ear, let him hear."

Focus Point

... What you see, write in a book and send it to the seven churches which are in Asia: to Ephesus, to Smyrna, to Pergamos, to Thyatira, to Sardis, to Philadelphia, and to Laodicea. (Revelation 1:11, NKJV)

This commission frames the entire section: one Lord speaking a complete word to a complete Church. The seven churches are historical congregations and a prophetic portrait of spiritual conditions through time. Christ's authority, His stars, His promises, and His corrections establish the standard by which He evaluates His people.

Main Theme

Jesus' messages to the seven churches display God's complete counsel to His people: praise, correction, command, and promise. Sevens mark the design—seven churches, seven stars, sevenfold promises "to him who overcomes." The names themselves carry meanings that echo their conditions; the sequence sketches a prophetic cycle from fervor to decline, with Philadelphia shining as a pinnacle of faithfulness and open doors. In every age and condition, the call is the same: hear what the Spirit says and overcome.

"Seven letters, one Lord: hear, repent, persevere—overcome."

Key Scriptures

- *He who has an ear, let him hear what the Spirit says to the churches. To him who overcomes I will give to eat from the tree of life, which is in the midst of the Paradise of God.* (Revelation 2:7, NKJV)
- *Because you have kept My command to persevere, I also will keep you from the hour of trial which shall come upon the whole world... Hold fast what you have, that no one may take your crown.* (Revelation 3:10–11, NKJV)

- *I know your works, that you are neither cold nor hot... Be zealous and repent... Behold, I stand at the door and knock... To him who overcomes I will grant to sit with Me on My throne...* (Revelation 3:15–21, NKJV)

Key Points

- **Seven Churches, One Complete Witness** The seven named congregations form a whole, revealing the full range of church health—love, suffering, compromise, perseverance, renewal, brotherly love, and lukewarmness.
- **Seven Stars in His Hand** Jesus holds the angels of the churches, showing His absolute authority and intimate care; nothing about His Church is outside His grasp.
- **Promises to Overcomers** Every letter ends with a promise—tree of life, hidden manna, white garments, the morning star, a pillar's place, and a throne—assuring that faithful endurance is met with eternal reward.
- **Hearing Is Holy** "Let him hear" is repeated to every church; revelation requires response. The Spirit still speaks, and obedience remains the measure.
- **Philadelphia's Open Door** Marked by perseverance and an open door, Philadelphia pictures brotherly love and peak faithfulness—heaven's endorsement amid global trial.
- **Laodicea's Lukewarmness** Self-reliance blinds; Jesus counsels refined gold, white garments, and eye salve as remedies for their condition. Love disciplines; zeal and repentance reopen fellowship.
- **Patterns That Preach** Names, numbers, sequences, and cycles reinforce that God governs history and hearts with design; sevens underline completion, and the ordered progression issues a sober call to return to Jesus.

Journaling Questions

Journaling through these seven letters helps you locate your heart before the Lord. Record where Jesus' commendations affirm you and where His corrections confront you. Note the repeated refrain—"He who has an ear, let him hear"—and write specifically what the Spirit is highlighting today. Track the promises to overcomers and connect each promise to a present obedience. As you do, you'll see patterns of drift or devotion and the open doors God sets before you.

Expect the Spirit to bring clarity about first love, purity, perseverance, and zeal. You may find you are Smyrna-faithful in suffering yet Ephesus-faded in affection; or Philadelphia-steady yet Sardis-fragile in substance. Answering honestly will position you to repent where needed and to hold fast where grace has kept you. This is how the seven letters become your roadmap to overcome.

Locate Your Church-Heart

Which church best mirrors my current spiritual condition—and why?

First Love or First Loss

Where have I substituted activity for intimacy, and how will I return to my first love?

Open Doors and Perseverance

What "open door" has Jesus set before me, and how will I persevere to walk through it?

Lukewarm Alarms

Where am I self-reliant or lukewarm, and what zeal-and-repent steps is Jesus asking of me?

____

____

____

____

____

____

Hearing to Overcome

What promise to overcomers most grips me today, and what specific obedience corresponds to that promise?

____

____

____

____

____

____

Actionable Steps

Return to First Love
Set a daily appointment to meet Jesus with no agenda but worship and affection. Read one church letter aloud and pray it back—confessing drift and choosing devotion.

Walk Through the Open Door
Identify one "open door" (service, reconciliation, mission, generosity) and take the next faithful step this week. Perseverance is proven in action.

Buy Gold, Wear White, Anoint Eyes

Practice Laodicea's remedy: invite refining (prayerfully surrender a comfort), pursue purity (repent and reconcile), and ask for sight (pray for Spirit-given discernment before major decisions).

PERSONAL REFLECTION

Beloved, Jesus still walks among His lampstands. He knows your works, your weariness, your wounds—and He calls you by name. Hear His commendation and do not despise His correction; both are love. Let His promises lift your eyes beyond the moment and anchor your steps in hope.

Surrender is your pathway back to fire. Ask for the counsel that heals drift, the perseverance that walks through open doors, and the zeal that refuses lukewarm living. He is knocking—not at a stranger's house, but at His Church. Open wide.

Will you let the Spirit search you and speak? Will you trade self-reliance for first love and faithful perseverance? Will you overcome—hearing, repenting, and walking through the door Jesus has set before you?

Closing Prayer: *Lord Jesus, You who hold the stars and walk among the lampstands, give me ears to hear and a heart to obey. Restore my first love, strengthen my perseverance, ignite holy zeal, and lead me to overcome. Write Your name upon me, and keep me faithful until You come. Amen.*

Chapter 68

The Seven Festivals of the Lord

And I John saw the holy city, new Jerusalem, coming down from God out of heaven, prepared as a bride adorned for her husband. And I heard a great voice out of heaven saying, Behold, the tabernacle of God is with men, and he will dwell with them, and they shall be his people, and God himself shall be with them, and be their God. (Revelation 21:2–3, KJV)

When God brought the Israelites out of Egypt, He didn't merely free them from bondage; He invited them into rhythm. He set appointments on His calendar and called them "My feasts." These were not man-made holidays but holy convocations—times when heaven met earth and the people met with their God. The seventh day, the seventh month, the sevens of Sabbaths—each cadence carried His signature of completion.

We in the Western church often assume these are "Jewish feasts" only, but the Lord plainly says they are His. That means they matter to everyone who serves Him. In these appointed times, He preached the gospel in advance. Jesus fulfilled the first four to the very day—Passover at the Cross, Unleavened Bread in the tomb, Firstfruits in the resurrection, and Pentecost in the outpoured Spirit. The story is not finished; three feasts remain.

Trumpets, Atonement, and Tabernacles point forward. The Feast of Trumpets announces awakening and the King's returning with the sound of a trumpet. Atonement speaks of judgment and the once-for-all High Priest. The Feast of Tabernacles promises God dwelling with His people forever. Even the "no one knows the day or the hour" language echoes the watchfulness required to sight the new moon that begins Trumpets.

So, what will you do with His invitation? He has set times, told His story in sevens, and aligned redemption with His calendar. Will you mark your life by His appointments and meet Him in the meaning He has revealed?

Focus Point

And the Lord spoke to Moses, saying, "Speak to the children of Israel, and say to them: 'The feasts of the Lord, which you shall proclaim to be holy convocations, these are My feasts.'" (Leviticus 23:1–2, NKJV)

This is the Lord's personal invitation. The feasts belong to Him, not to a culture alone. They are holy convocations—set times when God calls His people to remember redemption (spring feasts) and to anticipate the King's return and dwelling (fall feasts). Meeting Him on His calendar aligns our story with His.

Main Theme

The seven Festivals of the Lord reveal God's plan of salvation in two great movements: redemption accomplished in the spring (Passover, Unleavened Bread, Firstfruits, Pentecost) and redemption consummated in the fall (Trumpets, Atonement, Tabernacles). Jesus fulfilled the first four on their exact days; the remaining three point to His return with the trumpet, final judgment, and God tabernacling with humanity forever. Sevens declare completion; eights whisper new beginnings; fifties shout Spirit and Jubilee.

"God's calendar is the gospel in holy time—fulfilled, fulfilling, and soon to be finished."

Key Scriptures

- *For indeed Christ, our Passover, was sacrificed for us.* (1 Corinthians 5:7, NKJV)
- *But now Christ is risen from the dead, and has become the firstfruits of those who have fallen asleep.* (1 Corinthians 15:20, NKJV)
- *For the Lord Himself will descend from heaven with a shout, with the voice of an archangel, and with the trumpet of God.* (1 Thessalonians 4:16, NKJV)

Key Points

- **Passover—The Lamb and Deliverance** On the 14th of Nisan the blood speaks freedom; Jesus, the Lamb of God, fulfills Passover at the Cross.
- **Unleavened Bread—Purity and Separation** Seven leaven-free days picture sin removed; Jesus in the tomb seals the sign of holy separation.
- **Firstfruits—Resurrection and Promise** On the first day after the Sabbath, the first sheaf is waved; Jesus rises as the "firstfruits" guaranteeing our future life.
- **Pentecost—Spirit and Jubilee** Fifty days after Firstfruits, the Spirit is poured out; the Church is born on the very feast that celebrates God's giving.
- **Trumpets—Awakening and Return** The only feast beginning on a sighted new moon calls to watchfulness; many recognize in it the trumpet of the King's coming.
- **Atonement—Judgment and Mercy** The holiest day declares covering through the High Priest; Jesus provides forgiveness once for all.
- **Tabernacles—Presence and Joy** Seven days plus the great eighth day celebrate God dwelling with His people; Revelation 21:3 promises its ultimate fulfillment.

Journaling Questions

Journaling these feasts aligns your heart with God's storyline. Note how each appointed time reveals Jesus—Passover at the Cross, Unleavened Bread in burial, Firstfruits in resurrection, Pentecost in the Spirit's outpouring. Write how sevens (completeness), eights (new beginnings), tens (order and judgment), fourteens (deliverance), and fifty (Spirit/Jubilee) appear in your own walk. Record which remaining fall feast most stirs hope in you and why. Mark dates on your calendar and plan simple ways to remember Him on His days.

As you answer, expect awareness and awe. You may receive renewed gratitude for redemption, fresh resolve for purity, confidence in resurrection hope, hunger for the Spirit, watchfulness for the trumpet, sobriety about judgment, and joy in God's dwelling. The feasts will move from information to formation, from dates on a page to rhythms in your discipleship.

His Feasts, My Response

How will I respond to the Lord's personal invitation to meet Him at His feasts?

Cross and Cup

In what fresh way does Passover reveal Jesus to me right now?

Firstfruits Hope

Where do I need the promise of Firstfruits—resurrection life—to awaken my faith?

PENTECOST POWER

How is the Spirit inviting me to live the "fifty" of overflow and witness?

FALL WATCHFULNESS

How can I practice watchfulness for Trumpets, sobriety for Atonement, and joy for Tabernacles in this season?

ACTIONABLE STEPS

Put His Days on Your Calendar
Add the next occurrences of Passover, Unleavened Bread, Firstfruits, Pentecost, Trumpets, Atonement, and Tabernacles. Plan a simple Scripture reading or family meal for each.

Practice the Meaning, Not the Form
At Passover, read Exodus 12 and 1 Corinthians 5:7–8; at Firstfruits, celebrate resurrection with 1 Corinthians 15:20; at Pentecost, read Acts 2 and ask for fresh filling.

Lean Into the Future Feasts

On Trumpets, set time to watch and pray; on Atonement, fast and repent; during Tabernacles, create a temporary space (a simple tent or porch time) to thank God for His faithful presence.

Personal Reflection

Beloved, the Lord has written His gospel into time so you won't miss His heart. He finished what He started in the spring feasts and invites you to live awake for what is yet to come. Let the cadence of sevens settle your soul—He is complete in His works and faithful in His ways.

Lean into the grace that keeps appointments with God. Remember the Lamb, remove the leaven, rejoice in firstfruits, and welcome the wind of Pentecost. Lift your eyes for the trumpet, bow your heart for atonement, and rejoice that He will tabernacle with us forever.

Will you meet Him on His appointed days? Will you let His calendar form your worship and hope? Will you live ready for the trumpet, confident in the Cross, and joyful in the promise that He will dwell with us?

Closing Prayer: *Lord, thank You for Your feasts—Your appointments with Your people. Teach my heart to remember redemption, to walk in purity, to rejoice in resurrection, to welcome Your Spirit, to watch for the trumpet, to tremble at atonement, and to celebrate Your dwelling. Mark my life with Your holy rhythms. Amen.*

Chapter 69

The Sum of All Things

For by Him were all things created, that are in heaven, and that are in earth, visible and invisible, whether they be thrones, or dominions, or principalities, or powers; all things were created by Him and for Him: and He is before all things, and by Him all things consist.
(Colossians 1:16–17, KJV)

As I finish this book, I realize I'm nowhere near finished with this work. We could go on and on, but the point is really not about numbers at all. The sum of all things, including mathematics, is the person of Jesus Christ. The more I've watched the Lord preach through patterns, timelines, and prophetic markers, the more I've come to see this truth: numbers are a means, never the end.

God didn't give us numbers and order to entertain us or to make us obsessive arithmetic students. He gave us these things so we would be blown away by Him. He wants us fascinated enough to look for Him and to see Him. He wants us to pursue intimacy with Him, connect with His heart, and become attentive to His voice woven through the ordinary and the extraordinary.

Math and numbers were not created to be the point. They were created to illustrate that Jesus Christ is the point. The more clearly we see Him as the center of all things, the more everything else comes into focus. Colossians 1:16–17 declares that all things were created by Him and for Him, and that in Him, all things hold together. That includes the order behind the cosmos and the order He invites into our chaos.

So when you do the math, do what the Master Mathematician is telling you to do. It's okay to see the numbers on the chalkboard, as long as you're utterly fascinated with the Teacher doing the lesson. Will you let the equations lead you to the Face behind them, and allow wonder to escort you into worship?

Focus Point

For by Him were all things created...all things were created by Him, and for Him: and He is before all things, and by Him all things consist. (Colossians 1:16–17, KJV)

This passage anchors the chapter's heartbeat: Jesus is not merely an illustration within creation —He is the Architect, Sustainer, and Goal of it. Numbers, patterns, and order serve as signposts pointing to a Person. In Him, the universe coheres; without Him, even perfect mathematics lacks purpose. Our study only becomes worship when it returns to Christ.

Main Theme

This chapter concentrates our gaze where it belongs—on Jesus, the One for whom and by whom all things were created. Numbers, patterns, and prophetic alignments are valuable only to the extent that they illuminate the central truth that Christ is the sum and substance of reality. Colossians 1:16–17 is our North Star: creation exists through Him, finds meaning in Him, and holds together by Him. Therefore, the true goal of numerical discovery is not data but devotion; not arithmetic, but adoration. We do the "math," but we follow the Master.

"Jesus is the point—let every number return our hearts to the Name above all names."

Key Scriptures

- *For by Him were all things created...all things were created by Him, and for Him...by Him all things consist.* (Colossians 1:16-17, KJV)
- *And He is before all things, and by Him all things consist.* (Colossians 1:17, KJV)

KEY POINTS

- **Numbers Are Signposts, Not Destinations** God uses order and pattern to point to Jesus. When numbers become the focus, we miss the One they are meant to reveal.
- **Wonder Is the Doorway to Intimacy** The Lord wants us "blown away" so that fascination births pursuit—pursuit of His presence, voice, and heart.
- **Created by Him and for Him** Colossians 1:16 insists creation is not random; it is Christ-centered. Our studies should end in worship and surrender.
- **Held Together in Christ** Colossians 1:17 assures us that Jesus sustains all things. The same Jesus who upholds galaxies holds our lives together.
- **The Master Mathematician** Hearing Him is more important than solving the equation. The chalkboard points to the Teacher; relationship outruns information.
- **From Information to Transformation** Numbers inform, but Jesus transforms. Revelation becomes formation when it draws us closer to His heart.
- **Let the Lesson Produce Love** God's ultimate aim is intimacy. The outcome of study should be deeper affection and obedience to Jesus.

JOURNALING QUESTIONS

This chapter invites you to journal not about numbers themselves, but about the Person to whom the numbers point. Record where wonder has awakened worship in your story. Capture moments when study turned into surrender, when you sensed the Master Mathematician speaking through a pattern or a providential detail. Reflect on how Colossians 1:16–17 reframes your pursuits—career, calling, relationships—as created by Him and for Him. Write honestly about times the "chalkboard" distracted you from the "Teacher," and how you intend to turn back. Use your journal to map the shift from fascination to fellowship, from curiosity to communion.

Expect clarity about priorities—Jesus over everything. Anticipate renewed intimacy as you rehearse what He's already shown you. Welcome correction where study displaced surrender, and receive grace to re-center your life on Christ. Look for courage to trust the One who holds all things together, including you. Let your journaling become an altar where insight becomes obedience.

Christ at the Center

Where have I allowed numbers, patterns, or pursuits to eclipse the Person of Jesus, and how will I return Him to the center?

Held Together by Him

In what specific area of my life do I need to trust that "by Him all things consist," and what step of faith matches that trust?

From Chalkboard to Teacher

When has God used "the numeric on the chalkboard" to draw me to His voice? What did He say, and how did I respond?

Created for Him

How does "created by Him and for Him" reshape my goals this season? What needs to be surrendered or realigned?

____

____

____

____

____

____

Wonder Into Worship

Where is the Lord inviting me to move from fascination to fellowship—practically, this week?

____

____

____

____

____

____

Actionable Steps

Re-center Daily
Begin (and end) each day this week by praying Colossians 1:16–17 aloud, declaring that your work, relationships, and decisions are "by Him, through Him, and for Him."

Practice "Teacher First" Study
Before any study—Bible, project, planning—pause for two minutes of silence. Tell Jesus you prefer His voice to your insights, and invite Him to direct the "lesson."

Trade Fascination for Fellowship
Choose one area of curiosity (numbers, timelines, patterns) and convert it into a concrete act of devotion: worship, service, giving, or intercession that keeps Jesus central.

PERSONAL REFLECTION

If numbers have ever dazzled you, let them lead you now to devotion. Consider where Jesus is inviting you to trust Him more deeply: a decision that needs His wisdom, a schedule that needs His order, a burden that needs His sustaining grace. Ask yourself: Is He the point, or have I made the pursuit the point?

Surrender is the narrow road from insight to intimacy. Yield your need to master the "equation," and welcome the Master to lead you. Pray Colossians 1:16–17 over your life until your heart knows it: created by Him, created for Him, held together in Him. This is not about perfection; this is about ongoing "yeses" to His presence and leadership.

If Jesus is the sum of all things for me, what will I lay down, what will I pick up, and how will I practice His presence today?

Closing Prayer: *Lord Jesus, You are before all things, and in You all things hold together. Re-center my heart on You. Convert my fascination into fellowship, my study into surrender, and my insights into obedience. I confess that all things—my life included—are by You and for You. Be the point of everything I think, say, and do. Amen.*

About the Author

Pastor Troy Brewer, the senior pastor of OpenDoor Church in Burleson, Texas, is renowned for his prophetic insights and teachings that make complex Kingdom principles simple and practical. He is the author of 18 influential books, including bestsellers like *Numbers That Prophesy, Numbers That Preach (3rd Edition), Redeeming Your Timeline,* and *Looking Up*, along with many additional resources that equip believers to walk in freedom and revelation.

Beyond his ministry work, Troy is a passionate abolitionist and the founder of Troy Brewer Ministries, which has directly rescued more than 11,000 women and children from sex trafficking, providing them with essential care and a path to transformation through King Jesus. Through his efforts and partnerships, including SPARK Worldwide, founded by his wife, Pastor Leanna Brewer, over 4,000 children are currently under care around the world.

Troy continues to impact lives globally through his streaming platform, ODX.TV, which features podcasts and original shows including *The Pulse, Alter(ed) State,* and *The Counter.*

DESTINY IMAGE

Destiny Image is a prophetic Christian publisher dedicated to empowering believers through Spirit-led messages. Our mission is to equip and inspire individuals to fulfill their God-given destinies by providing transformative resources that resonate with the Charismatic and Pentecostal faith.

We specialize in books, blogs, and back cover copies that reflect prophetic insights, dynamic teachings, and testimonies of faith. Our commitment to fostering spiritual growth and kingdom impact makes Destiny Image a beacon for those seeking to deepen their relationship with God and embrace their calling in the power of the Holy Spirit.
